D1562342

FOR CHRIST
AND THE PEOPLE

EDITED BY
MAURICE B. RECKITT

FOR CHRIST
AND THE PEOPLE

Studies of four
Socialist Priests and Prophets
of the Church of England
between
1870 and 1930

THOMAS HANCOCK
by Stephen Yeo

STEWART HEADLAM
by Kenneth Leech

CHARLES MARSON
by Maurice B. Reckitt

CONRAD NOEL
by Robert Woodifield

LONDON
S·P·C·K
1968

First published in 1968
by S.P.C.K.
Holy Trinity Church
Marylebone Road
London N.W.1

Made and printed in Great Britain by
William Clowes and Sons, Limited
London and Beccles

© The Contributors, 1968

The title of this volume recalls that of the notable collection of sermons delivered by Thomas Hancock at St Stephen's Lewisham, where he served as curate from 1867 to 1873, and published in 1875.

HX
23
.R4

SBN 281 02255 0

CONTENTS

ACKNOWLEDGEMENTS

Thanks are due to the following for permission to quote from copyright sources:

Miss D. E. Collins, Hutchinson Publishing Group Ltd, and Sheed and Ward, Inc.: *Autobiography*, by G. K. Chesterton (copyrighted, 1936, by Frances Chesterton).

J. M. Dent and Sons Ltd: *The Life of Jesus*, by Conrad Noel.

John Murray (Publishers) Ltd: *Stewart Headlam: A Biography*, by F. G. Bettany.

NOTES ON THE CONTRIBUTORS

Stephen Yeo

Age 29. Teaches in the School of Social Studies at the University of Sussex. He is working himself on the period 1870–1914, with a special interest in the relationship between Religion and Society. He hopes to publish some work in this field before very long. He stood for Parliament for Labour in the 1964 and 1966 elections in Hornsey (Middlesex), on the last occasion narrowly failing to get in.

Kenneth Leech

Sambrooke Scholar of King's College, London, where he read History. Read Theology at Trinity College, Oxford. Trained for Priesthood at St Stephen's House. Doing research for Ph.D. on census data on migration for two East London wards. Assistant Curate of St Anne's, Soho.

Maurice B. Reckitt

Has been active in various departments of the Christian Social movement for half a century. Formerly an editor of *The Church Socialist*, he became in 1931 editor of *Christendom: A Journal of Christian Sociology*, and remained so for the twenty years of the periodical's life. His book *Faith and Society* was published in 1932; in 1946 he was invited to give the Scott Holland Memorial Lectures which were published in the following year under the title *Maurice to Temple: a Century of the Social Movement in the Church of England*.

Robert Woodifield

Started on the "Liberal Catholic–Christian Socialist" road in the early years of this century, under the influence of Percy Dearmer's teaching at St Mary's, Primrose Hill. On that road, in 1906, he met Conrad Noel, and between then and Noel's death in 1942 he got to know him intimately. He was associated with him in the Guild of St Matthew (which he joined in 1907 at the age of 21) and, more closely, in the Church's Socialist League, the Catholic Crusade, and throughout the years that he was vicar of Thaxted. His book: *Catholicism: Humanist and Democratic* (published in 1954) largely reflects Noel's theological and social outlook, which is expressed afresh in his essay in this book.

FOREWORD BY BISHOP BUXTON

It was a cold and foggy night when a group of young people, over fifty years ago, marched across from Westminster, to knock loudly at the great Gate of Lambeth Palace. Fr Conrad Noel and Fr Charles Marson were our spokesmen; and we carried the banner of the Church Socialist League. A Petition from the League was taken in by Fr Noel to the Archbishop (Randall Davidson)—urging him to espouse the cause of the unemployed.

Demonstrations of this kind, meetings in the Park, or in a hall, the issue of a journal: such were the normal activities of the C.S. League. Individual members of the League served the cause in other ways; several were called to the priesthood, some to research in sociology, one or two to parliament.

The Church Socialism of those days was not the State Socialism of modern times. The Catholic Faith was its basis. Its major prophet was Frederick Denison Maurice and the men about whom these essays are written owed their convictions mainly to his inspiration. Thus, the message which they stressed was founded upon—the Fatherhood of God and the common brotherhood of mankind; the identifying of God with humanity in the incarnation of Jesus Christ; the Kingdom, the supreme objective and God's Church, indwelt by Holy Spirit and taught by Blessed Mary and the Saints, instrument of the Kingdom; the divine purpose, not only the salvation of individuals, but also the redemption of the social order. For the individual will never be wholly redeemed while his environment remains poisoned by sinful, inhuman conditions.

No doubt the prophets about whom we shall read in this book had their peculiar foibles. Yet, on the main issues they are relevant for contemporary problems. For this reason, we owe a considerable debt to Mr Maurice Reckitt for planning the volume—the latest of his numerous services to "Church Socialism".

Conrad Noel, the subject of the fourth essay, was known to me from my early days; he was a frequent visitor at my home. I became his Curate at Thaxted during his first years as incumbent, i.e. before 1914. Mr Woodifield gives a careful summary of Fr Noel's thought and preaching, in which there was an unusual blend of "Tradition" and "Revolution". As I served him at the parish church, Sunday by Sunday, I became conscious of this fact. In the pulpit he was the fiery prophet, a Savonarola; then, at the altar, a man apart—deep in penitence, adoration.

A changed and changing world today! Once again, Holy Spirit, grant us prophetic voices.

> With thy living fire of judgement
>   Purge this realm of bitter things:
> Solace all its wide dominion
>   With the healing of thy wings.

✠HAROLD BUXTON

INTRODUCTION

If one were to ask the majority of well-informed persons who were the "Christian Socialists", one would be rather unlikely to find them replying with the names of the four Anglican priests with whom this volume deals. For some the phrase would suggest a small band of men grouped round F. D. Maurice and Charles Kingsley for half a dozen years after 1848—which, rather mysteriously, seemed to disappear from history after this. Others might recall a less sharply defined type of "progressive" reformer who early in this century related a rather idealistic collectivism to what they were wont to describe as "the Christian Ethic". A few, perhaps remembering references by their parents to a body called the Christian Social Union, might murmur the names of Scott Holland and Charles Gore.

None of these answers can fairly be described as incorrect. But they all leave out of account a school of thought which first crystallized in the early 1880s with the Guild of St Matthew, continued its development in the Church Socialist League, founded in 1906, and was perhaps most picturesquely exemplified after World War I in a somewhat esoteric body describing itself as the Catholic Crusade. It is in the belief that this movement should most certainly *not* be left out of account that this series of essays dealing with its most significant leaders has been assembled.

It takes this form for two reasons. In the first place because no satisfactory account of these men—indeed hardly any account at all in the case of two of them—has yet appeared.[1] And secondly, because "movements" move primarily because of the men who provide the main inspiration for them. It is the prophet rather than his disciples —and far more than the societies into which these organize themselves—who makes the essential bequest to history. This was pre-eminently the case with the man whose associates, though often at odds with him, specifically spoke of as "the Prophet"—Frederick Denison Maurice, from whom, if in varying measure, all those written about in this book knew themselves to derive.

[1] F. G. Bettany's biography of Stewart Headlam supplies a good deal of information about his activities but does not provide an adequate study of his theological outlook. Conrad Noel's "Autobiography", begun as his powers were waning, is not only incomplete but fragmentary and unreliable as to facts.

The movement, recovering his initiative after some twenty years
and henceforth carried forward by those with whom we are here
dealing, was roughly bisected by the opening of the twentieth century. Inspired by the preaching of Thomas Hancock in the late
1860s and early 1870s, it can be said to have petered out with the
arrival of the 1930s. It is perhaps significant that this period began,
as it ended, in that characteristically "capitalist" phenomenon—an
Economic Depression. Hancock becoming "unemployed" on leaving St Stephen's, Lewisham, in 1873 may be seen as typical of the
thousands who began to experience the same fate at this time,
especially in the textile industry. A large part of our movement's
concern was for that recurrently "waste product" of industrialism,
the Unemployed Man. In his fate the Church Socialist priest, at any
rate in the nineteenth century, often—and significantly—shared.
Like those for whose cause they stood, they were "not wanted" by
those in control of the system through which their efforts were
directed. After 1873 Hancock found no incumbent willing to employ him, and remained in this situation for nine years until H. C.
Shuttleworth, on being discreetly "shunted" from his Minor Canonry
at St Paul's Cathedral to the living of St Nicholas, Cole Abbey,
gave him a lectureship there and so, as Hancock wrote later, "re-
opened the doors of the House of the Lord to one of His ejected
priests". Headlam served briefly in four curacies, but was never
afterwards employed thus, still less was he promoted to a benefice.
Even in the new century Noel found himself unemployed for two
years. Judgement, these men felt, must begin at the House of God,
but on attempting to apply this truth they were to find it had but a
slender chance of being proclaimed there.

It is necessary to stress two points as applicable to all four of the
men dealt with in this book.

1. In the first place, as each of the essays makes abundantly clear,
their teaching was rooted in theology. This does not mean, of course,
that they were all great theologians; perhaps only Hancock was
that.[2] But both Headlam and Noel, and even Marson to a somewhat
lesser extent, were men with a conspicuous power of interpreting
theological truth as they understood it and of applying it to the

[2] See for confirmation of this statement the study of his theology provided
by A. M. Allchin in his book *The Spirit and the Word*, and elaborated in
Mr Yeo's massive exposition in the essay which follows.

social and political issues of their time. Nor does it require us to accept all their specific emphases as so important, or even so valid, as they themselves thought them to be. (I myself, for example, feel that the ultra-immanentalist standpoint of Conrad Noel, as so carefully and interestingly set out in Mr Woodifield's essay, went beyond the Church's "proportion of faith".) But their theological foundation, however we may regard it, is in striking contrast to the merely ethical idealism only too characteristic of the superficially religious Socialism of their times.

The term "Anglo-Catholic" is in itself so little satisfactory, and was in their day too often identified not merely with Ritualism but even with an introverted "churchiness", that it would be a little misleading to apply it to them. But what Mr Leech says of Headlam in the second section of his essay is true of all of them: they "saw themselves as standing within the tradition of the Oxford Movement [despite their differences with its upshot in Puseyism] and the Sacramentalist revival". It is significant that one with as little inclination to any type of ecclesiastical conformism as Noel had no hesitation in entitling the society of his followers as The Catholic Crusade.

2. Again, as Mr Leech says of Headlam, "Their crime was not unorthodoxy but unconventionality." If these men regarded themselves as rebels—and were happy to be so regarded—it was because they were seeking above all to redress a situation in which those left outside the Church had been neglected by that very Body of Christ which they regarded as "the representative of mankind".[3] They can surely be forgiven if seeing that the "chosen people" inside the churches were, if not so well at any rate so fully provided for, they turned to the "gentiles", the masses on whose banners Hancock rejoiced to find the words not of the Communist Manifesto but of the Gospels. The Church Socialists were, ecclesiastically speaking, Outsiders, and simply in being so bore an essential, if hardly a very influential, witness. Yet to see them as such ought not, I think, to be regarded as implying any aspersion upon such Insiders as those in the C.S.U. in the 1890s who, under the leadership of Westcott, Scott Holland, and Gore, were struggling to find ways of arousing a social conscience in the faithful. The tasks of G.S.M. and C.S.L. on the one hand and C.S.U. on the other were in reality

[3] See A. M. Allchin, op. cit., p. 62.

complementary, though their leaders did not always see them as such. If "rebel" priests were needed to "speak out loud and bold" to the man in the street, it was no less necessary for men who spoke with authority within the Church to "shake up" the man in the pew.

I venture to add here the name of one who, having been for long an Outsider himself, came to feel that with the changed situation created by the Great War the time had come for an effort in some degree to merge these two missions and link agitation with infiltration. This was Percy Widdrington, with the development and significance of whose life and work I have dealt with at some length in another book.[4] His initial inspirer had been Charles Marson with whose dynamic character and activities I deal here.

One characteristic of the men here discussed (though this is perhaps less true of Hancock than the rest)—with whom Widdrington may be included—is that along with their doctrinal outlook ran a strong streak of what can perhaps fairly be called romanticism. It was of course a duty, they felt, to *épater* the ecclesiastical *bourgeoisie*, but it could also be a good deal of a lark, and they thoroughly enjoyed themselves when engaged upon it. Indignation with the miseries and injustices suffered by the "humble and meek" justified them in doing what they could to pull down the mighty from their seats. This was a burden which might have been thought to lie heavily upon them, but in fact they bore it lightly. Their gusto and their wit, if sometimes perhaps appearing as merely impetuous and irresponsible,[5] often helped to commend their teaching to those ready to welcome vitality and *panache* in the proclamation of it.

These essays come from two very different age groups. It is all to the good that two young men, closely engaged in different ways with the problems of their own time, should offer us a fresh look at two prophets who were at the height of their powers some seventy years ago. For me Charles Marson, whom I might have met though I never did, has always been, as it were, an inspirer at one remove since I have heard so much of him from the lips of Widdrington

[4] *P. E. T. Widdrington: a study in Vocation and Versatility* (S.P.C.K., 1961).
[5] Scott Holland, very much a humorist in his own way, was fond of referring to the G.S.M. leaders as "Headlong and Shuttlecock".

who was—literally, but still more metaphorically—his pupil. That Mr Woodifield should have been willing to contribute to this book the essay which he has is fortunate indeed, for there is no man alive (indeed perhaps there never was) who has entered so thoroughly into the mind and character of Conrad Noel as he has.

The writers of these essays are encouraged to hope that what they have said here may lead any who read it to go to the writings of these prophetic spirits themselves. Here they may find inspiration to carry into future years, even perhaps into a new century, the effort to sustain an aspect of the Church's witness of which "affluent societies" and starving populations alike have as great a need today (and will tomorrow) as ever men have had in the course of Christian history.

January 1968   MAURICE B. RECKITT

Thomas Hancock, 1832–1903 "The Banner of Christ in the hands of the Socialists"

STEPHEN YEO

I

Brethren [proclaimed Thomas Hancock in 1859] *we* do not belong to ourselves, *we* are not our own witnesses, we belong to the whole world: our witness is in every man's conscience. Our cause is not Protestantism, Puritanism, Quakerism, Methodism—but ONE Body. Brethren, every man, woman, and child in this world was created by the Father, to be baptised into the Holy Catholic and Apostolic Church. Jesus Christ has given all mankind to her; he has given all mankind a claim upon HER. Our Charity, as her children, ought to be greater than the charity of other men, our toleration ought to be wider, more tender, more inviting, than the toleration of the separatists . . . the more the Charity of God is shed abroad in our hearts the more hateful schism will be to us. She, the living representative of JESUS in this world, ought to be to all men all that he was. No assumption, no pride, no untender or insulting phrases ought to pass her lips in her dealings with the Samaritans who surround her.[1]

This was at the age of 27, in a prize essay on "The causes of the decline of the Society of Friends". With remarkable intellectual persistence and integrity of personal life Thomas Hancock asserted the same faith for the rest of his days. Few people, least of all his employers in the Church of England, took any notice. He never rose above the rank of assistant curate, owed the only secure job he ever had to the sympathetic Henry Cary Shuttleworth (1850–1900), and in his forties and early fifties was largely unemployed. When he did at last get a position which approximately suited his talents, for much of the time he was forced to observe a world which was mov-

ing rapidly away from everything he stood for. It has moved further
since, and left Hancock almost totally unknown.

When Shuttleworth, a highly successful and popular priest, was
attracting much attention at the end of the nineteenth century,
Hancock admired his conduct in what he called "the flaming hell
of a rare popularity".[2] This was typical. Hancock suspected success.
He saw it as a temptation to be avoided. Religious men who courted
it did more harm than good, whether they were Wesley, General
Booth, Spurgeon, or Cardinal Manning. It tended inevitably to lead
men away from the already existing Kingdom within themselves
and within humanity towards the evils of self-centredness, sect, or
party. It tended to distract from "conscience towards God". Moreover, the means to its achievement in his own day were some of the
chiefest butts for Hancock's irony. A recurrent theme in his preaching was the pretentiousness and arrogance of "newspaper writers
and the autocrats of platforms and coteries".[3] Newspapers were
usurpers of the priestly function of education, prisoners of money
power, "the keys of the treasury by which a big journal lives are in
Mammon's hands".[4] They were typical of the age with its "super-
stitious credulity in wholesale self-advertisers and project adver-
tisers"—its "worship of a Barnum-like bigness". 'The age, or
world that now is, cannot believe that the saviour who shall
bring forth judgment on the nations must be one who 'shall
not cry, nor lift up, nor cause His voice to be heard in the
streets'." Instead of likening the Kingdom of Heaven to a mus-
tard seed, the least of all seeds, "it fancies the Kingdom of Heaven
grows like the most prodigious fungus".[5] Hancock knew the connection which exists between the nature of a society and the heroes
or "educators" it chooses. To adapt his message in order to get a
popular hearing would have been, in the age that he lived, to
abandon it.

Thus, that he was largely ignored in his own day was the result
partly of his own deliberate action. That he is unknown now would
seem to Hancock curiously appropriate. It fits his character. He
deliberately antagonized and disturbed, never comforted, those who
asked him to perform publicly. He always sought to get beneath the
assumptions of any public occasion and to examine them in the light
of God's nature. It did not matter whether it was Temperance
Sunday or May Day. When preaching to the respectable middle class
of St Stephen's, Lewisham, he would examine and dissect the

"sacred rights of property"; when preaching to the Socialist members and supporters of the Guild of St Matthew he would uncover the evil of man-made schemes for the salvation of society, in the light of God's purposes. Asked to write a study of possible reasons for the recent lack of success of the Quakers, for a prize given by one who wanted to reverse the trend, it is typical of Hancock that his entry showed how it was not only inevitable but desirable that such a sect should not flourish in the nineteenth century. Asked to preach on "Citizen Sunday", an occasion when the clergy were supposed to show their concern for social reform, Hancock devoted his sermon to showing how church reform was the only real reform. Asked to preach on Temperance Sunday he lauded the public house and showed how little temperance had to do with drink. The task of the Church, as he saw it in 1870, was "to take the scorned and hated side in those conflicts of our time in which we are obliged to share".[6] At that date this involved sympathy with the political aspirations of the people; it is typical of Hancock that when in the 1890s Socialism and Labour had become more fashionable, his sympathy became more qualified. Like F. D. Maurice, Hancock could have confessed that his nature was "very prickly and disputatious".

Nor was it merely inability to compromise which ensured obscurity for Hancock. In a sense obscurity was implied in his understanding of Christianity. Action to "get on" in the world was certainly wrong, but action of any kind which was not an affirmation of the central truths of the Incarnate God and his world was also wrong. An already existing Kingdom had to be realized. The only way in which this could be done was through assertion of its nature through the Church. This was to a great extent the responsibility of the ordained priests of God. They had not to build anything new, they had to reveal what was already there. In order to do this a basic requirement for Hancock was complete absence of the kind of self-will which led the Prodigal away from his Father.[7] Adherence to the incarnation should be the sole object of all wills. Hancock disliked the "gas-light and singing" conversions of the Salvation Army. He demanded instead a continual conversion to God and the view of creation God implied. There is in Hancock's own preaching an element of frightening intensity and awareness of the orientation of the will necessary to one who wants to practise the Presence of God. Some of his contemporaries, including Conrad Noel, recognized a difficulty about action which is connected with this intensity and which lies at the centre of Hancock's thought; it will be examined later; it meant that having uttered his faith, having declared "the Resurrection of Jesus Christ the Hope of Mankind",[8] having represented this in his own life as best he could, there was nothing else he could do. Church-building, social movements, personal leadership, philanthropic activity, even pastoral visitation were all possible ways of self-glorification, but none were adequate ways of worshipping God. Like a mentor of his, Matthew Arnold in *Culture and Anarchy* (1869), Hancock deplored all faith in mere "machinery". It is perhaps precisely for this reason that he is of interest now, at a time when there is much concern about alienation from "religion", much research into the history of that alienation, and increasing knowledge of the vast "religious" machinery to which previous generations pinned their faith to end that alienation.

It is in his preaching and writing that Hancock survives. Even here, however, he is elusive. One who knew him after 1897[9] said that it was in the study of history that he spent much of his time. His sermons were full of scholarly reference, no matter to whom he was preaching. In his later years he spent much of his time in the British Museum. His own library was rich in material on the seventeenth century, all of it carefully noted and cross-indexed. And yet, apart from the study of the Quakers (1859) and two small leaflets, on the *Act of Uniformity* (1898) and the *Puritans and the Tithes* (1905), none of his historical work, except for a number of anonymous newspaper articles, was published. He was planning a detailed history of the years 1640–60, mainly from the religious side, in his last years, "but the pity and the pathos of it all lay in the fact that as time went on and knowledge grew from more to more the power to restore life to the dry bones . . . was gradually slipping away from him".[10] Judging by his interest in religious and social movements, and his expressed desire for a history written from the point of view of the "common people" the twentieth century would have found anything he had written exceptionally interesting. But nothing survives. Little else of his was printed either. Hancock had a reverence for books and a rare conviction that none should be published unless they said things that could not be found in other books. Occasionally particular sermons were reprinted in his lifetime, mostly by the Guild of St Matthew; otherwise two volumes of sermons were published while he was alive and one the year after he died. Nowhere did he have time, although he certainly had the capacity, to write a work like *The Kingdom of Christ* (1837).[11]

2

It was a combination of the author of *The Kingdom of Christ* and of the essay on the Quakers (*The Peculium*) already mentioned which set the course of Thomas Hancock's life. F. D. Maurice was one of the judges of a competition initiated possibly by George Sturge, with a newspaper advertisement in March, 1858, offering 100 guineas for the best essay on the reasons behind the decline in numbers and importance of the Society of Friends.[12] J. S. Rowntree actually won the competition, but Hancock's essay was so commended that it too won 100 guineas. It also won him the lifelong friendship of Maurice, who guided him into ordination. He was recommended to Bishop Wilberforce, who made him a deacon in 1861 and a priest in 1863.

Before this Hancock's life is obscure. He does not merit an entry in the *Dictionary of National Biography*, his obituaries are uninformative, and few of his contemporaries go into any biographical detail about him. It is clear, however, that his decision to become a "Christian teacher" was not a long-matured, inevitable, childhood decision, nor did it stem from a conventionally clerical background.[13] His father was Charles Hancock, an artist who painted horses and, it seems, some fashionable portraits. Thomas remembers that his father used to go to the Derby in order to paint the winner, later to be "published in colours by Ackermann in Regent Street". He had a studio at "Tattersalls, Hyde Park Corner". There "he painted the walls with frescoes, life-size, sheep, a hurdle, blue sky. At end of room two knights in armour, life-size, fighting. Also a horse which was separable being painted on a tray of plaster". It was in this house that Thomas was born in June 1832.

His mother, Rebecca Hunt, was the daughter of a clergyman. But judging from the notes made by Thomas it was the artistic rather than the clerical side of the family which impressed him most. His mother's uncle was an amateur painter and took over the studio after Charles Hancock left. From him Thomas used to borrow books. "I walked round Hyde Park and read Pope's Homer with

delight. I remember reading it in bed . . ." There was also another
relative, John Hancock, a sculptor, who exercised great influence
over Thomas. He regarded John in 1850 as a "genius"; "I believe
I owe more to him than to any other living creature . . . I loved Art,
and from loving Art, loved Nature, Poetry and the world of lasting
things." Hancock went to at least four schools. The first, when the
family lived at Tattersalls, in High Wycombe, then, when they
moved to Knightsbridge, at "Mr Wright's" near-by, then for a
brief period he and his brother Charles went to Merchant Taylors',
before Charles died and Thomas was moved to Clarendon House,
Kensington. By the time he came to be so impressed by John Hancock he had been through the "School of Design" (1847–8) and
become apprenticed to a Mr Whitehead at "Hancock's Patent Gutta
Percha works at West Ham". When he started this work in March
1849, he noted: "Today I have begun my first essay in wood carving.
It is difficult and requires great care. Thank God I have stepped
even thus higher towards that great goal which I aspire to, to become an artist." At about the same time he was writing poetry and
having some published in *The People's Journal*. Later on he regarded his time at the works as "soulless". He was frustrated by the
lack of time he had for his own original work, which he brought to
show to John Hancock, whose good opinion he much valued. When
he had first set out for the works, his father had said to Thomas:
"You are entering the world. Be honest and upright." This provoked him in his notes to remember that "when I first came down
he said 'Be great'," and, he wrote, "Great I will be if I live."

Up to the age of 20 it was artistic greatness to which Hancock
aspired. There are few signs of his later preoccupations at this time
of his life. He mentioned in 1850 "the democratic ideas at that time
filling my brain"; he interpreted some events in his life in religious
terms; he placed some "texts of scripture" among his notes, but
there is nothing else recorded which is of interest for the rest of his
career. It is, nevertheless, interesting in the context of late nineteenth-
century Christian Socialism how un-Puritan a background Hancock
had. Interest in art was a feature held in common with many other
Anglican rebels of the day and was by no means confined to Headlam's activities with the Church and Stage Guild (1879–1900). Hancock himself regarded the "aesthetic" as one of the major tendencies
of the age. He hotly defended it in 1859:

The Incarnation gives sacredness to Art, because it is the vindication of the external world as the work of God's hands, as the object of His care, and the vindication of all human powers, faculties, pursuits, as the effects of His constitution of Mankind. Aesthetic faculties in all their forms of Picture, Sculpture, Music, Poem, Drama are provided inherently in His constitution of mankind. . . .[14]

There is no sign of how this continued interest in the things of his early training became joined to the kind of theological and historical understanding shown by the writing of *The Peculium* in 1858–9, for the Diaries end in 1850–1 when, owing to some financial difficulties, Hancock had to leave Mr Whitehead's apprenticeship. Thomas's own son, the Reverend Aidan Hancock, later told Stewart Headlam that his father was "at no college or university" before ordination.[15] This in itself was a remarkable background for a theologian and scholar. Presumably it must have been some time in the late 1850s that F. D. Maurice's influence was felt, in "leading me", as Hancock wrote "from a vague doctrinary Arnoldism to the sight of the real Church".[16] Certainly, although Maurice's influence was lifelong and pervasive, it must have made its major impact before 1859.

Hancock took his ordination supremely seriously and valued the chance to work as a priest more highly than anything else. It was no light-hearted rebelliousness which left him after four curacies, the same number as Headlam, without a permanent job in 1875. For four years (1861–5) he had been at St Leonards, Bucks; for one year each at St Mary's, Leicester and Holy Trinity, Westminster, and finally between 1867 and 1875 at St Stephen's, Lewisham.[17] Twice he was offered "higher" things. Once "a post of some honour and interest in the South African Church". The second time a living owned by Mr Wood, later Lord Halifax, at Hickleton, in 1872. The first he refused "not only because I had much more care for the national heart of England than for its imperialist extremities, but also because I agreed with *both* the opposed parties in the South African church, the Metropolitan and his suffragan of Natal".[18] The second he declined, again on principle, saying to Mr Wood, "You are the Lord and Patron . . . let the people elect me."[19] Compromise in order to advance was impossible to Hancock. How much it mattered to him that he should be properly employed was shown in 1883 when Shuttleworth offered him the "Lectureship" attached to St Nicholas Cole Abbey. "I cannot forget that night. He had given me my youth back again and re-opened the doors of the House

of the Lord to one of his ejected priests that he might go in again
and find his place in it. I went home astounded, feeling as if a new
age had come...."[20] From then on he worked as part of a large
thriving social parish in London. Shuttleworth was a man of "ex-
uberant and varied energy" and created a lively and typical 1890s
"institutional church" parish centred on St Nicholas, with a club
and parish rooms opened in 1889, flourishing guilds, and a magazine
read by ordinary parishioners as well as by church members. At one
time there was a chance that Hancock might have been able to do
the work he was most suited for—the training of clergy. A scheme
for a centre for ordinands within the parish was mooted, but it
never materialized. Even without this, for some years at St Nicholas
Hancock was able to preach and serve in a less than hostile environment.

This Hancock never enjoyed in his earlier curacies. His difficulties in these years seem to have been the result of three factors. His
own integrity must have been bewildering and at times must have
seemed like obstinacy to those around him. Together with this he
refused to identify himself with any recognizable faction or party
theologically or liturgically. This again was calculated to confuse
any normal nineteenth-century congregation of the respectable type.
Finally, there was his social teaching and democratic sympathies.
There is a little evidence that these caused misunderstanding and
hostility, but, judging from the sermons which were printed, they
were at all times implied rather than baldly stated. Of the three
factors they may have been the least cause of friction. It is impossible
to judge accurately since Hancock's biography can be filled in only
by odd references in the volumes of sermons. "Shame and misery"
were certainly caused him by the absence in his congregations of any
but the "well-dressed, respectable and decent". He spoke from
experience in 1872 in a sermon on "Property and Respectability, or
the idols which Englishmen are tempted to worship instead of the
Trinity in Unity"[21] when he said:

> The preacher of the Gospel may go a great way in attacking the preju-
> dices of his hearers, and be patiently tolerated, but let him even seem
> to lay an iconoclastic hand upon their most sacred idol, and he will
> find that the fanatical intolerance which he has aroused is fundamen-
> tally a religious intolerance . . . what the sepulchre of Jesus Christ was
> to our fathers in the Middle Ages, property is to us in this age.

For the most part he deliberately refrained from this sort of attack, thinking it much more important to lay the theological foundations than to help to build any social Tower of Babel. This aroused no less prejudice—sometimes even open demonstration, which to a man of Hancock's temperament can have caused no satisfaction and much discomfort.

In two of my curacies I have always entered the pulpit with some pain, conscious of the strain which I made upon the tolerance of the incumbent ... and the regular congregation. Both at St Mary's, Leicester and St Stephen's, Lewisham some persons used to give me weekly evidence of their disapproval of our relationship by rising from their seats and leaving the church as soon as I entered the pulpit.... The former thought I was not Protestant: the latter that I was not Catholic ... my main offence in each case was the same—my inability to submit to the fetters of party.[22]

To some priests continual controversy of this kind is welcome: not to Hancock.

Financial difficulties caused additional strain. These were not peculiar to curates of Hancock's views. They were common to all who had neither a rich living nor an inheritance of private means. "The life of a priest," observes Hancock in 1873, "unless he strives to be a keen man of business, rather than a teacher and helper of his nation, offers but a little brighter hope in our land than the life of an agricultural labourer."[23] Instead of doing the same as the agricultural labourer was doing in 1870 and turning to trade union organization (although the Curates Alliance was started in the 1870s), Hancock turned to journalism for a living. He acted as a reviewer for the *Saturday Review* and the *Church Quarterly* and later contributed to the *Echo* under Passmore Edwards and to some trade journal as well.[24] This cannot have been easy work for him. His articles were scrupulously researched and painstakingly written for a press whose presence and influence he profoundly suspected. All this was at a time when he might have been developing the talent for sustained historical and theological analysis displayed in *The Peculium* in 1859. The frustration felt at the gutta percha works must have continued into his curacies. If this was so, he rarely expressed it in writing. Once, introducing the volume of sermons called *Christ and the People* he allowed himself to comment, "The preacher of the Gospel in the richest church in Christendom cannot live off the Gospel. Therefore he must teach, let lodgings, or write;

if he writes it is for bread, he makes articles, not books ... he can tell men what it is to be tempted to make stones into bread. ...."[25]

It was said by one of his obituarists that Hancock was the prophet of the Guild of St Matthew (founded in Bethnal Green in 1877). It is true that he anticipated many of the attitudes of the Guild and was expressing its later concerns long before 1877. Certainly Hancock's activities during the years leading up to the formation of the Guild, towards the end of his time at Lewisham and after his departure from there, reveal much about its origins and nature. The rest of his life helps in the understanding of his thought; these years help in the understanding of his time, and especially the Guild of St Matthew as part of it.

The Guild is usually presented in the context of its later, post-1884, commitment to Socialism. It is seen as part of the Socialist "ferment" of the early 1880s. But Hancock's activities in the 1870s reveal that, in origin at least, the Guild was the product of a "ferment" among the London clergy of the earlier decade.[26] It was, certainly in the only sense in which Hancock can be regarded as its prophet, a church reform group preceded by other church reform groups. Indeed, as will be seen below, it was only as a church reform group interpreting rather than endorsing other socialist and reform groups, that Hancock was able to approve of the Guild.

1870 was the first year in which there is any sign of Hancock becoming involved in groups outside Lewisham, the area in which he was still working as a curate. In that year two other "Mauricians", Thomas Hughes (1822–96) and Llewelyn Davies (1826–1916), joined with others to form the Church Reform Union.[27] For a time Hancock acted as an "inefficient secretary" of the Union. It was founded, like the later Guild of St Matthew, partly in response to outside attacks upon the Church. In 1870 it was the Education Act, rather than Bradlaugh, which was causing the attacks. Hancock's commitment to the Union must have been uneasy, for he and Hughes differed in their reaction to the 1870 Act. Hancock would never, for instance, have joined the National Educational Union to fight against the National Education League. He resigned as secretary after deciding that its values were inverted, for it was predominantly clericalist, as he thought, while being anti-sacerdotalist. Then in 1872 Maurice, the inspiration of so many differing men and trends, died. Hancock was later moved to comment on how lonely this loss made him. "Though I had been in Holy Orders and served populous parishes in and near London, I had lived in a kind of isolation, for I had nowhere come into contact as yet with any brother priest who felt in what a particular sense Maurice had been sent forth by God to the Nation."[28] There were, by then, others who felt like him. He was able to meet them at the gatherings of the next group to which he was attached, the London Junior Clergy Society, founded in December 1873. This body helped Stewart Headlam to feel less isolated as well as Hancock.[29] It enabled Headlam to meet committed clergy such as Hancock and the Reverend G. Sarson (d. 1902). Llewelyn Davies was also a member and so was Shuttleworth, who joined soon after he came to St Paul's from Oxford in 1876. "There not a few of us first found, as I did,' wrote Hancock, a comradeship and community of purpose which brought a new gladness and freedom into our lives as clergymen."[30] It was at a meeting of the Society that he first met Shuttleworth, a priest to whom he felt he owed more than to any other clergyman of the time. Out of the Society came yet other movements and social groups which paralleled and preceded the Guild of St Matthew. There was the Curates' Alliance, of which both Shuttleworth and Hancock were active members and whose founder, the Reverend H. H. Hadden, started the *Church Reformer*, later to be taken over by Headlam. There were also the monthly suppers of the Clerical Social Club at one of which Shuttleworth rescued Hancock from the wilderness by inviting him to St Nicholas Cole Abbey in 1883. Already a member of these other groups, Shuttleworth joined the Guild of St Matthew in 1880 as a fashionable, charismatic young man about St Paul's with much "reputation" to lose. Hancock, less well known, was a member by that time, although it is not known when he joined. The context of the movement in its early days was a shared admiration for the theology and social views of F. D. Maurice among the younger London clergy and shared activity within a growing movement inside the Church of London directed towards reform.

3

The details of Hancock's life, like the details of his character, have for the most part to be inferred. The outlines of his teaching, how-

ever, can more easily be described. In two major volumes of sermons, *Christ and the People* (1875) and *The Pulpit and the Press*
(1904), and in one less important, *The Return to the Father* (1873),
can be found selections from his preaching between 1868 and 1895.
Contemporaries rated him highly as a prophet and theologian.
The almost universal comment is that he should have been given a
chair in some theological college.[31] Subsequent writers with an interest in the Christian Social movement when they have noticed him
at all have sought to place him between Maurice and Gore or
between Maurice and Westcott as the major prophetic figure of the
last thirty years of the nineteenth century.[32] Yet there has been no
attempt to analyse his message.[33] His more glamorous sermon titles
are often quoted, "The Banner of Christ in the Hands of the Socialists", "The Social Democratic Pentecost", "The Magnificat—the
Hymn of the Universal Social Revolution". These, at it happens, are
seriously misleading.

Hancock himself nowhere systematically expounds his beliefs. A
recent writer has warned that his work "nowhere claims to be a
complete and systematic whole". It would have been self-contra-
dictory if it had.   In a sense a sermon hymning the news of Easter
Day, such as he preached in 1868, was, for Hancock, the only legiti-
mate prose for a priest to compile. Anything else, any "system"
of theology, any carefully worked set of human arguments, might
serve only to stand in the way of the sight of the great objective
fact of God. To do this was to commit sin in the only real sense
in which Hancock understood that word. It is therefore appropriate
that anybody who wants to understand what Hancock had to say
has to go to scattered sermons in order to piece his ideas together.
This was Hancock's own method of exposition within individual
sermons. Rather than arguing from each established premiss to each
desired conclusion, he tended to repeat himself in a number of different ways until a composite picture had been built up. Like
Wallace Stevens, the poet of *Notes Towards a Supreme Fiction*, or
Michelangelo, the sculptor of the captives on the tomb of Pope
Julius, Hancock felt that he was chipping away in order to reveal
an already existing form rather than diligently constructing the form
himself. When he went to hear some scientist talk in 1872 he saw
the likeness of the scientist's activity to his own, rather than the
danger to his beliefs which he was expected to see; the scientist's
"whole business and end is to go through and through that which

merely *seems*, until he comes into actual contact with that which *is*, with some real work and word and thought of God".[34] This is what Hancock tried to do, no matter to whom he was preaching. The congregation of St Stephen's, Lewisham, to whom most of the sermons in *Christ and the People* and *The Return to the Father* were addressed, were not patronized. They were privileged to hear even more deeply felt theology than the more sympathetic later hearers of the sermons in *The Pulpit and the Press*. Incomprehension must have been not the least of the problems between Hancock and his congregations.

Hancock's sermons were always carefully designed, whether appropriately or not, for the audience he had in mind. As a result, when speaking to his congregation in Lewisham between 1868 and 1874 in the sermons reprinted in *Christ and the People*, he often preached about the nature of the real Church, in the same way as the later sermons for members and sympathizers of the Guild of St Matthew in *The Pulpit and the Press* were often about the "theology" of Socialism. In both books he was unlike modern preachers, perhaps especially those interested in "society" and the social implications of their message, in that he was never afraid to preach about God.

For him it was never a question of debating with the secularists or anyone else about God's existence or non-existence. He was uninterested in any apologetics apart from the apology contained in the day-to-day life and work of the Church. The philosophical and verbal definitions within which God could be contained and made intelligible were of no concern to Hancock. For him it was possible to make positive assertions about God's nature. God was known and real and could be talked about. "Theology is the science or knowledge of God. There can be no theory unless God can be known."[35] That he can be known is the starting-point of all other knowledge. Hancock did not look at the world with God and then at the world without God and decide which fitted his perceptions most appropriately. Like Maurice he started with a "great existing reality" and went on from there. He started from God and arranged his perceptions of the world and of humanity around him. There had been no alternative since God became Fact. When talking of God he does not apologize for talking of "something vague, dark, and confused", rather is it "something of divine clearness and lucidity".[36] Not only is it the single most important fact about the world that "it is possible for men to know God", he can be known in some detail. For this purpose we have Holy Week, which Hancock introduced in a sermon in 1868 with the words, "in this week we see the entire unfolding and disclosure of the innermost recess of the mind of God".[37] God does not depend on any feeling of ours towards him, nor does he need to be defended by us against the attacks of science, he can "look after himself", he has been "uttered" in his Son. This means that he is not something abstracted from a perception of the world, "the name God uttered by the co-eternal word does not stand as a mere synonym for the ultimate reality. It does not merely declare as our Teutonic word God does that the ultimately real is and must be the absolutely Good."[39] He is at the centre and start of the world whether we "realize" him or not. We pray to him whether we go on our knees in church and know all about the refinements of Trinitarian formulas or not. We may indeed worship him better without self-consciously knowing him, certainly without "feeling" him. In a beautiful phrase he used in 1870, "the passion is the epiphany of the tender feeling of God for those who did not and those who do not feel for Him. Be content not to feel. . . ."[39] It was the nature and meaning of God that for Hancock had to be explored on Passion Sunday, not human capacity for sympathetic "religious" emotion at the sufferings of Christ.

"The Word" tells us about God. Christ is our means of access to God. But at the same time he is God. He is also God's total identification of himself with Humanity, so that Christ, in a literal sense, becomes Humanity and Humanity only through him can become and has already become united in one. Hancock took the implications of the Trinity literally and seriously. He saw the world through his understanding of it. In common with other followers of Maurice he never allowed social awareness to imply "liberal" theo-logy: rather "orthodox" Trinitarian theology implied social aware-ness. Christ replaced the more ancient written word of the Hebrews, thus relegating the Bible away from the central position which most of Hancock's congregations must have been taught to give it. He did so not as a man (there is none of the Christ-the-man worship in Hancock which is found, for example, in Thomas Hughes) but as the revelation of God. In a way it is mistaken, however, to use this language of revealing God. The relationship between Christ and the Father, like the relationship between Humanity and Christ

in Hancock's thought is not an easy one to describe. The lines are
blurred and constant qualification is necessary. To him, as he explained in a sermon on "Science and Theology" in 1872, Christ did
not "discover" certain facets of the will of God which can be summarized in what is called "religion", he "came down from God
and revealed God's nature" which is the subject of the much more
permanent word "theology". It is important for the understanding
of Hancock's theology not to try to place God, the Son, Humanity
in consecutive order in time. Each reveals the true nature of the
other, but not stage by stage in sequence. Not one of them can
be understood except in terms of the other two. The best source
for an exposition of this idea is a sermon on the Trinity preached
in 1869—"The Fellowship in God the source of Humanity's Fellowship with God".[40] Here he explains how the nature of the Son
implies a particular nature which the Father has which, in turn,
finds an echo in human nature. "There is no certainty that God is
the Father unless it be true that He has, and ever has had, a co-
eternal Son. We might by a figure of speech call Him *a* Father, but
the eternal and absolute Father He cannot be, unless there is One
who is not merely *a* Son but the eternal absolute Son." In this way
we know that God is not "egotistic" or "solitary", for "there is no
likeness of such a God in ourselves". From that kind of God "all
that is best and godliest in the human heart necessarily shrinks".
The nature of God, known as it is, thus has implications for
Humanity. The fact that he is revealed through Humanity tells us
certain things both about him and Humanity. "If in finding access
to God we could only find an Almighty, a Creator, a Supreme Being, it is not certain that we should be any the better, it is certain
that we should be none the more glad . . . we do not really *know*
God*, until we know Him as 'Our' Father, until we realize that we
are indeed through Jesus Christ 'the children of God'." As will be
discussed later, this revelation of God is, to Hancock, the only
sanction we have for knowing that there is such a thing as
"Humanity" (a much used word in the sermons); without it we
could talk about different human beings as individuals but not as
a collective. Nothing, in Hancock, is what he would call "a mere
figure"; there are no analogies in theology; the central truths of the
Christian faith are to be taken literally. Their full implications are
to be understood and lived. Christ does not illustrate certain truths,
he embodies them. The commandment "Love thy neighbour as

thyself", for example, "is not only heard internally, it is seen externally in Jesus Christ".[41] It has not only been made possible as a commandment, it has been already fulfilled and in some way *exists*. Humans do not have to turn to God and ask for help to love their neighbour from time to time, they are in a situation where they and their neighbours are already part of a loved and loving whole, however much that whole is temporarily obscured. When General Booth of the Salvation Army produced his scheme for the regeneration of England in 1890 (*In Darkest England and the Way Out*), Hancock's reaction was predictable and consistent with this idea of the relationship between God and Humanity.[42] Booth, thought Hancock, was an autocrat. He sought to implement his scheme by his own action and that of his agents. Quite apart from anything else about the scheme which Hancock disliked, this in itself made it incompatible with catholic Christianity. There was only one Redeemer and he still existed and was still at work through the collective action of Jesus united with Humanity. Jesus is not "*a* son of God, as the heathen heroes and demi-Gods were thought to be. He is *the* Son" and "you and I and all sons and daughters of mankind are included in Him". There can be no individual usurpers leading men in man-made groups towards illusory paradise; "we are all in Him, and so are naturally partners and co-agents with Him and He with us in the work of saving men". Indeed such is the complete identification of God with Humanity that Hancock points out in the same sermon that when Christ says, "In as much as ye did it unto these ye did it unto me", he was speaking the literal and whole truth about Humanity. There is no question of "In as much as ye did it unto these . . . it is *as if* ye did it unto me".

God is thus known and he is identified with Humanity. He is continuously present. He is the moving force of History, the study of which, like the study of individual biography, is an important means of finding out about his will. He is potentially at least the moving force of the present. To rail against the age as a godless one, to teach that somehow in the nineteenth century God is further from creation than in the past is to mislead. To imply that "there was a time in which it (the world) was more Godly and believing than it is now"[43] is to misunderstand the nature of God. He does not appear and disappear. He has appeared once and is everywhere apparent; even "geology and astronomy and the like give to the patient enquirer a knowledge of the effected and effecting will of

God".[44] He is the foundation for all real knowledge of the universe, all things in the universe are in conformity with his will, even men. Leaves and stones conform without effort. Men can conform also; it is their highest purpose and real nature so to do.

Yet here a difficulty arises. For men to conform requires action on their part. They are already in conformity, through the incarnation. They have the assurance of conformity, through the Church. But still they have to act. It is in this area of action that Hancock is least helpful, except in so far as his life and thought raise in an acute form the problem itself. He did not in his own life solve it. An intellectual not an activist anyway, his intellectual position made activity doubly difficult. It is not easy to know what to do after reading Hancock's sermons and other writings except continually to reassert the central truths of his theology. Conrad Noel, in his obituary, thought it a weakness that so little is suggested in Hancock's thought about positive movement towards the Kingdom. He obviously felt some of the same frustration when confronted with his theology as a figure such as J. M. Ludlow felt when confronted with the "digger", not the "builder", F. D. Maurice. To quote Conrad Noel,

> His hatred of schemes, a hatred based on his belief that we are already in God's scheme, seems sometimes to have confused the mind of a thinker generally so conspicuous for his clearness. For surely, it is just because we are in God's scheme potentially that we shall always be devising schemes practical and outward, to correspond with the inward Mind of God towards men.[45]

Hancock disagreed, but never, in his printed sermons, self-consciously recognized the dilemma. The demands made upon one with his conception of God make any action difficult. Faith for him was "the constant sight of the invisible God by our reason and conscience". It was supremely important not to interfere with this "constant sight" by any self-will. In a sermon in 1890[46] he demonstrated what this meant. He had just met the epitome of the social problem of his day. An old man who, after "sixty years of honest fight, and the death of all his children, had been forced to choose between starvation and the workhouse for himself and his good wife". In other words, an individual member of "Darkest England" on whose behalf, and those far worse than he, General Booth had devised a "Way out" of which Hancock so disapproved in 1890.

Meeting the old man had forced Hancock to reflect: "Would it have been any help to such a man to read him a chapter of Mr Bellamy's *Looking Backward*. Ought I to have given him the Manifesto of the Communist Party? Should I have told him that a volume of Essays by the Fabian Society would treat his condition better than the Gospel of St John?" How should he meet this man's suffering? Not by these elaborate social schemes and visions. By any variety of Socialism? He then examines when and where Socialism does merit the "quality of Christian". His standards, as might be expected, are high. "Whenever and wherever it is at its best and highest, when it does not contentedly brag that it is scientific, or ignorantly brag that it is atheist, or self-complacently explain that it is only economic. When it is not the product of jealousy, or of irritation, or vanity, or malice, or unneighbourliness, or revenge for wrong, but is the product of 'conscience towards God'." This "conscience towards God" is more the concept of a mystic (although Hancock was not that), or at least that of a full-time theologian, than it is of a man who could do anything, immediate or long-term, for the old man about to enter the workhouse or for the society which built the workhouse. "Conscience towards God" does not simply mean "conscientiousness, or scrupulous tenderness of conscience. It means that conscience which the crucified and risen Son had toward the Father through always seeing Him as he is. It means our *consciousness* of God: the sight of the invisible and eternal unity: the possession of pure light on the Will of Wills and the relation of that Will to the world around us. . . ." Hancock spent his life studying and helping others to study in order to possess such "pure light". Both by intellectual conviction and as the objective result of that conviction social action was even more suspected and difficult for him than it was for Maurice.

It is a distortion of any thinker whose works are worth reading in themselves to separate the strands of his thought for individual summary. It is double distortion of a theologian, who in any case is bound to be dealing with concepts which merge and elide one into the other. When that theologian is Hancock, it is even more dangerous. The separate parts of his thought are unintelligible by themselves. As he warned in 1869,

> If we enter ever so little into the contemplation of the depths of the Catholic faith, that is the faith for all mankind and every creature—

we shall find it impossible to separate the unity of the church from
the unity of humanity; we shall find it impossible to separate the
unity of humanity from the unity of God in the Trinity.[47]

Nevertheless, of the three, God, Humanity, and the Church, it was
of the latter that he spoke most often, because it was to its members
in the narrow sense, to his regret, that he had to preach. His idea
of the Church is essential for the understanding of his idea of the
society in which it was contained.

The Church, for Hancock as for Maurice, was the Body of Christ.
It was catholic, i.e. universal, and existed whatever any man might
do about it. At the same time it was an institution, with doors,
ritual, and members who called themselves Christians. It is not
always clear which of these two aspects of the Church Hancock was
referring to in his treatment of it. It is clear that the transformation,
or rather the realization, of the ideal, universal, Church out of the
church with doors and members who saw themselves as different
from the rest of mankind, was one of the main preoccupations of
his life.

In one sense Hancock was a devoted and learned churchman. The
sermons in *Christ and the People* were printed not in chronological
order but approximately according to the cycle of the Church's year.
Each sermon was carefully arranged according to the theme suggested by that particular week or Sunday of the church calendar.
Even a sermon preached for the week of the 1st of May, Labour
Day, scrupulously related that secular feast to the coincident ecclesiastical feast of St Philip and St James.[48] The sermons were full of
learning about the rubrics of the Church and of comparisons between the practices of the Eastern and Western Churches. His
heroes were "simple ordinary parish priests" in their "daily work".

Perhaps because he had this reverence for the Church as founded
by Christ, he had scant reverence for the Church as understood by
his contemporaries. It must have been difficult for his congregations to understand his seeming indifference for the institution
which they had joined—more difficult when Hancock defended that
indifference on the grounds not that they took the Church too
seriously, but that they did not take it seriously enough. His attack
was not the one used by many socially minded clergy, that his congregation really ought to be looking outside the doors of their church
and involving themselves in local School Board elections and the

like. Hancock himself refused to participate in such activities; he would not have expected any Christian, as a Christian, to do so. He could not connect "religious" activity with the furthering of the purposes of God. He was aware of how few of the working class, although the description was not one he used, came to church. He was aware of how isolated the Church had become, " a few church-men stand almost alone in a warehouse, in a political assembly, in the ordinary society".[49] At the same time he had a fine understanding of the working of religious institutions in society. *The Peculium,* his work on sects as a whole, and scattered references throughout his sermons indicate that his theology gave him an instinctive feeling for categories which we should now call "sociological". His Church/Sect distinction is useful in social analysis as well as in theological understanding. He was therefore well placed, or so earnest well-wishers of the Church must have felt, to suggest "solutions" for the Church's situation. But, at least in terms of its usual activity, he refused. His distrust of man-centred activity extended to church work. He could see the enormous volume of "religious" activity which surrounded him in the Victorian age. Never before had there been parallel efforts to perfect the "machinery" of the Church. House-to-house visitations, meetings, missions, philanthropy, all were tried. All were ultimately futile. The Church did indeed have the respect of society to a great extent. Its endowments, its right to educate its and other people's children were attacked, but, by pressure-group activity, by concentration upon the interests of the Church as a corporation, no doubt they could be successfully defended. Hancock was uninterested in such defence; "the saddest characteristic of the Church in our age is an utterly preposterous faith in mere organization".[50] It might be successful, it depended on your point of view, but it was intellectually mistaken. How difficult it must have been for the burgesses of Lewisham to understand what he meant in 1868 when he said, "I do not think that the extension of the influence of the Church is a good thing merely in itself."[51] Ultimately, of course, the Church would not be truly catholic for Hancock, until every human was inside it; he could not see the connection between that desire and the success of places like, presumably, St Stephen's, Lewisham. "The Church complains, 'Men are departing from me'. The prophets say to the Church, 'Thou hast departed from God'."[52]

What then was the Church, properly understood? It was "the

outward social representative of His Son ... the mystical Body of
His Son, the Catholic Church". It was part of the Kingdom of
Christ, part of the future in which we already half live, but which
has yet to be fully revealed "when He shall appear". It was coextensive by its nature with mankind. Hancock refers quite frequently to "the church of the human-kind". To be admitted into
this Church, as he explained in a sermon called "Man's citizenship:
At once on earth and in Heaven", was not simple. It was "to
receive the sign and seal of our membership as human spirits in that
kingdom, that household, that family, that commonwealth, that
city (for each of these titles of human fellowship is at times applied
to the unseen fellowship which eye cannot see nor heart conceive,
nor words fully describe) which subsists 'eternal in the heavens' ".
As he explained in the same sermon,

> Everything that is eternal must be present. We shall not have the full
> fruition of it, we shall not enter into all its rights and immunities ...
> until the Saviour appears out of the heavens, and the City appears
> with Him, [but] though we have not yet the fullness of the state, we
> are in the state ... it does not yet appear what we shall be, but we
> know that when He shall appear we shall be like Him ... we are
> citizens, we need not say we hope hereafter to be citizens.[53]

The Church was the guarantee of this citizenship, the assurance
that it already existed and would later be perfected. When John
Stuart Mill, a thinker for whom Hancock had a reverential admiration, died in May 1873, he called his life, and the life of men such
as Proudhon, "one long confession that their ideal society does not
yet exist". Since there are such men who work devotedly for the
good of their nation, the question then arises:

> Does this society exist anywhere? Is it a city which hath foundations?
> Is it a dream? Is there a substance of things they hoped for? Is there
> anywhere yet the perfect master, the perfect servant, the perfect ruler,
> the perfect man? ... the sceptic says No, or Maybe, ... but Jesus
> Christ has sent His church to tell "all nations" and "every creature"
> of mankind that these things do exist, that they now *are*, where He
> is sitting the Son of Man at the Right Hand of God: that they are
> there that they may also be here.[54]

The Church is the hope for men, at the same time the sign that
their hope is already fulfilled.

The most original part of Hancock's idea of the Church, how-

ever, is not his criticism of the Victorian institution, nor the hope
and reassurance he derived from it as a representative of God, but
the blurred lines he drew between the Church and the rest of
creation. As A. M. Allchin has pointed out, Hancock's idea
of orthodoxy was based not upon common subscription to a set of
dogmas, nor upon "opinion" but upon common recognition of
historical and theological fact. Although this recognition in Hancock's own case, as was seen above, was an exacting process of
concentration and understanding, when elaborating what it meant
for the position of the Church in the world he almost abolishes the
distinction between categories which churchmen, certainly at that
time, held very fast. Hancock constantly referred to those "outside"
the Church. He saw the Church as existing for them, and they as in
some ways, for example the "catholicity" or comprehensiveness of
some of the social theories then popular, representing the Church
better than those inside its doors. He hated exclusiveness. He saw
the Puritan inheritance of the seventeenth century as disastrous in
its division of men into the elect and the damned. Men were sons of
God as men, not as members of a group of people all of whom had
the same ideas on baptism or church government. Christ had identified himself with Humanity, not with some humans. A proper
understanding of the Church made it difficult to say where it ended.
It certainly did not end where church congregations ended. It did
not even end where baptism ended, or where ability to understand
the Trinity ended, or where familiarity with the name of Christ
ended. It included all men, was "coextensive with humanity". But
here again Hancock's thought raises the problem of action precisely
at the point where the ideal and the actual meet. The Church already was coextensive with Humanity: but it was also a narrow,
self-interested corporation, the "prisoner of Caste and Mammon".

Furthermore, it was not only the Church, already established by
God, which was waiting to be realized. The organizations of men
and states were also divine units, part of God's constitution for
mankind. Hancock never thought beyond the mid-Victorian world
in this respect. Although in *The Pulpit and the Press* he tended to
refer more to the State, since by then the nature of the State was
being hotly debated in society outside, rather than to the nation, he
gave the two words the same meaning. He regarded the nation as
ordained of God. So also was the family, and other social units of
the day. Hancock was fascinated by social organizations, not just

sects, but parishes, and communes. He made Swiss social organization a special study. He was fascinated by them for what they told him of God, for he regarded them as being of parallel importance to the Church. Human effort, whether Socialists against the family or imperialists against the nation, directed against these divine units was evil and divisive. It was raising the human hand against the works of God. These units precede the Church in time, they are the fixed setting within which the Church has to work: "The parish system is simply the Church's pious and believing recognition and acceptance of God's own social and civil work in the parishes which he has made, the existing local communes...."[55] They are as "holy" as the Church. The Father had already established a complete godly and humane order in the earth before he sent his Church into the world. Not everything which existed was part of this order. There was "the world" set over against the Church, the family, and the nation. Hancock's use of this word was one of the most easily definable, most precise concepts with which he operated. "The world" was not the "materialism", irreligion, progress, and other characteristics which false church prophets give to their surroundings; most of what they refer to was for Hancock divine. "The world" was division, separatism, schism, selfishness, mancentredness.

> By the world, as opposed to the church we may mean any of the narrow and hollow fellowships, or the totality of those fellowships which men try to build up on the uncatholic or inhuman foundation of class or self, the world consists of those who mould and colour their lives as if they and their set were independent centres and self-owners and not the children of God and members of his family.[56]

This "world" is apart from the catholic, human-universal Church. It is quite distinct. Yet it is to be found inside the Church and Churches of the day quite as much as, if not more than, outside them. Just as the catholic Church is distinct from it, so too are the divine units within which men live other than the Church.

> The State or nation [said Hancock in a sermon on "Victory over the World"] may be enslaved by the world...but mankind, the State, the family and the individual man are of the Father, not of the world. The World may *spoil* a nation, or a family, or a man; it cannot *make* either. The Father made each man, each family, each nation, to be redeemed from the world. His revelation of himself began in his successive call and consecration of each of these to himself. The family

was the first foe God raised up against the world, the nation was the second, the church the third. . . .[57]

The Church becomes to Hancock a kind of prism through the refracted light of which the other units of mankind down to the individual should be seen and can become their true selves. It cannot be understood without them. It cannot exist without them. They cannot survive and develop without it. Thus in 1883: "To us the Church is an organic reality, founded not upon opinion, but upon the actual constitution of mankind into nations, communes, families, and persons—the whole of which the Son of God sums up in himself and represents as our second Adam, the Head of every man."[58] And in 1884: "The Church holds by the gift of the Son of God, and Son of Man, the one valid tradition and the only perfect ideal of personal manhood, the tradition and ideal of the family, the tradition and ideal of nationality, the tradition and ideal of organic neighbourhood, the tradition and ideal of Humanity."[59]

As with Christ and Humanity, so with the Church and Humanity, Hancock so merges the concepts as to obliterate the distinction between them. Human kind becomes the Church, as much as Christ becomes Human kind. Citizenship thus becomes as important as baptism. Both, as will be seen, imply certain rights, some of which were granted in Hancock's time (the vote), some of which were not (the election of God's priests). Whatever opinion Hancock held he held absolutely and stated sharply. It is not difficult to imagine the gasps of incomprehension which must have greeted a phrase of his in 1873 when he referred to "the modern anti-Christian theory of a citizen's allegiance to God".[60] But he meant it and proceeded to supply the arguments. There was no separation for him between the secular and the religious. There was no scale, along which could be ranged the religiosity of different classes of actions. Nationality in a nation was as serious an obligation carrying with it the duties of citizenship, as baptism in the Church with its obligations. "Our citizenship in England ought to be to us a means of using, manifesting, realizing, our citizenship in the heavens . . . we never so much need the recollection of our invisible citizenship as when we are called to exercise our visible citizenship."[61] In a sermon in 1870 on "Humanity and the Church", Hancock makes explicit the identification of the two. Baptism, he says, does indeed set apart. But more importantly it unites, "our union as the true Israel with the Gentiles, as the 'Holy Nation' with all nations, as church men with all men, is as divine an act as our separation from them. It is God who has united us. He has united us in nature by gathering us again into one new Adam—a new Father of all men—His Son Jesus Christ."[62] This broke down all distinctions, even that between the believer and the man, much cherished by Christian congregations then, as now. God is close; his hand is discernible in men's actions and their history; but there is no way of our telling, or reason why we should seek to try to tell, which man is chosen and which is not. Many are chosen who do not know the language of choice itself. There were no categories of "rationalists", "secularists", "believers" for Hancock; there were rationalists in the Church, indeed Hancock recognized the temptation towards rationalism in himself, there were believers outside the Church; the common category was "men". "By practical separation of the Christ from Humanity," he said, "of the Church from the state, of the Christian from the citizen, of the believer from the man, we may deny the Catholic faith in a far more terrible way than the Unitarian denies it."[63] In saying this, of course, the line broke down on both sides for Hancock. As well as saying that what his contemporaries called "the world" was holy and beautiful, he was also saying that what they called the Church was profane and ugly.

It has already been pointed out that the Guild of St Matthew should be seen in the context of the Church Reform movements of the 1870s rather than merely in the context of the Socialism of the 1880s. Already in 1859 Hancock had been excited about the agitation for church reform then apparent. At that time it had seemed to him "the great feature" of the Church. It remained the one line of positive action which he consistently advocated. His demands in this direction ran like a refrain through much of his preaching, so much so that he was clearly aware of how single track and monotonous he might have appeared by the mid 1890s. Having outlined, or as he would have preferred it, having drawn attention to the already existing outline of the comprehensive, human-universal, Church, he did think that specific measures could be taken in order to make that outline more widely visible.

Certainly it was implied in Hancock's identification of the Church with Humanity that there could be no other direction in which reform was valid. In a sermon in 1872 Hancock explained how "God sends his Prophets to rebuke the Church rather than the

World". Railing against the world was the great disease of the age
for Hancock. "The angry and senseless words of scolders of the
age are their own words...not God's word...for no word or
rebuke has a just claim to be called a prophetic word unless it is
uttered against the catholic church." It is no use complaining, as
some interpreters have done, how much of Hancock's ire is directed
against the Church. His definition of that body, and his idea of
Mankind meant that it could be directed nowhere else. The propheti-
cal office, which Hancock humbly saw himself as fulfilling, could
be exercised in no other way. The Church in its nature, then, was
catholic. What had happened to it?

Part of the trouble was that it had become successful. It had become "religious". It had come to be respected by "the world" because it was obeying the rules of the world. When "the world"
attacked it, threatened to deprive it of its established position, or of
its monopoly over the schooling of children, it replied in kind. It
began to organize as a separate "interest". It acquired a life of its
own aside from God's purposes—one of the main characteristics of
a sect. It began, for example, to ask its priests to organize for School
Board elections, a demand Hancock particularly resented. Reform
could never be achieved in that way, although success, the success
of the Scribes and Pharisees and of the Temple, might. Reform
could come only through restoring the Church to Humanity. Just
as the people had been deprived of their common lands by class
interest groups acting in the name of religion from the seventeenth
century onwards, just as they had been deprived of their common
enjoyment and "merriment" by exclusive, separatist, aristocratic,
anti-human groups (as, for instance, the Methodists), so too they had
been deprived of their right to own their own Church. This had
to be restored to them mainly through the return to the election of
priests. The Church was the prisoner of Mammon not only in its
external relations but in the very conduct of its own affairs. Livings
were bought and sold, distributed like goods. About nothing did
Hancock express so much indignation as this: "Until the Lord's
congregation in its primary and narrower senses has been organi-
cally restored in the parishes, and then in the dioceses, and then in
each of the nations, it will be impossible for the Lord's congregation
to assemble as one." When Hancock was asked to preach on the
Bishop of London's Fund Day in 1889, a day on which money was
raised for the building of churches in poor parishes, he conceded

that this cause might be helpful, but, for him it was not a priority. What was needed for the East End of London was not alms, but the concession of the right to choose their own ministers. "It is our great hope", he said, "and prayer that some day a Bishop of London, following the example of the holy apostles in Jerusalem, will go to the much 'murmuring' folk of the parishes of East London and say: 'Brethren, look ye out amongst you not only churchwardens and sidesmen and singers, but deacons and priests of honest report, full of the Holy Ghost and wisdom, whom we may appoint over this business.' "[64]

Here then was a positive line of action, based as it was on deep thought about the nature of the Church and God's purposes for it and its surroundings. But it is difficult not to feel that it was strangely unrealistic. 1889, of course, was the year of the Dock Strike as well as of Hancock's sermon for the Bishop of London's Fund. It is doubtful what the reaction, if any, among the people of East London would have been to such an action by the Bishop. Hancock, in this instance, was referring to a future hope. Nevertheless, he did advocate this reform as an immediate one. He did so on the basis of a symbolic view of "the people" rather than an actual one. This will be explored below. His faith was that "the common people can restore the Church", that "if the whole multitude of the disciples, the masses, the common people, will but reassert their claims and place in the Universal Spiritual Society in the common church of all the peoples",[65] all else would follow. This, surely, was placing too much weight upon an institution which was already less important than Hancock assumed. He saw the "ordinary parish priest" as holding the nation together, as stopping the divine units into which mankind was constituted from falling apart. It might be argued that they were already less important than that. The real controls had already moved elsewhere. In the same way Hancock argued against the Salvation Army *Darkest England* scheme because it stated the need for special agents for the collection and distribution of money for the poor. The Church already had the office of deacon, defunct as it was in its proper meaning, so what need, said Hancock, for the creation of any new posts for such a purpose? It may be doubted whether, in the circumstances of 1890, this was an adequate response. Undoubtedly, it followed from the idea of the Church already described. But perhaps Headlam's career after 1884 illustrated how by the end of the nineteenth century some other more effective, even if less intellectually rigorous, response was needed. As always, Hancock followed the argument wherever it led. It led to the Church and its reform by democratization as the *only* valid beginning for change. This left a yawning gap between the scale of the reform suggested and the reality of his times as they appear now and appeared then to some of his contemporaries. Hancock may have been right; if so, the world was a different place in his day from what it now appears to have been.

Most of what Hancock taught about "man" or "mankind", is implied in what he taught about God and the Church. Some of his teaching on the subject can more properly be looked at when Hancock is examined with more reference to his time than merely to the outline of his thought. But it is important to establish one main element of his view here. The centre of it, and the pivot around which many of Hancock's writings revolve, is the word "unity". Unity, of God with Jesus, of Jesus with the Church, of the Church with Humanity—but above all unity of men one with another.

Although Hancock fought against those who "scolded" the world, there were elements of that world which he continually reviled. They were the elements of division, of schism, of separatism, of sectarianism. Many words were used by Hancock to describe the one sin. It was, to him, a terrible sin, outweighing the good which sometimes accompanied it. Thus he did not completely reject Wesley, any more than he completely rejected Ignatius Loyola or Martin Luther (indeed he much admired them both). But in a sermon on the "Wesley centenary" in 1891 he was forced to conclude that "it would not be hard to maintain the thesis that the ambition of the good and religious, their too ready consent to be made kings by force for the best of purposes has done at least as much hurt throughout all Christianity as the ambition of the selfish and wicked".[66] This was referring to Wesley, in no spirit of party spleen, but in a spirit of sadness that he had set himself over against the Church; that he had set himself up as a leader, dividing men into his followers and the others; that even if he had not wanted to form a sect, some of his attitudes had been sectarian. As he had analysed the process with the Quakers in *The Peculium*, so he saw it being repeated in his own time with the Methodists, the Salvation Army, the Christadelphians. A prophet like George Fox or John Wesley could begin by making a protest on behalf of the "Universal Spiritual Society", but the evil starts when they or their followers claim that *their* society, their rule, their method, their teaching *is* this universal spiritual society. The form this claim takes is often the result of the character of the age by which they are surrounded, as in the case of the Salvation Army's bid for exclusiveness in the solution of material difficulties in society in 1890, but the claim itself is bad. It is based upon the motive power of "the world"—self-seeking. For Hancock there was none of the nineteenth century evangelical distinction between social good and individual virtue. Social arrangements were inseparable from individual conduct. The basis of sectarianism was therefore individual. The virtues he most praised were self-sacrifice, the preference for others above ourselves, "lowliness of mind", "looking on the things of others and not looking on our things". With these virtues the temptation to division, to separatism could be resisted. Christ, after all, was tempted. He was tempted to found "a new religion". He was tempted, and is sometimes treated as if he had yielded to the temptation, to act like a Mohammed or a Joseph Smith. Had he capitulated, the Scribes and the Pharisees, the Judases, would have welcomed him in absolute loyalty. But he would have betrayed the nature of God. Wesley, on the other hand, had fallen victim to "the temptation of popularity, the temptation to autocracy, the temptation to set up a kingdom for oneself, the temptation not to discourage the formation of a party or a sect of which oneself shall be the head, instead of bearing witness through the cross to the eternal Kingdom of God, the Kingdom of the Father, which was already set up through our nature and humanity, and was to be discerned, as he had told his disciples, within them".[67] That temptation had been too much for him. Instead of "striving to bring back their own mother to her own traditions", which was what prophets should do in the Church, men like Wesley had deserted her. Groups of Christians have their origin in the universal relation of men to God, not in the relation of some men to a leader, an emotion, or a doctrine.

The concept of division does not apply exclusively to "religious" groups. It is spread like a disease in the nineteenth century. The same sin has given birth to political parties. They fail to practise the virtues of which Hancock approved, their whole purpose is to avoid the beam that is in their own eye becoming apparent. They give themselves grand labels—such as Liberal and Conservative, as if they alone possessed the qualities their names suggest. They "pretend a monopoly of those qualities of which they so impertinently

usurp the titles". This, for Hancock, was the true meaning of the
word hypocrisy—"this monopoly of what is not exclusively ours".
It was shared by "Whig or Tory, Liberal or Conservative or other
such sects". Any organization not based upon the universal relation
of mankind to God was a sect. They do not and they cannot treat
men as brothers; "the Fatherhood of God and the consequent
brotherhood of men" are dependent upon each other. As Hancock
said in a sermon in 1893,

> The Father has made us all neighbours. He has joined every one of
> us unto a neighbourhood. But we have turned out of his way and
> have built up a number of social schisms, one or other of which we
> look upon as "Sion". There is the schism of the West from the East,
> or, as our fathers called it, the schism of the Town from the City,
> there is the schism of the rich few from the many poor, the schism
> of the nobles from the commoners, the schism of the Pharisees from
> the publicans and sinners, the schism of the employers from the
> workers, the schism of the cultured from the ignorant.[68]

In contrast to the sects stands the Church. In contrast to division
there is unity. The Church bears witness to this unity, "by bearing
witness to a common Father she demands that men should treat
each man as a brother and not as an alien". Three aspects of this
unity, partly reinforcing what has already been said, should be
brought out. First that it already exists. There is no need to create it.
The resurrection, as Hancock preached in 1869, confirmed "the
sight of mankind as a unity—the fresh perception that there is
somehow or somewhere the principle, the law or the person, which
does make the human race a unity".[69] Any attempts to build this
unity will be confounded by God, "whether they are made by
Popes, Emperors or Socialists. The latter are only the latest en-
deavourers to make a human unity". Secondly, there can be no other
basis, other than God and the Church, for thinking that the human
race is a unity.

> We may proclaim to all men that they are brothers, in the name of
> love or in the name of Right, but this will no more enable them to be
> brotherly, to forgive their enemies in the 19th century than it did
> in the 1st century. Unless we already have been made brothers ... we
> cannot be made so in Love's or Right's or in anything's name.[70]

People may try, the Positivists, for example, do try, thought Hancock in 1869. Their schemes were in many ways preferable to the
ideas of churchmen, since at least they did try to be catholic and

to involve all humanity; but without recognition of the true basis, they must fail. Later on (1891) the concept of the already existing unity was under severe strain in Hancock's mind, after the demonstrations of the unemployed and the threat which he, with his contemporaries, felt of revolution in England at that time, but he reasserted his faith: "The earth has not yet become a hell, though hell sends up its flames into it. The Common Brotherhood which makes the poor and the rich one is deeper and stronger than all the dividing accidents of life." Thirdly, Hancock takes quite literally this idea of the unity of all men. It means for him that all men will come to Christ, all men will inevitably form the catholic Church. He has the notion of those now outside coming inside as a single group. Just as *all* the publicans and sinners came and sat down to hear Christ, so, if only the Church were more church-like, *all* men now would come to it. This is a symbolic view of men as a real collective. It explains Hancock's indifference to efforts to attract some men here and some men there to the Church. *Mankind* will come: there is no need self-consciously to attract men. "Of nothing", said Hancock in 1869, "ought I to be more certain than this, that if I ever so feebly reproduced His teaching, according to my own time and my own countrymen, every aisle and every vacant place in this church would be uncomfortably crowded with the unclean, the ragged, the careless, the vulgar, the wicked—'all the publicans and sinners'." To Christ it was "not *some* of them—good specimens of a bad class—but it was the class as a class, that came".[71] Hancock throughout his preaching used the categories of "Scribes and Pharisees" and "publicans and sinners" more than any other descriptions of men; to him they were theological categories with literal application now as before. He used them, and what Christ said about them, without analogy, to apply to his own time. The publicans and sinners would come. In fact it was through them that the Church would be rescued, God's purposes vindicated, himself revealed, and unity realized.

4

The important years in Hancock's life were the years 1859–95. In 1859 he published *The Peculium*, in 1895 the last sermons of his which Headlam and the Guild of St Matthew chose to have re-printed were delivered. He lived until 1903, but there is reason to think that the mid 1890s were a watershed in the relation between Hancock and his times. So far Hancock's thought has been looked at largely without reference to chronology. Its relationship to the times and to other men and groups must now be examined.

1859 brought Hancock into personal contact with F. D. Maurice. Intellectually he must have been a considerable influence before that, when Hancock was in his middle twenties, but biographically his intervention in Hancock's life in that year was decisive. There is little doubt that Maurice is the thinker and the man to whom Hancock would most have liked to be related. Refusing, as always, to be identified with any party group or "schism" Hancock protested that he was no "Maurician".[72] The influence is, however, obvious and pervasive. It was often acknowledged by Hancock in his ser-mons and especially in the leaflet he wrote on the Act of Uniformity (1898).[73] His hatred of fame, his suspicion of all movements and parties, his reluctance to involve himself in anything that savoured of a challenge to the already existing Kingdom, his personal intensity and many-sided awareness of the connections between all sections of creation, all recall Maurice directly. Maurice's contribution to the dispute with Ludlow over the organization of the Christian Socialist workshops might have been written by Hancock:

> Every attempt to bring forth God's Order I honour and desire to assist. Every attempt to hide it under a great machinery, call it Orga-nisation of Labour, Central Board, or what you like I must protest against as hindering the gradual development of what I regard as the Divine Purpose ... an attempt to create a new constitution of society when what we want is that the old constitution should exhibit its true function and energies.[74]

There are differences, and developments, of Maurice in Hancock. These especially concern the nature of democracy. Some of what Maurice called "Democracy", for he used the word to cover much that he disliked in the liberal "progressivism" of the age, was also rejected by Hancock, but in Hancock's interpretation of the forces of his age there was a commitment to the idea of democracy in its narrower sense which Maurice never had. Yet the similarities between the two thinkers are more striking than the divergences. The difference was partly owing to the changed character of the age after Maurice's death in 1872: what was happening in both Headlam and Hancock's life and thought after that date was the application of Maurice's basic theology to entirely new "signs of the times". These were in themselves, for Headlam as for Hancock, new revelations of God's purposes. Hancock's feeling of isolation and despair after Maurice's death was only lightened when he came into personal contact through the groups of London clergy in the 1870s with other men who felt as he did about the great prophet. There were other mid-Victorian thinkers as well as Maurice to whom Hancock's debt is clear. Much of his work recalls Thomas Carlyle (1803–55) both in style, ironical and prophetic, and in content. Hancock had in common with Carlyle a firm idea of the naturalness of "organic" (a word much used by Hancock) units of community and neighbourhood which were under strain in the nineteenth century, and a sense also of reaching back before the seventeenth century to find natural values extant. Matthew Arnold (1822–88) was also one of the "advanced thinkers" with truly "catholic" conceptions of mankind who were putting the narrowness of the Church to shame whose ideas Hancock, to some extent, endorsed. At times, particularly in the 1870s when Hancock was defending the Board schools arising in working class neighbourhoods against the petty, self-interested, fears of his fellow-churchmen, he put forward an idea of "culture" which is entirely Arnoldian. More commonly he used the word with the extra element of relationship between every man and God. It was less of an individualistic, self-perfecting, self-cultivation, ideal to Hancock than it was for Arnold. Hancock once wrote that Maurice had rescued him in his youth from "a kind of literary Arnoldism".[75] Elements obviously remained, to Hancock's advantage. His hatred of narrow Puritanism, his respect for the finest achievements of the human mind and art, his assumption that these achievements were the universal birthright of men as men, not of élites as privileged classes, all relate to Arnold.

In the neat chapters and chronological sequences into which historians for their own convenience like to arrange the past, Hancock at first sight appears to be "early". He should, first, be placed firmly in the context of these mid-Victorian thinkers like Maurice, Arnold, Carlyle, and, another man whom he much admired, John Stuart Mill (1806–73). Was he, nevertheless, an anticipator of the late nineteenth-century growth of social awareness among Christian groups and individuals? As far as the "Christian Socialist" strand of activities after 1854 is concerned, he seems to have played no traceable part. Convinced as he was in 1868 of the hopefulness of artisan activity, there is no sign that he came into any direct contact with it. Friendly Societies, Trade Unions, the Co-operative movement, Adult Education—these are the usual headings under which historians try to trace the continuation of the burst of Christian Socialist activity of 1848–54.[76] Under none of them does Hancock, a thinker not an activist, a parish priest not an agitator or organizer, fit. The most appropriate sphere for him would have been the Working Men's College. Neither the histories of that institution, nor Hancock's own writings, record any contact. The people involved in these activities were his contemporaries. He was nearer in age to Ludlow (1821–1911), to Hughes (1822–96), to Llewelyn Davies (1826–1916)[77] than to Shuttleworth (1850–1900) or to Headlam (1847–1924). With the two last he came into contact over the Church Reform Union and the Guild of St Matthew, but not, it seems, in any more secular bodies. The various branches of post-1854 "Christian Socialist" work were dissipated within the wider society rather than concentrated within the Church; Hancock's suspicion of activity of this kind has already been brought out. Did he then anticipate the growth of social consciousness, to put it at its vaguest, within the Church itself? Here it is a mistake to look at the Lambeth conferences from 1888 onwards, at the Church congresses in the 1880s with their invitations to speakers such as Tom Mann and Westcott, at the official pronouncement of ecclesiastical bodies in the last quarter of the century, and to conclude from these that all developments of this kind were crowded into the "ferment" of those years and caused by the new creed of Socialism, developing guilt among the middle classes, and the other factors which were producing late nineteenth-century social changes. The change in official attitudes had a background. It is as part of this that Hancock's work should be seen. Hancock's *Christ and the People* sermons were delivered between 1868 and 1873. From the vantage point of the Guild of St Matthew this may indeed seem "early". But they were part of a wider intellectual development. Westcott's *Essay on Comtism* appeared in 1864. Llewelyn Davies published his *Morality According to the Lord's Supper* in 1867, and his *Gospel and Modern Life* in 1869. Even earlier he had written *Social Questions from the point of view of Christian Theology* (1864). In the parishes also developments were taking place. Lowder and Machonickie were at St George's-in-the-East in Stepney, denouncing the sweaters in 1862. In the same parish the Reverend Arthur Stanton (1839–1913) founded the "Brotherhood of Jesus of Nazareth" after the Paris Commune in 1871. Elsewhere the Reverend W. R. Corbet had founded "The Society of the Holy Spirit for studying Social Questions in the light of Christian Realities" in 1869.[78] So Hancock is not to be seen as standing in an entirely vacant gap between the mid-century and the Guild of St Matthew period. He said that after Maurice's death in 1872 he had felt isolated; this may be more a comment upon his own position and habits than upon what was going on at the time. Hancock belongs very much to this earlier phase of the development of the Anglican conscience. Far from anticipating later developments, as will be seen, he tended latterly to warn against them, to preach *at* them not *for* them, to distance himself from them rather than to encourage them.

Hancock was forty-five years of age when the Guild of St Matthew was founded in 1877. A year later it moved out of its original local context and became a national movement. In 1884 it changed direction once more and, in the year that Toynbee Hall was founded and the Democratic Federation became the Social Democratic Federation and the Fabian Society started, it became publicly committed to Socialist ideas. The Guild reached its peak of success in 1893–5, by which time Hancock was over sixty; by the time he died (1903) there was discussion inside the Guild about the usefulness of its further existence.[79] The Guild lived on, latterly a much decayed body, until 1910.

Unfortunately, little has been written about the Guild as an institution in the context of its times rather than as an episode in the history of Christian Socialism. All who write about it assert that it was entirely, and to the detriment of its ultimate health, dominated by Headlam. This may have been so. Unfortunately, Hancock's career does not help in the understanding of the internal history of the Guild, for little is known about his "physical" relations with it. He certainly joined before 1880, preached often for it, wrote articles and published sermons in the *Church Reformer*, and, once, but only once, invaded Headlam's stamping ground to write the leading article for that paper. Other than that nothing can be said, which is unfortunate, because the Guild is more interesting than merely as a chapter or two of Headlam's biography. It seems likely that Hancock would have had little to do with organization, would

not have dominated the "politics" of the Guild, and that the role
he played for the members was that of teacher, prophet, and theologian. Although Hancock had been in parishes for many years
as a curate and was to be in a thriving parish with Shuttleworth
after 1883, the response he made to the social changes of the day
was primarily an intellectual one, not the result of personal contact
with "the poor". When the journal of the Charity Organization
Society (*The Charity Organization Reporter*) noted in January 1884
that "the Socialist movement appears to be gaining a great hold
upon the clergy owing to the fact that they, more than any other
of the educated classes, are brought into close contact with the evils
which Socialism desires to remove",[80] this may have been true for
some members of the Guild, but it was not for Hancock. His was
no case of dramatic conversion to Socialism in the mid 1880s coinciding with the change in professed aims of the Guild. His
response to society did indeed get sharper in *The Pulpit and the Press*
as compared with *Christ and the People*. This was because outside
changes appeared to be arriving at some sort of a crisis. But there
was a basic continuity which he shared with the Guild. There was
the continued assertion of the primacy of theology and the Church
over Socialism and society. The Guild was never a body which
spotted a Labour bandwaggon and attempted to join it. It was never
a body which uncritically identified itself with the Labour movement in any of its specific forms. As Maurice Reckitt has written,
"the widespread if often tacit assumptions of most of those who
were soon to follow that noble idealist Keir Hardie into the I.L.P.
(founded 1893) was either that the doctrinal aspect of Christianity
was a matter of indifference or that religion was a private affair
which could be indulged in without reference to political opinions.
Nothing could be more flatly opposed to the theology of Headlam
and Hancock and to the whole standpoint of the GSM than such
assumptions: indeed the Guild might almost be said to have been
founded to contravert them."[81] In Hancock's own case he was
preoccupied with most of the Guild's concerns before 1877 and
preoccupied with the same concerns after the change in 1884. The
change, if there was one, came in the history of the Guild in the
mid 1890s, and with it a possible change, although it can only be
inferred from sermons, in Hancock's attitude towards it.

With all the original aims of the Guild in 1877 Hancock would
have been in profound agreement: "To popularise the church and

its services, combat secularism, promote education, social intercourse and recreation among its members." The Church and its services, as has been seen, were of great importance to him, even if not for the same reasons as those who fought so viciously about what particular forms they should take. They were the best and only form of combating secularism. Here also Hancock would have been in agreement with the emphasis Headlam gave to this phrase. Open and dramatic debates in the Halls of Science were to him, and certainly to Hancock, only the smallest part of the fight. Their main intention was to reveal the goodness in secularism and the purposes the movement and the Church shared. The principal weapon was to reform the Church in order to expose its true nature against those whose livelihood inside it depended on keeping that nature obscure. As Hancock had said in 1874, "there is no need for us to swell the yelling chorus raised around us against external disbelief".[82] In many references to the meaning and nature of current disbelief, secularist and otherwise, in his sermons in the early 1870s Hancock's theme was to recall the Church to "a keener sense of our own inward heresy". This was precisely what the Guild tried to do after 1878. Its defence was positive and actual, not narrow and verbal. If "social intercourse and recreation" in the original manifesto meant a total rejection, as it did, of Puritan attitudes to enjoyment, art, and the Sabbath, Hancock had decided on that course as far back as 1859. Education, the remaining element of the manifesto, throughout the 1870s had been the national theme to which Hancock most often returned. A little later the Guild moved even closer to Hancock's principal interest. Headlam called the last six words of the revised formula "to promote the study of social and political questions *in the light of the Incarnation*", the *"raison d'être* of all our Christian Socialism and efforts towards social and religious reform". They were the basis of Hancock's view of the world.

When the Guild adopted its formula of 1884, more care has to be taken in relating Hancock to it. The *Church Reformer* of October 1884 and March 1885 printed the revised aims.

> Whereas the present contrast between the great body of the workers who produce much and consume little and of those classes which produce little and consume much is contrary to the Christian doctrines of brotherhood and justice, this meeting urges on all churchmen the duty of supporting such measures as will tend (*a*) to restore to the people the value which they give to the land; (*b*) to bring about a

better distribution of the wealth created by labour; (c) to give the whole body of the people a voice in their own government; and (d) to abolish false standards of worth and dignity.

With some of these aims Hancock's ideas are in complete conformity: with others qualifications have to be made. This should not be surprising, for although members of the Guild including Headlam looked up to him as a great teacher, he was on many occasions preaching at least as much with the idea of undermining simple Socialist ideas, with the idea of getting his hearers to examine their assumptions in the light of God's purposes, as with the idea of rallying them behind their agreed aims. Since the Guild has usually been presented as an appendage to the life of Headlam, it is interesting to look at the interpretation of its ideas in the thought of another who was revered within it, but who was not afraid to challenge any received opinion.

The language Hancock used in the discussion of social problems was biblical, not economic, and was more apt to refer to the vineyard than to the labour market. Occasionally, in *The Pulpit and the Press*, he used the word "capitalism" to describe the economic system, but more usually the words he chose were "commercialism", the society of Mammon and Caste. He recognized that "the English for Mammon in our present condition of social development is capital",[83] but chose to call it Mammon none the less. Class is not a word he used in its economic meaning. For him it meant any selfish, separatist sectarian groups who were concerned more for their own organization, ideas, and interests than for the "catholic" interests of the whole nation. The "working class" were for him still "the poor", "the outcasts", when antagonized the "vultures"; the sections of them he tended to draw attention to were more those of Mayhew's "characters" of the mid-century than the "industrial army" of his day. The "London crossing-sweepers", the "London sandwich men", the "East End seamstresses", "the poor men and women who will try to sleep tonight on the stone streets of London"—these were the people on whose behalf Hancock felt most deeply. Divisive language, as he explained in a sermon in May 1891 on "Labour Day and the Red Flag", was repellent. The language of ultimate brotherhood was Christian. Carlyle and R. H. Tawney are in the tradition to which Hancock belongs, not Marx and Hyndman. Thus when Hancock, in 1886, wanted "a fair statement in better words than I can formulate of the hopes and objects of the Guild of St Matthew", it was to the Magnificat that he turned.[84]

> He hath shewed strength with his arm: he hath scattered the proud in the imagination of their hearts
> He hath put down the mighty from their seat: and hath exalted the humble and meek.

The contrast between the mighty and meek, the rich and poor, concerned him, but the language of production and consumption and the mass of technical, specialized, prudential, "Fabian", administrative, decisions necessary to end the contrast was never any concern of his. "Property" was indeed an idol whose worship Hancock wanted to end. But it was because it was worshipped not because of its economic effects that Hancock was against it. Anything put in its place, such as State Socialism or economic equality, or anything else which was worshipped apart from God, would have been equally obnoxious to him. "Machinery" of all kinds, as we have seen, was anathema to Hancock. There is no record of his reaction to the questions Headlam put in the name of the Guild of St Matthew to candidates at the election of 1885, but it is reasonable to deduce that such matters as the rating of unoccupied land, the rating of land values exclusive of house values, and even increased power for municipalities to undertake industrial work for the purpose of relieving distress (three of the eight questions), were not regarded as of primary importance by him. He had faith that when the reign of Mammon was ended, questions of employment and remuneration would solve themselves under God. Thus in attacking the reliance of General Booth's scheme of 1890 on money as an agent of social change Hancock declared,

> By the Father's will as it is done in Heaven there is, and cannot but be, certainty and sufficiency of bread in the earth for everyone who needs. So whenever and wherever the Son sets up his Kingdom in its fullness in the earth there and then ... there is immediate sufficiency of bread for all the hungry, and more than sufficiency ... where Mammon's kingdom is still in possession and men and women are subjects to it, there can only be certainty and sufficiency of daily bread for the rich and competent. All the rest must depend for their bread in a nearer or more remote degree upon the will of the landlord and the money lord.[85]

It was God who would "bring about a better distribution of the wealth created by Labour", not the schemes of man.

The Guild gave high place to the land question. It was an issue upon which many Radicals of the period found themselves making the transition towards a more fundamental, less piecemeal, critique of society, than earlier radicalism had allowed. Hancock was too outraged, in a sermon for Harvest Festival in 1888, that "Caste and Mammon, idle fashion and busy competition, demand prodigious quantities of food for their horses, yet the land cannot be spared to grow corn and fruit for English men, women and children, and wholesomely employ them on its culture". "No English priest", he thought, "can hold an ideal Harvest Festival until all English land really belongs to England."[86] His phrase for what needed to be done rather than "nationalize" was "recommonize" the land, since "bread" was "the gift of God to the whole nation"; yet he was not a Georgeite. Henry George presented the land question in *Progress and Poverty* (1879) as the single key the turning of which would rescue the collapsing machine of political economy. The single-tax was an economic, administrative, solution of the whole social problem. This was not Hancock's perspective. His was much more the perspective put forward by the Hammonds in works such as *The Village Labourer* (1911). The key word was "common". The English people had been deprived of their common enjoyments, their common worship, even their Book of Common Prayer. The common land was part of this deprivation and should be restored to them. "To give the whole body of the people a voice in their own government", and to "abolish false standards of worth and dignity" —the third and fourth aims of the newly constituted Guild—were entirely Hancock's own. Both in Church and State a central aim of his was, from 1868 onwards, to move towards universal enfranchisement of the English people. Without it they were not citizens of the divine units of Church and nation; it was their right as people created by God. All the labourers had to be admitted into the vineyard before its Keeper could work satisfactorily. At first, in the 1860s and 1870s Hancock's advocacy was in both directions, religious and secular. Later, when advances had been made towards admitting men into the citizenship of the nation, he joined with the Guild in pressing, through the *Church Reformer*, for their admission into the rights which membership of the universal Church implied.

One of the themes of the *Church Reformer* and the Guild of St Matthew was the attempt to interpret the age to itself. Where others in the Church saw only antagonism to their beliefs, the Guild saw the existence of shared purpose. Where others saw decline, the Guild saw the possibility of renewal for the Church. Where others saw salvation, if it was to come, coming from their own methods magnified, the Guild knew that it would come from a proper reaction to the methods and movements of others. What was going on outside the Church was for them and supremely for Hancock crucially important; God was at work in the world then in exactly the same way as at any other age in history. The "signs of the times" had therefore to be read. In Hancock's case they were read in the light of his understanding of the incarnation, of God, of the Church, and of Humanity. His reaction to the events of the day relates perhaps more to that understanding than to the events themselves. It was a matter of continually keeping a "conscience towards God" who, as Providence, was revealing himself in the history of the time, but who had once and for ever fully revealed himself in Christ.

Events in Europe and elsewhere reinforced Hancock's idea of the nation as a divine unit and the only proper setting for the Church. The only possible basis of human unity was national unity with a national Church. "This very week", Hancock noted in 1868, "He has cast down the Spanish dynasty." This is one among other "judgments with which he has visited the dynasties which have lent their authority to force the Christian peoples into that unity which is made by submission to the false father on earth".[87] It is in events like these that God is forwarding the recovery of faith in the Church's unity. Similarly, the victory of the North in the American Civil War and the Bulgarian struggle against the Turkish Empire were God-given and good. In the case of the former Hancock asked in 1873: "Do you think it was one God who broke the chains of the slaves in Egypt, but another God who broke the chains of the slaves in America. . . . Do you think it was one God who took the throne from Saul and gave it to David but another God who took the throne from Pio Nono and gave it to Victor Emmanuel?"[88] In many respects Hancock's reaction to his time was that of a mid-Victorian liberal. As well as believing in nations he believed in "civilization" unquestioningly. He would never have put the word in inverted commas as Henry George, William Morris, and others were to begin to do in the 1880s: he was still sure that it would make "progress" from its existing base in Western Europe.

The new factor in the post-1867 English scene was, of course, "the people". Their presence it was, together with the panic reaction to their presence by "the classes", which was towards the end of the century imposing most strain upon mid-Victorian categories. They it was who had most to be interpreted to the Church, as the Guild saw it, and the Church interpreted to them, as other more superficial minds saw it. "The people" were getting the vote by stages, were seeking to enter politics and to rely upon organizations of their own against those created for them by others. At various dates their activity caused stir. One such was the early years of the 1880s, the years leading up to the reorientation of the Guild of St Matthew in 1884. All the time what they did or were thought to be capable of doing threatened concepts like that of "Unity" and "Brotherhood". Often the threat came in the name of these noble words, but that did not make it any the easier to understand. A pervasive feeling of crisis, of the newness and unpredictability of the situation is characteristic of the years during which Hancock flourished.

His own assimilation of the changing force is worth examining. It is also worth quoting in some detail. It helps in the understanding of his theology, of which it was a part; it helps to "place" him in his time; it makes possible comparison between Hancock and the other figures treated in this book. Unfortunately, it is impossible to be precise about the development of his thought over time. Scattered sermons are not enough. But even from what material we have interesting patterns can be made out, for even at times when he was not explicitly addressing himself to a social theme Hancock's unceasing preoccupation with those who are "without" the Church was apparent. His most pastoral, biblical, expository sermons for his congregation at Lewisham are no less interesting for this theme than the more colourful "Labour Day and the Red Flag" sermons in *The Pulpit and the Press*.

In the first few years of his preaching (1868–71) Hancock showed himself to be aware of the situation immediately following the Reform Act of 1867. It was a time for stocktaking. Social and political thinkers, aware of a great change, were looking to see what history and the present could tell of where the change was likely to lead and what the result of it might be. Fear and hope were expressed in about equal proportions. Bagehot, in the second edition of *The English Constitution* (1872), was hopeful that "deference" would keep the new entrants in the club of English politics obeying the rules; Matthew Arnold, in *Culture and Anarchy* (1869) was unsure but hopeful that the rising working class would not ape the existing Philistine holders of power, but would represent something genuinely new and exalted; J. M. Ludlow, a follower of F. D. Maurice, in *The Progress of the Working Class (1832–1867)* used past experience as a sign that the newly enfranchised possessed in their institutions and ideas the power to conduct themselves within the voluntary society which he wished to see continue. Many, however, were determined to stop democracy where it had now arrived, lest anarchy followed. It is not just an historian's cliché to echo Derby in calling the 1867 measure "a leap in the dark"; nobody knew what might happen. At this time of speculation Hancock was unequivocal about the merits of enfranchisement. He made no qualifications about "respectability", or income level, or preparedness to decide the nation's future. On theoretical grounds total citizenship was essential. Every man, as a man, not as a householder, has the right to citizenship.

> An unenfranchised man [he said in 1868] is still in our nation a mere subject...wherever the catholic and human idea of a state is still at strife with the feudal notion of a state there citizenship and nationality are not yet correlative terms...there every man is not a citizen as a man.... That each native must become at last a full member of the nation or that the nation must perish, we are taught both by the providential word of the Father manifested in history and by the words said to each child by the same Son of Man in that Sacrament of Baptism which he instituted for all nations and every creature.[89]

In exactly the same way as baptism implies the right to full citizenship in the Church, which means election of priests by parishioners, so nationality implies the right to full citizenship in the State. In spite of this commitment to democracy, "Socialism" at this date meant to Hancock an attempt by humans to create an artificial unity as bad as "the great empires" or "the Papacy" with their attempts to do the same. "Caesarism, Ultramontanism, and Socialism are nearer often than their disciples take them to be. Each is an implicit contradiction of the Catholic faith. Each is a virtual insinuation that God has not already constituted us one body."[90] This did not mean that Hancock was antagonistic to social justice at this time. On the contrary, in 1869 he was convinced that "the present way to the intellect, the conscience and the heart of the great mass of the English people lies ... through political and social truth and equity".[91] The Spirit of the Son of Man, he thought, was speaking to the English Church "through the artisans and labourers of our time". He was asking for "justice" and rights: the Church was only giving him "alms and charities". Already, as he would repeat later to the Guild of St Matthew, Hancock was declaring,

> I do not shrink from saying that in the ordinary politics and social doctrine of the thinking mass of the English artisan I see something which is already far more Christian, far more catholic, a far more faithful reflection of the mind and law of the crucified and risen Christ for the nation, and far more at one with the doctrine which we ourselves are teaching in the church by the ministration of the all-levelling and all-exalting sacraments than I discern in the political and social doctrines of the majority of the English priests of Jesus Christ.[92]

As yet there had been no major social movements among the artisans or labourers to which Hancock felt he could respond, but within the Church were hopeful signs. In an interesting sermon preached on the Sunday after the confirmation of Temple as the Bishop of Exeter in December 1869, Hancock showed how much he hoped of those "outside" the Church. Dr Temple had contributed a piece to *Essays and Reviews* (1860), which he was later to withdraw. As a result there were hostile ecclesiastical moves against his confirmation as a bishop. These "party" moves had provoked demonstrations of popular support for Temple which led in turn to more alarm than the original appointment. Hancock was excited by the demonstrations; in support of them he preached a sermon in 1869 which was later printed separately as a leaflet. They led him to assert his belief that the Church already was, if only it was allowed to be, the democratic society:

> The crowded city church, even the unseemly hisses with which the people greeted the report of those who opposed the election, the loud and welcome cheers of the great mass of those that were literally "without" standing in the streets, bear testimony to the hopeful fact that Christ Jesus has not left the Church of England but that the Consecrator of Bishops who holds the hearts of the people in His hands, is again offering these English hearts to His bishops, priests and

deacons in this nation. The church exists for the sake of them that are without.[93]

Soon Hancock's reactions had to become more specific. After the French Commune of 1871 it was no longer a question of merely speculating about the new popular forces and interpreting them hopefully for the Church. Actual clashes, in various different forms, between them and established society took place. "The people" became a real presence, not a future unknown. This change, and in the sermons it occurred in 1871–2, may be said to introduce a second phase of Hancock's interpretation of his time. It was a phase which lasted until about 1890, thus spanning the major part of his working life. This is a more natural division, as we shall see, than to suggest that 1884, the year of the Guild of St Matthew's new formulation of its aims, constituted a real break for Hancock. Once class clashes occurred a sense of crisis quickly developed. From the 1870s onwards in England, there was quite widespread fear of a "general over-turn". It reached climaxes in individual years, but was generally present amongst sections of the articulate middle class. In Hancock's own case, in sermons preached on three consecutive Sundays in 1872, reprinted in *Christ and the People*,[94] there is a discernible note of greater urgency in his words, which had not been there between 1868 and 1871. His central idea of the unity of men was under strain. There were increased dangers of schism and false unity. For example, in the sermon called "Property and Respectability, or the idols which Englishmen are tempted to worship instead of the Trinity in Unity", Hancock referred to "the threatened war of classes throughout Christendom—which I believe nothing can avert but the conversion and repentance of the clergy in every nation, and our determination to abstain because we are priests from consecrating Party and to reassert our mediatorial function as the social bond of union between classes". On Whit Monday, 1873, a "great procession of artisans" took place in London. Again Hancock called upon the Church to avoid identification with the selfish, oppressive forces of class; he fully supported the procession. In 1874 in a sermon on the Son of Man appearing "as a thief in the night" to his Church, he warned how "the Son of Man, the everlasting redeemer of slaves, came unexpectedly, as a thief in the night, upon the house of Egypt . . . so He came upon Rome . . . so He has twice appeared in flaming fire in Paris . . . so He may appear in

London ...". Revolutions, like the unseating of dynasties, were God-sent. Moreover, it gradually became clear in the 1870s where Hancock stood in any possible clash. The forces of class, of disunity were the forces in possession of power; it was they who constituted a threat to the unity of mankind, not the challenge being made to them nor the challengers. "In every household of God," he said in 1874, "whether a civil society or an ecclesiastical society, there will be on one side those who are for the Son of Man and for Humanity. There will be those on the other side who are for self or for their class or their party."[95] It was the "outcast" people, the disinherited, who represented the Son of Man. They even, in the procession of artisans in 1873 and in the unemployed demonstrations of the 1880s, carried his words on their banners and made their demands for justice in his name. They even, in the 1880s, came to church in order to demonstrate. In so doing they revealed how God was to save his body from corruption. Hancock in the 1870s and increasingly in the 1880s saw in the social ideas and movements of the working class "the wild and eager protest of the redeemed conscience and reason of Humanity against the false and narrow theories which the reign of Pharisaism has taught men to identify with the Kingdom of Christ".

The General Election of 1874, coinciding as it did with a parish mission in Hancock's church, inspired him to preach the most typical sermon of this period.[96] He interpreted the events around him in terms of the parable of the Labourers in the Vineyard. He drew an analogy between the labourers hired at various times during the day with the "classes" used by God in the world at various dates in history.

> Some, like ancient aristocracies, have been entrusted with the culture of Humanity from early in the morning of the history which is God's day; some, like the great plutocracies from the 6th hour of God's day; others, like the middle classes, from the 9th hour of the history of peoples. Now it is the 11th hour—the last hour but one, a critical hour. The Lord sees his glorious work of universal human culture is not done ... God looks upon his dear vineyard of Humanity and sees the moral degradation of millions, the unredeemed slaves, the ignorant who are perishing for want of knowledge, the despairing suicide, the total absence of any possible hope in life for whole classes of men and women, the waste of noble faculties in low drudgery, the horrible rule of the incompetent and the mediocre ... God therefore de-

scends among the dregs of society, amongst those whom we call the enemies of society, that He may fetch forth real saviours and culti-vators of Humanity.

God goes down into the market place, sees those who are standing idle, allows them in, gives them work, enfranchises them. This, for Hancock, was an absolutely necessary process. All have to get into the vineyard before God's work is completed. "The remainder" are being let in, in Hancock's own time. This is the purpose and excitement of the age; "the thing to be dreaded is not the admission of new classes and new men into the vineyards but the suspicious temper with which they are regarded by the earlier possessors".

In the 1880s Hancock's awareness of the people outside the vine-yard gets sharper, his sense of social crisis more persistent, and his identification with one side in the struggle, as the side of God and unity, more complete. The language of the sermons in *The Pulpit and the Press* is full of denunciation and vividness of image which contrasts with the cooler exposition of most of *Christ and the People*. There is no immediate change of view, rather an intensification of view already expressed in response to more dramatic outside events. There has been a change, but it is a change from the time before 1871. Thus the word Socialism no longer has the same meaning for Hancock as it had in 1868. He admitted in 1884 that "that which is anti-social, separatist, or sectarian in our kind, according to the apostolic writers, is fundamentally anti-spiritual. Socialism, however materialist or sensual its temporary manifestations may be, is Born of the Spirit".[97] The mid-1880s were years of passionate debate about the proper way of meeting poverty. They were the years of un-employment demonstrations, occasional violence, debate about the Mansion House Funds, labour disturbance, and the beginning of the realization by politicians such as Chamberlain that governments would have in the end to assume a positive initiating role in social legislation. Hancock responded with powerful words: "Now that the civilised world is becoming crowded more thickly with the hungry, naked, homeless, helpless workers without work, the for-gotten social doctrine of the Lord is coming forth with a fresh confirmation." The sense of crisis he had earlier felt he now expressed more vividly: "The richer that the rich become and the poorer the poor, the faster the nation develops into the likeness of the Apocalyptic Babylon, which is contrary to the heavenly Jerusa-lem, the City of God and of Mankind."[98] A little later, in a sermon

on "The Social Carcase and the Anti-Social Vultures", he proclaimed that

> In the capital of our Western island, the "East" has become a symbol
> of misery and despair . . . in the East is generating the anti-social force
> by which those whom God made to be men and women are being
> dehumanised into the vulture . . . If we English people, like the people
> of Jerusalem, refuse to be gathered together by the Son of Man—
> united rich to poor, educated to ignorant, as one family of equal
> brothers and sisters in Him—our day of judgment, the end of our
> world, the consummation of our age cannot long be delayed. Unless
> England repents, and rises out of her moral and social death, the Son
> of Man must appear and let loose the "vultures" by whose dreadful
> ministry He will destroy the carcase of a corrupt and putrid civilisa-
> tion.[99]

At the same time as warning the "carcase" about its attractiveness
for "vultures" Hancock at this date shows his most complete identification with the social forces of the day. This was the time when
the movements of the people seemed to coincide most completely
with his understanding of the nature of God. There is no doubt in
his mind in 1885 that the poor are "God's social mediators between
him and the other classes into which Society is divided".[100] In the
often quoted sermon on "The Magnificat as the Hymn of the Universal Social Revolution" Hancock is encouraged by the banners
they are carrying. "Have you, my brethren," he asked, "looked at
the banners of the mob? Have you observed whose image and super-
scription they bear? It is not Caesar's, not Victoria's, not Glad-
stone's, not Schnadhorst's, not Hyndman's." They carry biblical
texts. "You can see to whom they have felt obliged to go in order to
find the fullest expression of their faith." Whether this was an
accurate description of the state of the people in the mid-1880s does
not matter. This is how they appeared to Hancock with his symbolic, not economic, view of "the people". Although not personally
involved so far as is known, as Headlam was, in demonstrating on
the streets, Hancock was fully decided that the forces for which God
stood, the forces of unity, were on one side of the struggle which he
was witnessing.

> The theories of society which are thought out by slaves under the lash
> of Egypt, by labourers sweating in the fields and workshops of the
> modern nations, and not those elaborated in the prudential councils
> of statesmen, or by comfortable professors of political economy, are

those which exhibit the fullest reflection of the Kingdom of God's son which God has foreordained to prevail and to be realised.

The last sermon preached in *The Pulpit and the Press* was in 1895, ten years after this peak of excitement in 1885–6. Thereafter, as will be recalled, there is reason to suppose that Hancock spent much time in the British Museum in the study of history, in an effort to communicate some of his knowledge of the seventeenth century. This break in 1895 is not just an accident of selection for the volume of sermons printed after his death in 1903. It also constituted a turning-point in Hancock's reaction to his time, the culmination of a third phase of his interpretation of the age. As might be expected from his theology and its implications for social action, already discussed, there was bound to come a time when the optimism and intellectual identification with the poor of the years 1871 to 1886 was questioned by Hancock. For the most part these years of the 1870s and 1880s saw little, and this only the beginning, of direct organization of "the poor" for the purposes of capturing political power. Sporadic appeals of "outraged humanity" combined with the mid-century base of voluntary class organization in the Friendly Societies, the Co-operative movement, and the Trade Unions, were still the norm. It was not until the early 1890s, with the foundation of the Independent Labour Party in 1893, that a different kind of challenge began to be made. The potential and unknown force of "the people" began to assume definite shape, backed as it was by an idea of "Socialism" which was given firmer definition and intellectual respectability by work like that of the Fabian Essayists in 1889. Around this time there was a definite change of tone in Hancock's preaching, a change which helps to make clear that it was to the world before the 1890s that he really belonged. Its passing left him by, and it has never returned to win new notice for him.

One of the first signs of a new mood in Hancock were the two sermons, privately printed by the Guild of St Matthew, in answer to General Booth's *In Darkest England and the Way Out* in 1890. It seemed to Hancock quite typical of the age which, owing to "the excitement of fear and responsibility, the dread of a great social catastrophe, and the conviction of guilt" was now turning to massive material, mammon-based, schemes for the rescue of society. In the same year he had woven around his encounter with the old man going into the workhouse a sermon attacking reliance upon future visionary schemes such as those of Edward Bellamy in *Looking Backward* (1887) and the Fabian Essays (1889) for the relief of present social ills, and urged Socialists to turn to "the sight of God" as "the source of Endurance under suffering". At this time "so deeply has the necessity of immediate social reform, and the fearful looking for judgment in the shape of a social catastrophe seized upon the mind of our age, that a sect is now bound to be Socialistic or a failure". He admitted that in the case of Booth he had not actually read the book with its elaborately worked out rescue Utopia; it seemed to him a scheme by one of those "practical" men whom he so distrusted and of whom there were now more and more around. In 1891 there is increasing disillusion in the sermon already quoted on "Labour Day and the Red Flag". Socialists, in so far as they were good, had been anticipated by Christ, and in so far as they were "agitating Scribes and Pharisees, who reject Christ and his Church", they were evil. The creed they put forward was that all men were brothers, but how far did they live up to it?

> In the actual, political-social, exposition of their creed, in newspapers and at meetings, do they not set up a privileged aristocracy, a schismatic semi-fraternity, an uncatholic church, a kind of Atheist-calvinist sect . . . all men are *not* brothers, the Sacred privilege is restricted to wage earners.

It was not only their behaviour and their theory, which previously had seemed so hopeful to Hancock, which was disappointing. A further danger had arisen—the evil of party. Once this became part of the programme of the poor, Hancock's placing of all his virtues of unity and catholicity on their side was seen by him to be mistaken. He then started preaching quite definitely against the new tendencies. They had ceased to fit into his theology. Thus in 1892 he is still "glad" that "He has in these last days called into the field of politics the long silent and oppressed estate of Labour". But the foundation of a Labour Party is quite different:

> Labour is for *all*, by it we all live. So I can no more regard the godly estate of labour than I can regard the holy order of the priesthood as a mere party . . . if the wage worker sells his soul to a party he will have the same condemnation as a priest who becomes the slave of a party. Has not the Lord already given us signs . . . that to this estate of Labour He has entrusted the redemption of all other estates in the Commonwealth from their present miserable captivity to the immoral

and anti-social parties of the Ins and Outs. Oh may they be faithful as
the apostles were to so great and world-wide a trust.[101]

By 1894 it looked to Hancock as if they might not be faithful. In
response to developments he returned once more to the root of all
his teaching—the individual man's relationship to his God as a son.

The Ideal Commonwealth, [he said] the kingdom of heaven on earth
is for the multitudes as its King declares. But it cannot be realised or
entered into by the multitudes . . . through the immoral and mechanical
processes of any one party outwitting, outcrushing, outbribing, out-
voting, confounding and crushing any other party. . . . It can only be
realised by the new creation of ideal men, women and children. That
new creation is the evolution and education of the new man which
is largely each one of us, through the man-becoming of the eternal
Son of God . . . in proportion as the new birth of Humanity grows
and thrives within us we shall detect those dangerous and fertile roots
of all social evils which are within ourselves, we shall grow in a Godly
scepticism of the braggart promises of any and every party, and we
shall look more and more for the light and grace of God in all men,
women and children, chiefly in such as are least agreeable to us and
most opposed to ourselves and our class and party prejudices.[102]

This was a noble ideal and consistent with Hancock's beliefs, but
inconsistent with the way politics was going. Finally, in the next
year, 1895, in a sermon on "Citizen Sunday", Hancock referred to
an area of politics in which Headlam was active, that of London
Government. He did not endorse the "sectarians" at work in this
field. He did not find in this work, as he had found in the artisan
organizations of the late 1860s, the most hopeful signs for the rescue
of the Church. On the contrary, he distanced himself from those
crying for reform in London and defended those who abstained
from such activities "lest they should involve themselves in the
bondage and unrighteousness of Party". It is church reform alone
which will make any appreciable step towards the realization of
God's Kingdom. Even here, where action of a kind had been taken,
it was, sadly, the wrong action. Ludlow could welcome Fowler's
Parish Councils Act of 1894, Hancock could not. It could have been
a real effort to democratize the Church but "instead of a whole and
generous parochial reform, embracing the spiritual as well as the
secular aspect of neighbourhood, we got nothing better than that
lame, blind and decrepit Parish Councils Act, by which they
blunderingly attempted locally to tear aside the universal Christian

Society from the civil society".[108] Thus even in the sphere where the only valid progress could be made, the true path which it had seemed as if "the people" might force the authorities of Church and nation to follow, was rapidly being lost.

Halevy in Volume V of his *History of the English People in the Nineteenth Century*, recalled how "it was generally felt . . . that the election of 1895 marked a turning-point in the moral and political history of the British people". It was a huge victory for the Conservatives and Unionists, for an alliance between Lord Salisbury and Joseph Chamberlain. It thus formed the setting for a phase of English history in which along with the "Rise of Labour", "Imperialism" was to be a dominant theme. This was to last beyond Hancock's death in 1903. It was to become as important a part not just of foreign politics but of the domestic popular scene as the unemployed demonstrations and social tensions of the 1880s. It was to produce similar demonstrations of feeling as the ones Hancock had assimilated into his theology and seen as part of God's purpose between 1871 and 1890. It was to happen with the aid of new organs of mass opinion. In May 1896 Alfred Harmsworth brought out the first number of the *Daily Mail* as a halfpenny paper. Hancock's views on the newspaper press, long before the new developments, have already been quoted. The changes can only have been even less to his liking: with these, combined with the jingo views and "sensations" which the papers now started to peddle, he must indeed have felt as if the values he had striven for had less and less chance of realization. It is in fact natural to make a break at the date of the last printed sermon of his in 1895. Parties, even of labour, the Press, and Imperialism, that false attempt to break God's natural boundaries of nations, were all at this time bigger and had more grip on the future than Hancock. An index of the change can be found in Headlam also. He too had felt "the divine excitement" of the earlier period—the 1880s. By 1893, in the first editorial of that year in the *Church Reformer*, his mood had changed. He considered the possibility of folding up his lively paper altogether. The people on whose behalf it had been produced did not appear to be interested.

In that vast area we call the East of London there is hardly a bookseller to be found [he wrote] but there are, we suppose, literally thousands of purveyors of newspapers and little magazines, now after a steady canvass this year we have found that even friendly newsagents ridicule the idea of selling a serious monthly which costs 2d. Something smart, spicy, crisp, sensational is wanted. The large majority of the people for whom we are working are completely indifferent to our work one way or the other. It may be that until their material conditions are better, their hours of work shorter, their time for education longer we were foolish to expect that they would attend to us.[104]

Hancock could never desire to supply anything "smart, spicy, crisp, sensational", nor, on the other hand, would he have thought it a Christian vocation to work for better material conditions, shorter hours, or even more schooling so that a demand for something better might be created. He therefore turned to his original preoccupation of 1859, the writing of history. More widespread feeling of an analogous kind may have been the reason why the Guild of St Matthew never advanced beyond the point it had reached in 1893–5. It had belonged, as Hancock described the earlier period, to the age of "evangelical anticipation" of ten years before. To this age Hancock, in a contribution he made to a memoir of Henry Shuttleworth published shortly before he died in 1903, was able to look sadly back. For him the roots of England's sin in the last years of the nineteenth and first years of the twentieth century went back to 1876 and to Disraeli, a politician whom he disliked more than most. In that year Shuttleworth had come to St Paul's for the first time, and the Christian Socialist spirit had shown signs of resuscitation among the younger clergy of London.

> It was the year in which the still national heart of England was astir and petitioning, and the wisest of English patriots, thinkers and historians were taking up arms against the turgid bill of our semi-oriental Prime Minister, for manipulating our old English kingdom into a brand new Empire after the model of Asiatic imperialism. His idea of a monarch was not an Alfred but a Nebuchadnezzar.[105]

At that time, thought Hancock, the fight had been successful. The English people had not yet been corrupted. They still represented the greatest hope for the Church. They were still the clear agent of God's purposes and had not had time to be unfaithful to their trust. The 1880s were "a hopeful generation".

> The Devil had scarce begun to infect the poor in our dear fatherland with his anti-Christian plague of Imperialism, there were still wage workers serious enough to be secularists, too serious to be gamblers and jingoes, and with sufficient love for their neighbours and their

nations to look for some great revolution, like that promised by the
Blessed Virgin to the poor, the humble and the hungry and still pro-
fessedly anticipated by the church in the daily recitation of the Magnificat.[106]

They were days when churchmen and "good men who never
dreamed of going to church" met and talked together in the Guild
of St Matthew. Since then there had been sad changes, noticed by
Hancock since about 1890. The "hopeful generation", in his view,
was passed by the time he wrote this memoir in 1902–3. One of its
members, James Adderley, complained later how Hancock, "one
of the greatest prophets of the Church", had been "left unrequited
all his days"[107] by the Anglican authorities. It was not only the
Anglican authorities who left him thus—so too did his times.

NOTES

1. Thomas Hancock, *The Peculium: An Endeavour to throw light on
   some of the causes of the decline of the Society of Friends, especially in
   regard to its original claim of being The Peculiar People of God*, 2nd edn
   revised (London 1907), p. 33.

2. G. W. E. Russell, ed. *Henry Cary Shuttleworth: A Memoir* (London
   1903), p. 65.

3. Hancock, *The Peculium*, pp. 170–1.

4. Hancock, "The Pulpit and the Press" (1884), in *The Pulpit and the
   Press and other Sermons* (London 1904), p. 3.

5. Hancock, "The Heaven from whence we expect the Saviour of our
   body" (1890), in *The Pulpit and the Press*, p. 177.

6. Hancock, "Fellowship with Christ in his sufferings is not to be sought
   in our feelings but in Fellowship with Humanity" (1870), in *Christ and
   the People* (London 1875), p. 203.

7. Hancock, *The Return to the Father*, 3rd edn (London 1908), p. 20. The
   first edition of these sermons was in 1872.

8. The title of a sermon preached at St Stephen's, Lewisham separately
   printed in 1869.

9. W. E. Collins, Bishop of Gibraltar. He wrote an informative introduction to the 1907 edition of *The Peculium*. See Hancock, *The Peculium*,
   pp. 9–30.

10. W. E. Collins, op. cit., p. 28.

11. A clergyman of the Church of England (J. F. D. Maurice), *The King-dom of Christ* (London 1837). Like *The Peculium* Maurice's work had reference to the Society of Friends. It was written as "letters to a member of the Society of Friends".

12. W. E. Collins, op. cit., pp. 16–18.

13. The biographical information about Hancock up to 1850 is taken from a transcription of some of his early diaries kindly lent me by the Reverend Ieuan Davies. The transcript is headed "Book One of the Life and Diaries of Thomas Hancock, copied from his notes up to 1852 and written out by Kate Hancock from 1903–1906".

14. Hancock, *The Peculium*, p. 165.

15. F. G. Bettany, *Stewart Headlam* (London 1926), p. 116.

16. In an introduction to an edition of *Christ and the People* which I have been unable to trace. It is quoted in *Sobornost: The Journal of the Fellowship of St. Alban and St. Sergius*, Series 3, No. 5, Summer 1949, p. 167. The editorial of this periodical contains some interesting remarks on Hancock.

17. See *Crockford's Clerical Directory* (1900).

18. G. W. E. Russell, ed. *Shuttleworth Memoir*, p. 40.

19. See obituary of Hancock in the *Church Times*, 2 October 1903.

20. G. W. E. Russell, ed. *Shuttleworth Memoir*, pp. 85–6.

21. In *Christ and the People*, pp. 210–322.

22. See *Sobornost*, loc. cit., p. 166.

23. Hancock, "The presentation of the First-born: a law for the English as well as for the Jews" (1873), in *Christ and the People*, p. 154.

24. F. G. Bettany, *Stewart Headlam*, pp. 155–6.

25. *Sobornost*, loc. cit., p. 167.

26. The best source here is G. W. E. Russell, ed. *Shuttleworth Memoir*, pp. 36–65. These pages were written by Hancock.

27. See E. C. Mack and W. H. G. Armytage, *Thomas Hughes: The Life of the author of Tom Brown's Schooldays* (London 1952), p. 199.

28. G. W. E. Russell, ed. *Shuttleworth Memoir*, p. 36.

29. See F. G. Bettany, *Stewart Headlam*, the chapter on "Bethnal Green 1873–1878".

30. G. W. E. Russell, ed. *Shuttleworth Memoir*, p. 46.

31. See, for example, James Adderley in *The Commonwealth*, November 1903; Stewart Headlam quoted in G. C. Binyon, *The Christian Socialist Movement in England* (London 1931), p. 46.

32. See, for example, Maurice B. Reckitt, *Maurice to Temple: A century of the social movement in the Church of England* (London 1947), p. 130.

33. This is not quite true. A. M. Allchin in *The Spirit and the Word* (London 1963), devotes two chapters, pp. 51–87, to a consideration of Hancock's theology. Allchin seeks to rescue Hancock theologically as "one who in time, will surely be recognised as one of the great teachers which God gave to the Church in the course of the 19th century".

34. Hancock, "Science and Theology" (1872), in *Christ and the People*, p. 463.

35. Ibid., pp. 456–7.

36. Quoted in A. M. Allchin, op. cit., pp. 176–7.

37. Hancock, "Everyday Morality and the Theology of the Days of Christ's passion" (1868), in *Christ and the People*, p. 219.

38. Hancock, "The worship of Mammon" (1885), in *The Pulpit and the Press*, p. 8.

39. Hancock, "Fellowship with Christ in His sufferings is not to be sought in our Feelings but in fellowship with Humanity" (1870), in *Christ and the People*, pp. 198–9.

40. See Hancock, *Christ and the People*, pp. 291–309.

41. Hancock, "The Religion of the State requires the Theology of the Church" (1885), in *The Pulpit and the Press*, p. 174.

42. It was expressed in two sermons, "The Common Salvation and schemes of salvation", and "The Heaven from whence we expect the Saviour of our Body", both preached in 1890. See *The Pulpit and the Press*, pp. 161–187. These sermons were also privately printed as a leaflet by the Guild of St Matthew. They contain some of Hancock's most important thinking.

43. Hancock, "God sends His Prophets to rebuke the church, rather than the world" (1872), in *Christ and the People*, p. 62.

44. Hancock, "Science and Theology" (1872), in *Christ and the People*, p. 457.

45. Conrad Noel on Hancock in *The Commonwealth*, August 1904, quoted in G. C. Binyon, op. cit., p. 90n.

46. Hancock, "The sight of God the source of Endurance under wrong" (1890), in *The Pulpit and the Press*, pp. 143–6.

47. Hancock, "The Fellowship in God the source of Humanity's Fellowship with God" (1869), in *Christ and the People*, p. 306.

48. Hancock, "Labour Day and the Red Flag" (1891), in *The Pulpit and the Press*, p. 200.

49. Hancock, "Humanity and the church" (1870), in *Christ and the People*.

50. Hancock, "The Judgement Parties fear at asking questions of the truth" (1873), in *Christ and the People*, p. 392.

51. Hancock, "Everyday morality and the Theology of the Days of Christ's passion" (1868), in *Christ and the People*, p. 216.

52. Hancock, "God sends His prophets to rebuke the church rather than the world" (1872), in *Christ and the People*, p. 68.

53. Hancock, "Man's citizenship at once on Earth and in Heaven" (1868), in *Christ and the People*, pp. 39–43.

54. Hancock, "Christ's ascension and its utility: the things above are the things needed on the earth" (1873), in *Christ and the People*, pp. 267–70.

55. Hancock, "My duty towards my neighbour" (1895), in *The Pulpit and the Press*, p. 292.

56. Hancock, "The hatred of the World to the church" (1873), in *Christ and the People*, p. 437.

57. Hancock, "Victory over the World" (n.d.), in *Christ and the People*, p. 227.

58. Hancock, "The church and the Commonwealth as national educators" (1883), in *The Pulpit and the Press*, p. 153.

59. Hancock, "Christ uniting His church to the state and endowing his clergy" (1884), in *The Pulpit and the Press*, p. 107.

60. Hancock, "The presentation of the first-born: a law for the English as well as for the Jews" (1873), in *Christ and the People*, p. 143.

61. Hancock, "Man's citizenship at once on earth and in Heaven" (1868), in *Christ and the People*, p. 55.

62. Hancock, "Humanity and the Church" (1870), in *Christ and the People*, p. 238.

63. Hancock, "The presentation of the First-born: a law for the English as well as for the Jews" (1873), in *Christ and the People*, p. 145.

64. Hancock, "The Apostolic fund is not silver and gold, but the name of Jesus of Nazareth" (1889), in *The Pulpit and the Press*, p. 124.

65. Hancock, "The Banner of Christ in the hands of the socialists" (n.d., mid-1880s), in *The Pulpit and the Press*, p. 36.

66. Hancock, "Jesus overcoming the temptation to popularity" (1891), in *The Pulpit and the Press*, p. 194.

67. Ibid., pp. 188–9.

68. Hancock, "My duty towards my neighbour" (1895), in *The Pulpit and the Press*, p. 295.

69. Hancock, "The Resurrection of Jesus Christ the hope of mankind", a sermon preached on 4 April 1869 at St Stephen's, Lewisham, p. 4.

70. Hancock, "The social-democratic pentecost" (1884), in *The Pulpit and the Press*, p. 99.

71. Hancock, "Jesus Christ the irresistible attractor of the people" (1869), in *Christ and the People*, p. 3.

72. *Sobornost, loc. cit.*

73. Hancock, *The Act of Uniformity (1662): a Measure of Liberation* (London 1898), pp. 26 and 54.

74. F. D. Maurice, quoted in N. C. Masterman, *John Malcolm Ludlow the builder of Christian Socialism* (Cambridge 1963), p. 98.

75. *Sobornost, loc. cit.*

76. See, for example, D. O. Wagner, *The Church of England and Social Reform since 1854* (New York 1930).

77. For interesting biographical details of the Reverend J. Llewelyn Davies see an obituary of him by his son in *The Contemporary Review*, June 1916, pp. 782–8.

78. For these developments see G. C. Binyon, op. cit. They need exploring in more detail than has yet been done.

79. D. O. Wagner, op. cit., Chapter V, "The Reformers Organize (1877–1895)", see pp. 187–93 and G. C. Binyon, op. cit., Chapter XVI, "The Guild of St. Matthew", pp. 143–54.

80. *Charity Organisation Reporter*, January 1884, quoted in Helen Bosanquet, *Social Work in London 1869–1912: a history of the Charity Organisation Society*, p. 74.

81. Maurice B. Reckitt, op. cit., pp. 128–9.

82. Hancock, "The witness of the creation to the promise of the Son of Man's appearing" (1874), in *Christ and the People*, p. 72.

83. Hancock, "The worship of Mammon" (1885), in *The Pulpit and the Press*, p. 10.

84. In the sermon "The Hymn of the universal social revolution" (1886), in *The Pulpit and the Press*.

85. Hancock, "The common salvation and schemes of salvation" (1890), in *The Pulpit and the Press*, p. 167.

86. Hancock, "Bread the gift of God to the whole nation" (1888), in *The Pulpit and the Press*, pp. 117–18.

87. Hancock, "The unity of the church is to be kept not made" (1868), in *Christ and the People*, p. 376.

88. Hancock, "The presentation of the first-born: a law for the English as well as for the Jews" (1873), in *Christ and the People*, p. 149.

89. Hancock, "Man's citizenship at once on Earth and in Heaven" (1868), in *Christ and the People*, p. 37.

90. Hancock, "The unity of the church is to be kept not made" (1868), in *Christ and the People*, pp. 364-5.

91. Hancock, "Jesus Christ the irresistible attractor of the people" (1869), in *Christ and the People*, p. 17.

92. Ibid., p. 18.

93. Hancock, "A bishop must have the good report of those who are without the church", a sermon preached on the Sunday after the confirmation of Dr Temple, 12 December 1869, pp. 10-11.

94. Hancock, "Property and Respectability are the idols which Englishmen are tempted to worship instead of the Trinity in Unity", "The excuses which Christians offer to God for not entering into fellowship with Him and Humanity", "The false fellowships to which the religious world invites the members of the universal fellowship" (1872), in *Christ and the People*, pp. 310-52.

95. Hancock, "The Son of Man revealing Himself to his church as a thief" (1874), in *Christ and the People*, p. 129.

96. Hancock, "The Election and the Mission" (1874), in *Christ and the People*, pp. 20-33.

97. Hancock, "The social democratic pentecost" (1884), in *The Pulpit and the Press*, p. 92.

98. Hancock, "The worship of Mammon" (1885), in *The Pulpit and the Press*, p. 11.

99. Hancock, "The Social Carcase and the anti-social vultures" (n.d., mid-1880s), in *The Pulpit and the Press*, p. 15.

100. Hancock, "The poor are God's elect and the world's creditors" (1885), in *The Pulpit and the Press*, p. 45. This sermon interestingly reflects the national mood of 1885 and echoes the speeches made in that year by Joseph Chamberlain. Hancock pleaded with his listeners to "remember what we owe to the poor . . . we must pay our debts . . . if we do not pay . . . He will come to us as He came to other nations, as the Judge of the poor . . . the poor are in every nation the majority, and they multiply faster than all other classes. If they willed and if they were to organise themselves, they could at any moment destroy the whole fabric of society that now is." For a comparison with Chamberlain and for the mood of 1885 see Helen Lynd, *England in the Eighteen Eighties* (Oxford 1945).

101. Hancock, "Priests and political parties" (1892), in *The Pulpit and the Press*, p. 238.

102. Hancock, "The Lenten Fast" (1894), in *The Pulpit and the Press*, pp. 248-249.

103. Hancock, "My duty towards my neighbour" (1895), in *The Pulpit and the Press*, p. 294.

104. Quoted in F. G. Bettany, op. cit. For the chronology of the Guild of St Matthew see the chapter on "The Church Reformer 1884–1895".

105. G. W. E. Russell, *Shuttleworth Memoir*, p. 41.

106. Ibid., pp. 59–60.

107. James Adderley, *In slums and Society* (London 1916), p. 199.

Stewart Headlam, 1847–1924 and the Guild of St Matthew

KENNETH LEECH

I

Stewart Duckworth Headlam was born at Wavertree near Liverpool on 12 January 1847. He went to school at Wadhurst, Tunbridge Wells, and then, from 1860 to 1865, at Eton. From an Evangelical home background, he learnt a love of religious controversy which remained with him to the end. (It was told of his father that he used, at Tunbridge Wells, to waylay an old-fashioned High Churchman and argue with him about Baptismal Regeneration.) Stewart was brought up in an atmosphere of debate and discussion, and its effects were very soon apparent. "Stewart talks and argues well," his father was reported to have said, "but the worst of him in argument is that he is less keen on finding out the truth than in demolishing you as his opponent." At Eton, both his religious devotion and his political consciousness received impetus. He began to go to early Communion in one of the local churches. His political views may well have developed through his having been taught by William Johnson, a friend of Maurice and Kingsley. It was Maurice whose thought was crucially to shape his life and beliefs.[1]

At Trinity College, Cambridge, from 1865 to 1869, Headlam read Maurice's work and heard him lecture, and Cambridge and Maurice became inseparable. Maurice had in 1860 been made Professor of Moral Philosophy in the University, seven years after he had been deprived of his chair at King's College, London, on grounds of unorthodoxy. "It was his theology which drew me to Maurice at first", Headlam told his biographer, F. G. Bettany. In particular, Maurice's insistence on the Fatherhood of God and the Brotherhood of Humanity through the Eternal Sonship of Christ came as an immense liberating experience to Headlam. Pusey's theology he found dreary by contrast. This devotion to Maurice did not meet with approval from his father who sent him for help to one Herbert James, an Evangelical clergyman at Livermere. But in February 1870, James wrote to confess his failure. "His thoughts still run in the same grooves of Maurice, and from what I know of his character I do not think that they will be lightly given up." C. J. Vaughan, later dean of Llandaff, was no more successful in "curing" the young Headlam of his affliction with Maurice, and told Headlam that he was tired of Maurice's "jargon about righteousness and peace".[2]

Headlam's first curacy was at St John's, Drury Lane, where he worked from 1870 to 1873. It was a parish consisting largely of artisans, shopkeepers, actors, and market-porters. In the St Martin's National Schools nearby—the parish had been carved out of St Martin-in-the-Fields—Headlam was able to develop his lifelong interest in education. At the same time he began to attend the theatre, opera, and ballet. Bettany records an incident of some importance which belongs to this period. One evening, Headlam had recognized on the stage a couple of girls who were communicants, and had spoken of his discovery that they were dancers when he met them subsequently. They implored him not to let other church attendants know how they made their living, because if the nature of their work became known, they would be cold-shouldered in the church. The experience doubtless had a deep impact on the young curate and was to inspire his later work for the Church and Stage Guild. "His whole career", Bettany wrote, "might have been different, his quarrel with the Bishops might never have reached an acute stage, had he not met these two dancing girls and listened to their story." Eventually, his passionate concern for a wholesome and just attitude to the stage was to bring about a crisis in his pastoral work. But it was his devotion to Maurice's teaching which produced the first crisis and delayed his ordination to the priesthood. He had spoken in sermons of the possibility of pardon in the future state. His vicar, R. G. Maul, was unhappy and so was the Bishop, and in 1873, soon after he had been priested, Headlam left Drury Lane for Bethnal Green.[3]

Bethnal Green became in a real sense Headlam's home. The years at St Matthew's under Septimus Hansard (1873–8) were the happiest and yet the most critical years of his life. To this period can be traced the flowering of his sacramental social theology, his quarrel and dialogue with Secularism, his famous lecture on music-halls, and his foundation of the Guild of St Matthew. Here too he met Frederick Verinder, then a pupil teacher at the National School, who was to have a tremendous effect on his thought. Headlam established himself in a flat at 135 Waterlow Buildings, where he would hold study evenings for teachers and others. It was out of these local study groups that the Guild of St Matthew emerged, originally a parish guild. Soon it was to spread its influence over a wide area and to become "the red hot centre of Christian Socialism" in England.[4]

The idea of a guild occurred first to one of Headlam's class-girls as a means of ensuring that some people were always present at the early Celebration. But its objects, in their final form, were of a much broader significance. They were:[5]

1. To get rid, by every possible means, of the existing prejudices, especially on the part of Secularists, against the Church, her sacraments and doctrines, and to endeavour to "justify God to the people".

2. To promote frequent and reverent worship in the Holy Communion and a better observance of the teaching of the Church of England, as set forth in the Book of Common Prayer.

3. To promote the study of social and political questions in the light of the Incarnation.

Members pledged themselves to communicate at all great festivals, and to be present at Holy Communion on Sundays and Saints' Days, and to meet together for worship on St Matthew's Day. After Headlam had left Bethnal Green for Charterhouse, he kept close contact with the Guild, and their objects were adopted in the above form. From its beginnings on St Peter's Day 1877, with forty members, the Guild grew to 364 by 1895, though it fell to 200 by 1906. Among its priest members (priests numbered 99 in 1895) were H. C. Shuttleworth, W. E. Moll, Thomas Hancock, C. W. Stubbs (later Bishop of Truro), Conrad Noel, Charles Marson, Percy Dearmer, and Percy Widdrington. Its secretary was Frederick Verinder.

The Guild was a society at once intensely religious and intensely political. It appealed primarily not to the intellect, as did the Christian Social Union, but to the conscience, and its theology led directly to its political action. Rooted in the belief that men could only approach God in community, it laid great stress on the Catholic Church as the divine community. Christ, it held, became not "a

man"? but Man, and Christians could therefore only be united as
parts of mankind to the Head of the Human Race. Central to the
achieving of this unity were the two divine sacraments of equality
and brotherhood. The Guild too was a firmly socialist body and
could justly claim to be the first socialist society in England, having
adopted a socialist basis in 1884 several months before Hyndman
turned the Democratic Federation into a *Social* Democratic Federation.[6] The theology and social outlook of the Guild will be considered later.

A major role was played during Headlam's time at Bethnal Green
by his visits to St Michael's, Shoreditch, a Tractarian stronghold.
Here he experienced the glory of the eucharistic liturgy in the rite
of the Western Church. "It left a great impression on my mind,"
he said, "and if the label of Ritualist as applied to me has any
justification, the justification dates from my curacy at Bethnal Green
and my visits to Father Nihill's church." When some years later he
was forced to leave St Thomas's, Charterhouse, it was to Father
Nihill that he went. At St Michael's Headlam learnt the beauty
and the value of Catholic ritual, and this was at the heart of his
future ministry. He was to see the intimate link between the ritual
of the Mass and the social process by which the material order was
to be redeemed. It was no moderate Catholicism that he saw at
St Michael's. It was there that Charles Merion, a Roman Catholic
music-hall manager, asked him about the differences between the
Anglican and Roman Communions, and received the answer, "Not
much to talk about, apart from the Pope".[7] But the happenings
which eventually led to his removal from Shoreditch began during
the years at Bethnal Green.

In these years he began to visit the Hall of Science in Old Street
where the Secularists held their meetings. Headlam believed himself
to be a Secularist and the Church to be "the best and the largest
Secular Society".[8] Indeed, his views on the secular role of the
Church have a curiously modern ring. Jesus Christ, he used to
insist, "revealed himself not as the teacher of religion but as the
Servant of Humanity". "The work of Jesus Christ and of His
Church is then ... shown to be secular work: all work for
Humanity, material as well as spiritual, is today revealed as being
'of Christ'."[9] It was this wide viewpoint which led him to admire
and respect a man like Bradlaugh. Headlam wrote on 4 April
1875, after one Old Street meeting:

Next Sunday Bradlaugh lectures on Christian Culture, and is sure to say some nasty things about Christians and we deserve it. How much nearer to the Kingdom of Heaven are these men in the Hall of Science than the followers of Moody and Sankey![10]

Out of these meetings arose his concern for the repeal of the Blasphemy Act, and there is not the slightest doubt that, as he himself admitted, "the Church itself has gained from my Bradlaugh campaign."[11] The Bishop of London, however, did not see things in this light.

The occasion was Bradlaugh's committal into custody in 1880 for his defiance of the House of Commons' ruling on the oath. Headlam at once sent a telegram to Bradlaugh, wishing him good luck "in the Name of Jesus Christ the Emancipator". The Bishop of London was furious, and Headlam's reply to his objection did not improve relations between them.

I have always thought that it was a Christian duty to have sympathy with all "prisoners and captives", and when a man who has worked hard in the cause of freedom is suffering from the injustice done to him by professing Christians, a Christian priest who knew him well would, I think, be failing in his duty if he did not express his sympathy.[12]

In the period which followed later when Headlam was under episcopal censure, a clergyman who had dared to invite him to preach pleaded with him, "I do beg you not to talk about Bradlaugh or Our Lady." Both were dynamite. When the Bishop queried his vicar at Charterhouse about the ridiculous rumour that Headlam did not believe in the Divinity of our Lord, the Vicar replied, "Of course he does, and I think he believes in the Divinity of Our Lady also!"[13]

Headlam's clashes with the Secularists too were vigorous and entertaining. On one occasion Bradlaugh had been lecturing on the atonement. At the end of the lecture, Headlam rose and announced calmly that he proposed to smash Bradlaugh's argument to pieces. He then took out a Book of Common Prayer and began to read from the Athanasian Creed, "Such as the Father is, such is the Son, and such is the Holy Ghost". This was the teaching of the Church, he declared, that everything that was the Father's was also the Son's. Bradlaugh had, if not confounded the Persons, certainly divided the Substance. There were not two Gods, one of whom could only be reconciled to the world by the death of the other, for

6—F.C.P.

the will of the Father was the will of the Son. He sat down. Bradlaugh's only comment was that this was the first time he had heard
a defender of Christianity use the Athanasian Creed in its support.[14]
Headlam, while he defended Bradlaugh and at times supported his
position, was never reluctant to criticize and condemn what he felt
to be the reactionary aspects of his social outlook:

> Mr Bradlaugh's arguments against Land Restoration range him on
> the side of the landlords and of the landlord-appointed Tory parsons
> who quote the eighth commandment against Henry George... Mr
> Bradlaugh and some Secularists are still fast tied and bound with the
> chains of the Malthusian theory of poverty.[15]

He was scathing about what he considered the irrelevance and
fossilized nature of many of the Secularists' discussions:

> It is quite pathetic to hear that the Bethnal Green Secularists have
> lately been occupied for several evenings in discussing "whether the
> Israelites crossed the Red Sea" and the "Epistle of St Barnabas"....
> Indeed, if it were not for the Guild of St Matthew's lecturers, we
> doubt whether the "Secularists" would get much secular teaching at
> all.[16]

Their narrow sectarian outlook, too, he scorned mercilessly. "I
have been told over and over again by your leaders", he said, "that
I am better than my creed: but I cannot return the compliment. I
tell you that you are worse than yours."[17] Yet he clearly believed
that Bradlaugh was a God-given ally in rooting out bogus religious
attitudes, that he was "fighting .... as a free-lance on our side" and
"clearing the ground for us". He helped to destroy "the burden of
an infallible book, the horror of a God who can be bribed and who
torments vindictively". He exposed the foul caricature which passed
for the gospel and, by so doing, he helped to vindicate the true
gospel. Because Bradlaugh had no God to love, Headlam believed,
he loved humanity the more. He would stand out in future ages as
a monument to the folly of false religion, and through him God had
taught the Church a terrible lesson.

> To Mr Bradlaugh we said, "Inasmuch as you took pains, to the best
> of your power, to improve the secular conditions of the people, you
> did it to Christ: though you may not know God, God knows you."[18]

After Bethnal Green, Headlam had moved to Charterhouse (1879–
81), but it was his championship of the Old Street science classes

which led to his removal from here. He then spent a short time working under Malcolm MacColl at St George's, Botolph, a phase which was brought to an end when he spoke with Michael Davitt at a meeting in Hyde Park. Bishop Jackson had by this time despaired of the troublesome curate. "I am sorry I must refuse, as at present advised, to license Mr Headlam. Both in doctrine and discipline he goes beyond the bounds of the most lenient interpretation."[19] So Headlam became more isolated, though W. E. Moll allowed him to assist at St Mary's, Soho.

Headlam's years in the wilderness were not made happier by the suggestions from time to time that he should become a dissenter. "No Bishop or Vicar ever ventured to accuse me of doing or saying anything contrary to the doctrine or discipline of the Church", he pointed out. "My Priesthood was my most valued possession."[20] Headlam's crime was not unorthodoxy but unconventionality. Although the Australian atheistic paper *The Liberator* once described him as "extremely broad in his religion", yet Headlam was no modernist in the present-day sense. His radicalism was firmly based on the Bible and the creeds, and was characterized by "an intense orthodoxy of belief in the Gospel".[21] It was to the literary defence of this gospel that he now turned his attention. His major work was *The Laws of Eternal Life*, first published in 1884. This was a series of studies in the Church Catechism (which he held to be "the best manual of Socialism").[22] Like all his work, it was grounded in the most uncompromising dogmatic teaching. "There is no need for a new Socialist Religion," he wrote later, "no need for a new Theology, no need for a new Church . . ."[23] What was needed was the liberation of orthodoxy from the false interpretations and distortions which hid its glory and beauty. Father Adderley wrote of his theology shortly after his death:[24]

> Headlam based his gospel on theology. There were old doctrines to be re-stated and properly understood in view of the new learning if the Church was to take its proper share in social reform. . . . It did not interest him to further political reforms as such. What did interest him was to make Christians orthodox and to persuade them to recognise the implications of their religion. . . . He wanted to get the mind of Church people right on religion. He had faith that when once that was secured, the Church would take its place in social reform. . . . Baptism was the entrance of every human being into the greatest democratic society in the world. The Mass was the weekly

meeting of a society of rebels against a Mammon-worshipping world-order. Let the working men of England claim their rights as Christ's members and do their duty as Christ's soldiers and the present order would crumble. . . . It was because England had ceased to be Christian that injustice and sweating and cruelty stalked the country. Let the true Church, the baptised democracy, enter it and reign.

Headlam died in 1924, six years after the ending of the war, and his words about the war in many ways typify his approach to society. It was, he said, a "great and righteous War", and he rejoiced that his evening classes had been reduced in number because many had gone to fight, that "God's just wrath may be wreaked on a giant liar".[25] The liberation of France, the crushing of Prussian militarism and bureaucracy, and the deliverance of other nations from these evils, were to him spiritual ideas. The allies were engaged in a spiritual combat. Headlam was therefore no pacifist and warned against what he considered hasty generalizations from the Sermon on the Mount. Christ had his eight woes as well as his eight blessings. He wrote:

How then can we best show our love for the Germans? By carrying the War to such a conclusion as will set them, too, free from a military tyranny. By making them realise that they have made a huge mistake in letting Prussian landlordism and bureaucracy dominate them. . . . Not peace at any price, not a temporary peace, but a peace founded on righteousness which will enable each nation to live its own life to the full, which will deliver the nations, including Germany, from Militarism and Bureaucracy.[26]

Liberation from slavery: it was his aim in the war years, and it was his aim throughout the whole of his hectic and God-centred life. It is to the theology which drove him on and formed the throbbing heart of his activity that we must now turn.

2

Was Headlam an "Anglo-Catholic"?[27] It is a difficult question to answer. Certainly he saw the movement for church reform, the "New Church Movement" as he called it, as being "for the most part the logical outcome of the Oxford Movement of 1833".[28] Some of his fierce opponents linked together as twin evils his Catholicism and his Socialism. Thus an Evangelical clergyman wrote to the *English Churchman* in 1886:[29]

> I am well and sadly aware of the existence of a small section (I had almost said sect) in the Church, which professes to hold opinions both "Catholic" and Socialistic. Such is the body of men composing the "Guild of St Matthew" and constituting, as I believe, one of the most dangerous elements in the Church. Plausible, as all Socialism is, winning over High Churchmen by its professed "Catholicity" and Broad Churchmen by its similarity with Atheism and the Secularists (for whom its precepts doubtless smooth and widen the narrow way, with the facility of a Jesuit missionary), this Guild has from small beginnings advanced of late with threatening rapidity. Indeed I believe the Evangelicals alone have been uncontaminated by its spirit.

Headlam, there is no doubt, saw himself as standing within the tradition of the Oxford movement and the sacramentalist revival. He saw the work of the Ritualists who continued and extended that of the Tractarians to be of "the widest national and political significance". For it asserted the validity of a full Catholic life within England and the English Church, a life which was not dependent on communion with a foreign prelate. Headlam firmly rejected the Roman claims, but saw that they could be resisted only by the restoration of "those full Catholic privileges which the English Church used to enjoy before the so-called Reformation. Then, but not till then, can there be a real unity of Christendom, with the Holy Father at Rome as the natural ancestral head among his episcopal equals."[30]

Yet it was F. D. Maurice who, more than any other, shaped Headlam's theological outlook. He believed that the time would come when Catholics would set to work to build the sepulchre of Maurice. He welcomed *Lux Mundi* which he hoped would serve as a schoolmaster to lead Oxford churchmen to Maurice. "It will introduce the younger Catholics at Oxford to a theology more like that of the Catholic Church than Canon Liddon is wont now-a-days to dole out to them." The association of Maurician theology and Socialism with Anglo-Catholicism was one of the crucial features of Headlam's life, and his permanent legacy to English Christianity. It is certainly in great part the result of his work that the Anglo-Catholic movement inherited a tradition of vigorous social action. It is deeply to be deplored that the "extreme" wing of the movement today has almost entirely lost its grip on this tradition, and has more and more degenerated into an effeminate and sectarian pietism. In 1884 Headlam went to speak at Pusey House, Oxford, during the first term of its existence, and his appearance led to the following lines, written by an Oxford observer:

> Sing a song of thousands,
>   Thirty, say, or more,
> Spent in subsidizing
>   Brightman, Stuckey, Gore.
> When the house was opened
>   Straightway Headlam came—
> Was not that a pretty thing
>   To do in Pusey's name?[31]

It would be hard to overstress the influence of Maurice on Headlam's theology. What can be exaggerated is the extent to which Maurice and his circle committed themselves to the principles of Socialism which Headlam espoused. It has been said of Maurice, Kingsley, Ludlow, and Hughes that "the one thing they never did was to commit themselves to the growing working class movement of Britain".[32] While some may find this a misleading judgement, it is no doubt true that their chief significance lies in their theological approach which made possible the formation of a soundly based Christian Socialism by men of Headlam's generation. For it is clear that before Maurice the Oxford Tractarians drew hardly any conclusions for social policy from their doctrine. Only Pusey was prepared even to warn of the danger of riches.[33] It was the fusion of Anglo-Catholicism with the theology of Maurice which led to the Social Catholicism of later years, which was to become embodied, albeit in a modified form, in the Christendom Group.

Sacramentalism was at the heart of Headlam's social theology. He saw the ritual of liturgical worship as embodying the most explosive social and political doctrine. A church full of men and women taking their part in the Mass and worshipping Christ the Emancipator would be a greater power for the conversion of London than all the missions and other agencies.[34] One Evangelical suggested (scornfully) that the *Church Reformer*'s motto ought to be "The Mass and the Masses".[35] For the Socialism of Headlam and the Guild drew its power from its sacramental life and doctrine. The Guild held that "the great Sacraments of the Church, but especially that Sacrament which we call the Lord's Supper, the Holy Eucharist, the Holy Communion, or the Mass, are powerful for working this social and secular salvation".[36] Headlam longed for the restoration of the one great Christian service to its proper place in every church in England.

> We have from the beginning in this Guild, and rightly, connected the restoration of the Mass to its proper place with our secular and political work: our Sacramentalism with our Socialism ... we are Socialists because we are Sacramentarians.[37]

Headlam made no bones about this uncompromising sacramentalism:

> Now we of the Guild of St Matthew ... say that that [i.e. the Church's] work cannot progress unless both the Church's sacraments and doctrines are maintained in their fullest strength and efficiency.... We are not true to ourselves, not true to doubting humanity, if we do not maintain the Church's sacraments and doctrines in their fullest strength and efficiency.[38]

The Lord's Supper he saw as "the Feast of National Emancipation", "the Great Emancipator's Supper", "the service which tells of brotherhood, solidarity, co-operation". "Now it is to this idea of international brotherhood," he wrote, "that the word Mass specially bears witness."[39] He realized that the Holy Sacrifice had effects upon the whole world, and beyond this world upon the souls in Paradise.

> I conclude therefore by reminding you that the Sacrifice which we offer is of Redemption for *all* mankind, not only of the pious few who may come to take their part in it. And so the importance of offering that Sacrifice for the dead is not only of private and individual value, but it is essential for the getting rid of dark narrow notions about God which too often have been current. It is impossible for those terrible denials of our Lord's great statement "I, if I be lifted up, will draw *all* men unto Me" to survive when the Host is elevated for the dead as well as for the living.[40]

One of the finest expositions of the social significance of liturgy was Headlam's statement before the Royal Commission on Ecclesiastical Discipline (1904–6). Evidence had been given of illegalities in his celebration of the Eucharist at St Margaret's-on-Thames. He appeared before Sir Michael Hicks-Beach and Archbishop Davidson, and, after apologizing for having a primatial cross carried before him (by a music-hall manager!), he delivered a vigorous defence of his actions. Thus on the Confiteor he said: "I was confess-

ing my sins to them in accordance with the Apostolic injunction—
they were not priests; one is in a builder's merchant's office, the
other, I believe, is a coal merchant, and the two men, simple laymen
as they are, had the audacity to ask Almighty God to have mercy
upon me, forgive me my sins, and bring me to everlasting life."
On the last Gospel, he said: "The reporter is right when he says
that I read [it] to myself and genuflected thereat . . . when I read to
myself the words which are the centre of all life and civilization,
which abolish all class distinctions and unbrotherly monopolies, 'the
Word was made flesh'. The most stupendous fact in history! I
acknowledge that it brought me to my knees." But it was his final
judgement on the Commission itself which was devastating: "My
main object in appearing before you is to submit that these little
meticulous details are not matters which demand Ecclesiastical
Discipline one way or the other, they simply want a little good feeling and common sense. Ecclesiastical Discipline should be directed
against the *real disorders in the Church; these disorders are social
and industrial and not ritual, and they are terrible.*"[41]

The Mass and Catholic worship were revolutionary in their social
demands. Headlam repeated these sentiments over and over again.
He was certain that "a Socialist is not doing his best for the spread
of Socialism unless he is a thorough Catholic Churchman",[42] and
that a quiet parish priest who attended diligently to the sacraments
and doctrines of the Church was doing more for the Socialist cause
than the most brilliant lecturer or pamphleteer. For the Church itself
was "the Socialistic community which Jesus Christ founded",[43]
"the organ of the Kingdom of Heaven upon earth".[44] He dismissed
as irrelevant the accusation that churchmen had been and still were
violently anti-social in their conduct and teaching. What mattered
was whether the basis, the constitution, the essential brotherhood
documents of the Church were or were not in favour of co-operative
brotherhood and against anarchic competition. And he never tired
of pointing out that "the character . . . of the Christian Church is
distinctly and essentially democratic".[45]

It was his conviction that all men were called into this great
brotherhood which formed Headlam's approach to the issue of infant baptism. He believed that "the Priest, no matter how narrow
his teaching may be, is bound to baptize every child brought to him,
simply because he is a human being".[46] Baptism was the sacrament
of equality. Headlam saw his attitude to baptism as exposing in its

acutest form the fundamental difference between the Church and the sects.

In the teeth of those sects which insist on conversion or on intelligent appreciation of Christian doctrine as a preliminary to Baptism; in the teeth of those disloyal Churchmen who would refuse Baptism to those children whose homes and environment are such that they are certain not to be properly brought up; in the teeth of those emotional missionising clergy who practically deny that the baptized, simply because they are baptized, are regenerate, are children of grace, are united to Jesus, are present inheritors of the Kingdom of Heaven, the Church insists that infants shall be baptized. Could you possibly conceive a better witness than this against sin and for humanity.[47]

Infant baptism was the surest safeguard against exclusiveness and the sectarian mentality which Headlam saw to be subversive both of Catholicism and of Socialism.

Nothing distressed Headlam more than the perversion of the Church's doctrinal and liturgical formularies in the defence of injustice and reaction. It was, for instance, claimed during the lock-out of the agricultural labourers that the low condition of the workers was in part due to the teaching of the Catechism about submissiveness. Headlam soon stressed that the Catechism spoke of "that state of life into which it *shall* please God to call him", not "*has* pleased", thus encouraging, as he said, "a divine discontent". Submission was called for, not to the higher classes, but to one's *betters*. In fact, he argued, the Catechism was "a most important document against oppression and for liberty".[48] But the rot had spread further, for Christians had not only used particular formularies in an evil sense. They had warped major doctrines. In a lecture to the East London Secular Society in 1876 he drew attention to "popular mistakes" about the doctrines of atonement, inspiration, punishment, heaven, science, priestcraft, and the Word of God.[49]

Headlam's spirituality was deeply Catholic, rooted in the sacraments and the divine office. A note in the *Church Reformer* for 1894 welcomed the *English Missal* and urged its readers to see that their churches had it.

Not a book on ceremonial with the Mass thrown in nor a plain copy of the Prayer Book service with a high church exterior, nor a volume with the English and Scotch Office sandwiched with the Office of 1549 to the confusion of the faith, nor a garbled and ineligible altar card. All these we have known and lamented, till we had come sorrowfully to the conclusion that the English priests who desired to say Mass as the Church directs were so few that no publisher could be tempted to make the venture.[50]

His personal prayer showed a strong devotion to our Lady. "By cultivating a real reverence for the Blessed Virgin Mary", he said, "you are helping to make the Church once more, and more fully than ever, the great secular society." "I regularly say the 'Hail Mary' ", he pointed out on another occasion, "and I strongly advise you to do the same."[51] Mary's role in the Church was of the utmost importance, for he saw the end of neglect of her to be individualism. A narrow religion, a cruel theology, a vindictive eschatology were impossible for those with whom Mary was a real power. The cultus of our Lady he saw as the most important of Catholic rights and privileges.

Liturgy was dynamic to him. His comments on the much neglected Commination Service were penetrating:

> The Commination itself, if "the general sentences of God's cursing" were brought practically home to people, must either result in a huge increase of Christian Socialism, crowded meetings in the west-end in support of Mr George, and an earnest attempt to get the workers a full share of the profits resulting from their work; or else in a large number of rich and aristocratic people leaving the Church.[52]

He had a similar view of the Commandments. They were glorious and emancipating, the commands of One who worked a great political deliverance, who led a horde of slaves out on strike against their masters, and educated them into a great nation.

Schism was abhorrent to him, and he hated dissent.

> Indeed, if it were not for the Dissenters and their middle-class adherents there would be but very little opposition to the Church's work.... The Secularists do not effectively oppose, for the Church has proved that what is secular is sacred. The Socialists do not oppose, for the Church is distinctly pledged to Socialism. It is Dissent which chiefly hinders the spread of this secular socialistic Society. It is Dissent which prevents the Church from being a strong united body in each parish and diocese for the subjugation of the proud, the mighty, and the rich, for the exaltation of Christ, for the deliverance of the workers.[53]

He once wrote of "Wesleyans, Baptists, Congregationalists, Salvation Army Officers". "They are, undoubtedly, all of them committing the sin of schism; a terrible sin, an individualistic, anti-democratic sin."[54] By separating from the Church of the nation and forming societies based on opinion or character instead of humanity, such men were denying the sacredness of the national life. More than this, by thinking that the churches should be founded on opinion and not on humanity, the sects tended to view beautiful and human things as somehow wrong. They thus became Puritan as well as anti-national, and Puritanism to Headlam was a great evil.

To him, Catholicism involved the redemption of the created world at every point, and, holding to this ideal, he was saved from the danger of concentrating attention only on the ultimate vision of the Kingdom and to the neglect of the immediate tasks. The new world was to be built within the structures of the old, within the structures of parish, district, and borough. It was wrong, he stressed, to use big phrases, whether religious or socialistic, about God's Kingdom coming, or about the universal brotherhood, or about the complete emancipation of the workers from the tyranny of the capitalist and the landlord, unless it was realized that a common saved, or a playground made, or a swimming bath built, or a footpath preserved, by means of the united action of the parishioners and maintained out of the common purse, were partial realizations of the ideas which the big phrases conveyed.[55]

The relationship of Headlam to his bishops was affected by numerous factors. Historically, it was his enthusiasm for Maurice which instilled doubts into the mind of Bishop Jackson and led to a delay in his ordination to the priesthood. But it was the question of theatres and, in particular, the ballet, which led to the most serious and prolonged clash with episcopal authority. Bishop Jackson had been sent a copy of Headlam's lecture on "Theatres and Music Halls". His response was horror. "Not for the first time has it caused me to ask pardon of our great Master if I erred, as I think I did, in admitting you to the ministry." He went on, "But I do pray earnestly that you may not have to meet before the Judgment Seat those whom your encouragement first led to places where they lost the blush of shame and took the first downward step towards vice and misery."[56] Headlam, never the most tactful of mortals, decided that he should publish in pamphlet form not only the lecture but also the Bishop's letter and other correspondence. It was the end of his Bethnal Green career.

The whole issue of the stage was to burst up again when Frederick Temple succeeded Jackson as Bishop of London. The Church and

Stage Guild had then been in existence for six years, and Ben Greet had suggested that Dr Temple should be invited to one of its meetings in Drury Lane. Temple declined, but agreed to see Headlam, who was honorary secretary, and at the interview he proceeded to denounce the stage, and especially the ballet, with fervour. To Temple, the ballet was a cause of terrible harm to young men. He was particularly concerned about the length of ballerinas' skirts, which he considered indecent. The interview with Headlam was long, but the Bishop remained unimpressed. "As well have a Church and Publican Guild as a Church and Stage Guild. Not that individual publicans *and even barmaids* might not be very good people."

It was not surprising, therefore, that when Headlam appealed to Temple for a licence, the answer was negative.

> The Bishop of London regrets that Mr Stewart D. Headlam appears to him to be doing serious mischief, and holding that opinion, the Bishop is not able to give Mr Headlam facilities for doing more mischief.

His chief offence was, of course, "a tendency to encourage young men and young women to be frequent spectators of ballet dancing". Headlam's reply was scathing and sarcastic.

> How ridiculous the Bishop's new ecclesiastical test is. In order to obtain a licence in his Diocese the poor curate has not only to form a correct opinion on the dress proper for ballet dancing—presumably without seeing a Ballet, for that would lead him into temptation— but also to persuade the ladies to adopt the dress he has selected. This opens altogether a new sphere for the Professors of Pastoral Theology.[57]

It was not until 1898 when Mandell Creighton was Bishop of London that the ban on Headlam was removed.

The Church and Stage Guild had been founded on 30 May 1879. As far back as the early days of his curacy at Drury Lane, Headlam had been disturbed by the prejudice within the Church against the theatre, and the controversy sparked off by his notorious lecture only made him more determined to fight the prejudice. The immediate idea of a guild came from Mrs Nina Cole. Headlam became the honorary secretary and its first chairman was Mark Marsden. Within a year it had 470 members. Meetings were held monthly, and there were two dances each year at St James's Hall to which came dancers from the Empire and the Alhambra. The dances lasted till 4.30 a.m. Headlam later gave dances at his house in Upper Bedford Place. Relations with the Alhambra management were particularly cordial. Headlam described the purpose of the Guild:

> The objects of the Guild were to break down the prejudice against theatres, actors, music-hall artists, stage-singers and dancers, in those days only too common among Churchmen; to promote social and religious sympathy between Church and Stage; to vindicate the worthiness of acting and dancing as arts, no less capable of being dedicated to God's service than any other work of man conscientiously pursued; and to claim for religious persons the right to take part in theatrical amusements, whether as performers or spectators. There was one thing we always repudiated as a Guild, and that was having any idea of undertaking a mission to the dramatic profession. Such a notion would have seemed to us an impertinence. Rather, we used to say, should there be a mission among the clergy to teach them a right understanding of the stage and the player, and to preach to some of them a broader charity.[58]

Further light is thrown upon his ideal in forming the Guild by his four points in reply to the Bishop of London's criticisms in 1877. They express a whole dimension in theology.

1. I hold it as an eternal truth that the Incarnation and Real Presence of Jesus Christ sanctifies all human things, not excluding human passion, mirth, and beauty, and in this firm conviction I am constantly strengthened by the fact that so many regular and devout communicants, both here and elsewhere, enjoy heartily the drama, music and dancing.

2. I hold that the clergy are bound as officers of the Christian Church, to consider well the question of Public Amusements: and while facing the fact that there are evils connected with theatres and music-halls, to use their influence to support what is good in them, and to rid them of those who misuse them.

3. I hold that the religious world has done a grievous wrong in refusing to recognize the calling of a Dancer or Public Amuser as a virtuous and honourable one. For this reason I have spoken at length in my lecture of the goodness and public usefulness of such callings, and have not confined myself to the praise of tragedy, or Shakespeare.

4. That some coarse and low people frequent Music Halls I do not attempt to deny: but one who has seen as much as I have of the conditions under which, in our present social state, certain classes of the population are forced to live, knows better than to put down their

want of culture or their evil living to the account of the Music Hall Manager. . . .[59]

Above all, Headlam insisted that his activity within the field of the theatre was rooted in theology. "The Athanasian Creed", he said, "teaches us that the manhood has been taken into God; that it is necessary to everlasting salvation that we believe rightly the incarnation of our Lord Jesus Christ; that the Holy Spirit is incomprehensible, immense, boundless in His influence. These are the theological facts on which I base my vindication of the stage."[60] Sound theology was indispensable to his whole approach to the world, and it was supremely through the other guild, the Guild of St Matthew, that Headlam's theological outlook found expression.

3

The Guild of St Matthew was essentially a Catholic body, rooted in Catholic Orthodoxy and in the sacramental life of the Church. It saw the main function of the Church to be the realization on earth of the Kingdom of Heaven.[61] The mission of Christ was to bring about the reconciliation of heaven and earth, and to liberate humanity from all sin and oppression. So he was "the Carpenter of Nazareth, the Divine Revolutionist, the Emancipator of the Oppressed, the Founder of the Democratic Church".[62] Those who were admitted into the Body of Christ were present inheritors, not future heirs, of the Kingdom. But it was not only within the visible Church that the rule of Christ was manifested: "The revolutionary Socialist of Galilee is the force which rules the world."[63]

It was Frederick Verinder who, more than any other single person, gave the Guild's particular concerns a biblical and theological basis. The Guild, and Verinder himself, saw the key issue for social theology to be the ownership of land. In his works, Verinder stressed that the Mosaic Law was alien to the whole development of the landlord system. "The principle which underlies the Mosaic agrarian legislation is absolutely fatal to what we know as landlordism. Jehovah is the only landlord; the land is His because He and none other created it: all men are his tenants."[64] The Hebrew did not have to pay a landlord for permission to till the soil, for the law forbade landlordism: no capitalist could levy a tax upon him for the use of the instruments of production, for manufacture had hardly an existence. There was, moreover, no privileged class to support in idleness and luxury, and no indirect taxes to be paid on food and drink. Even in the vastly more complicated problem of modern industrial organization, Verinder saw, the land question was fundamental. In England, the landlord, while levying his rent-tax upon capitalists and workers alike, actually created the conditions which enabled the former to fleece the latter. Landlordism was responsible for that continued migration of population into the towns, to which the ever-increasing bitterness of competition for work was due. The abolition of landlordism would lessen this bitterness which was the life-blood of the capitalist system. But for the Guild the demand for the ending of the landlord system was basically a theological demand: "Their position—their very existence as landlords—is grossly immoral."[65]

Verinder's thought on land doctrine is summarized in a small volume *My Neighbour's Landmark*,[66] and this can be taken as a characteristic expression of the theology adopted by Headlam and the Guild. Verinder argued here that the principles of the Hebrew land laws were fatal to the idea of private property in land. The earth belonged to God, he was the only Landlord, and God had given the use of the land to all generations of man. The equal division of land gave to each family of Israel direct access to the soil, so that, by his own labour under the Law, the Israelite could produce all that he needed. The Landmark set the seal upon these rights, and the Year of Jubilee was provided to secure the restoration of equal access in each generation. The Year of Jubilee was in fact the climax of a great cycle of Sabbatical periods: "The whole series of Sabbatical holidays were threaded on one string and formed so many links in the chain of a just agrarian system."[67]

The social theology of the Guild demands a closer attention than has been given to it. There were writers who accused the Guild of going beyond the teaching of Maurice and Kingsley, but Headlam would reply by saying that the principles which Maurice had brought to bear upon Chartism, co-operation, and the question of *his* time could only land the Guild where it now stood with regard to contemporary questions. And here the significance of the Guild lay in its stress on the land. Headlam said, "We feel that the LAND is the point at which the attack must be begun."

Were the land nationalized, the return of the workers to the land would relieve the congestion of the population in our great towns which at present enables the ground landlord and the capitalist alike to take advantage of competition for their own benefit. We think therefore that those are the best Socialists who concentrate their attention on the fundamental evil by which all others stand or fall.

For its time this was very advanced thinking, and many indeed saw the concern for "land reform" to be obsessive. "The *Church Reformer* is sometimes blamed for the large proportion of space which it gives to the consideration of the Land Question, and for the persistency with which the restoration to the people of the value which they have given to the land is advocated in its columns", the journal observed in 1885.[68] Indeed, the following year a correspondent complained that "the attempt to whitewash Music Halls, the alliance with foul-mouthed Secularists, and the advocacy of Utopian schemes of Land Law Reform are not the kind of Church reforms in which I take much interest."[69] But to Headlam and the Guild, private ownership of the land was the fundamental cause of social evil, for it embodied that individualism and isolation from God which was the effect of the Fall. The abolition of private ownership and its replacement by a just land system was therefore of the utmost theological and political importance. "The restoration to the people of the whole of the value which they have given to the land . . . should, I take it, be the primary object of all Socialists."[70]

At the heart of the Guild's theology of land was the theme of the Year of Jubilee, the Acceptable Year of the Lord. Thus the achievement of common ownership was firmly set within the sphere of redemption, the political aspect of that cosmic process by which Christ was restoring all things to himself. When, on Trinity Sunday, 20 June 1886, Queen Victoria began the fiftieth year of her reign, the *Church Reformer* hailed the day with these stirring words:

> The *Queen's* Jubilee is good; but the *People's* Jubilee is better. Why may not the year upon which we now enter be the Jubilee of both Queen and People?
> For the Jubilee of the Hebrews, as ordained by the great statesman, whom God for their deliverance raised up and inspired, was the Jubilee of a whole People; and its observance was founded upon, and was expressly designed to conserve, a divinely ordained system of Land Nationalization.[71]

It continued:

"Liberty throughout all the land unto all the inhabitants thereof":
That is the ideal of a true Year of Jubilee. Liberty to the wage-slaves;
liberty to the landless English labourer; liberty to the landlord-ridden
Irish people; restoration to the disinherited of their share in the land
which the Lord their God giveth them, and of which the injustice
of their brother man has despoiled them.

Thomas Hancock described the Jubilee as "a great national sacrament of regeneration, a new birth of the secular Commonwealth
by which it returned to the image of the eternal Kingdom of God
after which it had been originally constituted".[72]

But the effects of the Guild remained largely intellectual. "It
never showed the slightest sign of becoming a popular society or of
attracting the interest of the working classes".[73] Mr Reckitt attributes
its limited influence in part to its "reliance on shock tactics and its
identification with a mood of 'revolutionary defiance' where a more
persuasive outlook might have succeeded".[74] But, clearly, as one
of its members admitted, it "was not destined to convert the Church
of England to Socialism or anything like it".[75] Its indirect effects
should not be underrated. Dr Inglis has shown how there was a
marked change in the attitude of English Christians towards social
issues after about 1890. Before that, even the Tractarians "still saw
the poor as individual souls to be saved and not as members of a
society to be transformed".[76] The Guild certainly helped to thrust the
problem of Socialism upon the Church, and its "shock tactics" ought
not to be deplored. Nothing less than shock tactics could have
shaken a Church which for the large part of the century remained,
like Bunting's Methodists, "as much opposed to democracy as to
sin", and given it a concern for the social order. At least by 1888,
the respectable Canon Fremantle could write that "the time is past,
I think, when socialism should be spoken of merely as 'an enemy' ".[77]
The real weakness of the Guild was pinpointed, in somewhat
exaggerated form, years later by Conrad Noel. He claimed that "beyond a general support of the working-class movement, it confined
itself to land reform and was dominated by the teaching of Henry
George".[78] The first part of this claim is nonsense, but it is true that
the Guild was tied too much and too uncritically to George's
theories. So it moved ominously towards the very sectarian mentality which its later leader had denounced so vehemently in earlier
years.

4

I have devoted most of this essay to the discussion of Headlam's general theology and religious position. But it would be wrong to omit reference to the many-sidedness of his activity, and so it is appropriate to end with some observations on Headlam as a man of action in Church and society. The most important vehicle for the expression of his position and that of his disciples on current issues was the *Church Reformer* which Bernard Shaw once described as "one of the best of the Socialist journals of that day". Headlam was its editor and leader-writer for twelve years, and by 1895 he estimated that he had spent around £110 a year on it. But it never succeeded in reaching a very large public. Described as "an organ of Christian Socialism and Church Reform", it had part of Blake's "Jerusalem" as its motto.

The *Church Reformer* concerned itself with wider issues than mere changes in the ecclesiastical structure, but it did deal at length with "church reform". Certainly by the end of 1887, Headlam felt that the time had come for the Guild of St Matthew to do what it could towards the abolition of the system of appointment of bishops and beneficed clergy. Headlam said in a sermon at St Luke's, Kentish Town, on 23 September 1894:

> We feel that the best traditions of the Church are being violated and that the whole principle on which the Church is founded is being contradicted by the way in which at present the Church in each parish is allowed no voice in choosing its parish priests. The patron we know in old times was at first the military and then the legal defender of the Church's rights, and as such of course did good and necessary work, but now all that is done by the State, which protects the Church and all other institutions from violent or illegal encroachments. Therefore we feel that the patron is useless and that his claim to force the priest on the parish is a violation of the rights of the Church in the parish. . . .[79]

But there was no issue of social significance which was regarded as outside the sphere of the *Church Reformer*. Teetotalism soon incurred the wrath of Headlam's pen. To him, the temperance campaign was simply diverting attention from the key social problem, that of land reform. "The 'Drink Question' ", he conceded, "has indeed all the vital social importance which teetotallers claim for it but not for the reasons which they usually put forward. The greatest social question—we had almost said the only social question —is the Land Question, to which the housing question and the drink question and the taxation question all add up."[80] In the same way, he viewed the concern about vice and prostitution as isolating one facet of the wholesale corruption of society. It was absurd to express horror at sexual vice whilst acquiescing in a vicious economic and social system. So when in 1885 the *Pall Mall Gazette* printed a series of "revelations" entitled "The Maiden Tribute of Modern Babylon", the Council of the Guild of St Matthew met and passed the following resolution:

> That in the opinion of this Council the recent "disclosures" show that it is the duty of all Churchmen
>
> 1. To support the Criminal Law Amendment Bill now before Parliament, at least so far as the raising of the age up to which girls are protected is concerned; while opposing the clauses which confer additional power over women upon the police;
>
> 2. To support such measures as will give women a voice in the making of the laws under which they and their children live;
>
> 3. To encourage parents and others to give plain teaching to their children on sexual matters;
>
> 4. To promote all such measures of social reform as shall tend to get rid of the tyranny of wealth over poverty, which is the main cause of the special crimes now brought to light.[81]

The *Church Reformer's* scope and concern was as wide as Headlam's. In the early days, he recalled being told "that it was hopeless to attempt to support Mr Bradlaugh, the Ballet, Socialism, Sacramentalism, and the Cultus of our Lady all together".[82] But he saw such a combination as perfectly consistent, indeed as a necessary result of the fact that the incarnate Lord had sanctified the whole of human life. The *Church Reformer* came to an end in September 1895 for purely financial reasons. It was impossible to run the magazine practically without advertisements, and if its death had a moral, it was the excessive dangers of the influence of advertising over the press.

A major sphere of Headlam's activity was education, and he was particularly concerned about the place of the Bible in the schools—

that is, about the teaching of the Bible *as literature*. Dogma he regarded as the business of the Church, not of the schools. Undenominational teaching degraded both religion and literature. In theory, the London School Board rejected all forms of dogma, but there was the dogma, in Headlam's view a most pernicious one, which lay behind much of their religious teaching—the dogma that the Bible and the Bible alone is the religion of Protestants. This belief, he saw, was irrational and unintelligent, and substituted an infallible book for the life of the Church. "The Church existed long before the Bible and could go on without the Bible." He did, however, hold that "the Bible left to itself leads inevitably to the Catholic Church" and that this was why many were afraid of it, and would like to take it out of the schools. Headlam insisted that there should be Bible teaching in schools, but that "if the Bible is to be taught at all in the Public Schools, there must be no treating it as the infallible Word of God".[83] Indeed, he was prepared to admit that perhaps nothing would help more to capture the Church for the people than the compelling of the State to end its impertinent attempt to teach religion.

Headlam was a revolutionary. For this reason he was almost as much a misfit in the circles of the Fabians, "the patron saints of reformism",[84] as he was in those of conventional religion. He had very little historical perspective, and he often lacked a sense of balance. But in his approach to society, to what modern writers tautologically describe as the "secular age", he was way in advance of his time. Many of the battles which Headlam fought are still being fought; the Establishment in the Church of England is still in many ways in a pre-Headlam condition. But for much of his time even he was addressing an in-group, and Christian Socialism was to remain very much a sectarian group on the fringes both of the Church and of the working-class movement. This has been an appalling tragedy for which Headlam must share very little of the blame. His Christianity was perhaps more sound and orthodox than his Socialism, which was dominated by the somewhat esoteric teachings of George. Yet he saw the whole of his witness as a unity. And so when one of his acquaintances once asked him, "How is our old friend who believes in the Mass, the Ballet and the Single Tax?", he replied, "Yes, these have been my preoccupations."

NOTES

1. F. G. Bettany, *Stewart Headlam: A Biography* (John Murray 1926), pp. 7, 12.

2. Ibid., pp. 20, 24, 25.

3. Ibid., p. 28.

4. G. C. Binyon, *The Christian Socialist Movement in England* (S.P.C.K. 1931), p. 119.

5. *The Guild of St. Matthew* (1890).

6. M. B. Reckitt, *Faith and Society* (Longmans 1932), p. 83.

7. Bettany, op. cit., p. 76.

8. S. D. Headlam, *Priestcraft and Progress* (John Hodges, London 1878), p. 81.

9. *The Service of Humanity* (John Hodges, London 1882), pp. 2–3.

10. Bettany, op. cit., p. 50.

11. Ibid., p. 55.

12. Ibid., pp. 60–1.

13. Ibid., pp. 53, 63.

14. Ibid., pp. 51–2.

15. *Church Reformer*, Vol. IV, No 4 (15 April 1885), p. 86.

16. Ibid., Vol. V, No. 4 (April 1886), p. 76.

17. *Priestcraft and Progress* (1878), p. 84.

18. *Church Reformer*, Vol. X, No. 3 (March 1891), p. 47; Vol. XIV, No. 1 (January 1895), p. 3.

19. Bettany, op. cit., p. 64.

20. Ibid., pp. 73–4.

21. Stephen Liberty, "Stewart Duckworth Headlam, I", in *Christendom*, Vol. XV, No. 72 (December 1948), p. 269.

22. *The Laws of Eternal Life* (London 1905), p. 9.

23. *The Socialist's Church* (London 1907), p. 29.

24. J. G. Adderley in *The Commonwealth*, December 1926, cited in Reckitt, op. cit., p. 86.

25. *Some Old Words About the War* (1915), pp. 5, 6.

26. Ibid., p. 16.

27. Lord Wemyss once described Headlam in the Lords as a Jesuit. His comment was based on a curious report in the journal *Jus,* and the Editor, in a letter of apology, wrote: "Lord Wemyss forwards to me your letter to him of the 16th inst.; from which I gather that it is incorrect to describe you as a member of the Society of Jesus. . . . I wrote the paragraph myself and I am afraid I confounded the said Society with another of which I was told you were a member—I think it was the Society of the Holy Cross. I know nothing of either Society, and trust that the mistake imputed nothing of an objectionable character" (*Church Reformer,* Vol. VI, No. 9 (September 1887), pp. 205–6.

28. *Church Reformer,* Vol. IV, No. 3 (16 March 1885), p. 49.

29. Cited in *Church Reformer,* Vol. V, No. 10 (October 1886), pp. 236–7.

30. Ibid., Vol. IX, No. 9 (September 1890), p. 197.

31. Stephen Liberty, op. cit., pp. 269, 273; Binyon, op. cit., p. 104.

32. Stanley G. Evans, *The Social Hope of the Christian Church* (Hodder 1965), pp. 153–4.

33. A striking exception to this, however, can be found in W. G. Ward's once-famous book *The Ideal of a Christian Church,* published in 1844, four years before Maurice, Ludlow, and Kingsley came together, which has been described as "England's first volume of catholic sociology".

34. Annual Address to the Guild of St. Matthew, 23 September 1889 (*Church Reformer,* Vol. VIII, No. 10 (October 1889), p. 220).

35. Ibid., Vol. IX, No. 3 (March 1890), p. 54.

36. S. D. Headlam, "The Guild of St Matthew: An Appeal to Churchmen", *Church Reformer,* Vol. IX, No. 11 (November 1890), p. 244.

37. Ibid., Vol. X, No. 10 (October 1891), p. 221.

38. S. D. Headlam, "The Need for Tangible Sacraments and Definite Doctrines", ibid., Vol. XI, No. 1 (January 1892), pp. 9, 10.

39. S. D. Headlam, *The Meaning of the Mass* (S. C. Brown, Langham and Co., Ltd. 1905), pp. 18, 20, 29, 44.

40. Ibid., p. 14.

41. Cited by Stephen Liberty, "Stewart Duckworth Headlam, II", in *Christendom,* Vol. XV, No. 73 (March 1949), pp. 12–13.

42. "Socialism, Liberty and the Church", in *Church Reformer,* Vol. XIV, No. 10 (October 1895), p. 222.

43. *The Laws of Eternal Life,* p. 11.

44. *The Socialist's Church,* p. 22.

45. Cited by Binyon, op. cit., p. 120.

46. *The Laws of Eternal Life*, p. 14.

47. Ibid., p. 68.

48. *The Church Catechism and the Emancipation of Labour* (London N.D.), p. 3.

49. "Some Popular Mistakes About the Church's Teaching", in *Priestcraft and Progress*, pp. 81–97.

50. *Church Reformer*, Vol. XIII, No. 12 (December 1894), p. 268.

51. *The Service of Humanity*, p. 58; *The Meaning of the Mass*, p. 41. Cf. "The Holy Rosary", in *Church Reformer*, Vol. X, No. 8 (August 1891), pp. 71–2; "A May Address to the Union of the Holy Rosary", ibid., Vol. XI, No. 7 (July 1892), pp. 152–4.

52. *Church Reformer*, Vol. III, No. 3 (15 March 1884), p. 49.

53. Ibid., Vol. X, No. 2 (February 1891), p. 27.

54. Ibid., Vol. XI, No. 10 (October 1892), p. 220.

55. Ibid., Vol. XIII, No. 10 (October 1894), p. 219.

56. Cited in *Church Reformer*, Vol. IV, No. 10 (October 1885), p. 236.

57. Ibid., Vol. VI, No. 9 (September 1887), pp. 193–5.

58. Cited by Bettany, op. cit., pp. 101–2.

59. *Church Reformer*, Vol. IV, No. 10 (15 October 1885), pp. 236 ff.

60. *The Service of Humanity*, p. 16.

61. *Church Reformer*, Vol. XIV, No. 10 (October 1895), p. 219.

62. S. D. Headlam, *Lessons from the Cross* (London, 2nd edn 1892), p. 18.

63. *The Laws of Eternal Life*, p. 27.

64. Frederick Verinder, "The Bible and the Land Question", in *Church Reformer*, Vol. V, No. 7 (15 July 1885), p. 152.

65. S. D. Headlam, "The Land for the People", ibid., Vol. VI, No. 8 (August 1887), p. 177.

66. Frederick Verinder, *My Neighbour's Landmark* (Andrew Melrose, London 1911).

67. Ibid., p. 69.

68. *Church Reformer*, Vol. IV, No. 6 (15 June 1885), p. 129.

69. Ibid, Vol. V, No. 9 (September 1886), p. 196.

70. Ibid., Vol. VI, No. 8 (August 1887), p. 176.

71. Ibid., Vol. V, No. 7 (July 1886), p. 146. It should be noted that Headlam was not a monarchist. He held that "the Hebrew Prophet's protest again

monarchy is as necessary, now as ever, and on the same grounds, viz., that under a monarchy bishops become flunkeys", but he felt that "the time is not yet ripe for a Republic in England" (ibid., Vol. VI, No. 7 (July 1887), p. 145; No. 6 (June 1887), p. 122). He believed that "a democratic Republic is the Christian ideal of government" (ibid., Vol. XI, No. 2 (February 1892), p. 27), and accepted "the divine right of insurrection".

72. Thomas Hancock, "The Jubilee or Obligatory Revolution in the Commonwealth of Israel", ibid., Vol. VI, No. 8 (August 1887), p. 185.

73. M. B. Reckitt, *Maurice to Temple* (Faber, 1947), p. 135.

74. Ibid., p. 210.

75. J. G. Adderley, *Slums and Society,* p. 204.

76. K. S. Inglis, *Churches and the Working Classes in Victorian England* (Routledge, 1963), p. 251.

77. W. H. Fremantle, *The Present Work of the Anglican Communion* (1888), p. 27.

78. Conrad Noel, *An Autobiography* (1945), p. 60.

79. *Church Reformer*, Vol. XIII, No. 10 (October 1894), p. 231.

80. Ibid., Vol. IV, No. 5 (15 May 1885), p. 102.

81. Ibid., Vol. IV, No. 8 (15 August 1885), p. 186.

82. Ibid., Vol. XIV, No. 1 (January 1895), p. 3.

83. S. D. Headlam, *The Place of the Bible in Secular Education* (London 1903), pp. 12, 19; *The Socialist's Church*, p. 32.

84. E. J. Hobsbawm, *Labouring Men* (1964), p. 255.

Charles Marson, 1859–1914 and the Real Disorders of the Church

MAURICE B. RECKITT

I

The name of Charles Marson is not one that is now at all widely remembered. This is both an injustice and a misfortune, for few more vigorous personalities have appeared in this century in the Church of England, of which he was at once a devoted lover and an astringent critic. When the present writer mentioned his name to perhaps the most wise and perceptive prelate on the bench of bishops, he replied at once and with enthusiasm, "Ah yes, Huppim and Muppim and Ard." This was not surprising, for no one who has had the good fortune to light upon that excoriating pamphlet is likely to forget it. But he frankly confessed that this was all he knew of the man. Yet the now surely almost incredible defects of much that passed for religious education, both of the Church's children and of their pastors, in the first decade of this century, was far indeed from being the only, or the principal, theme to which Marson devoted his unflagging zeal, zest, and wit. Paul Stacy, one of his disciples, well said of him, "He let light in all round."

Yet that Marson should be so generally forgotten is understandable. Part of his early ministry was spent overseas, and his short, meteoric blaze in metropolitan curacies in the early 1890s was soon succeeded by what proved to be for him a wholly satisfying pastorate in the heart of the west country. His books (save for a few pamphlets) were never widely circulated and are now almost unobtainable; they tended to be either too fiery or (on rural themes) too placid for most readers to welcome or cherish them. This was a man who lived most vividly in the memories of those who knew him best, and these are now dead.

Moreover Marson, dynamic, dogmatic, contentious, had what it is perhaps more justifiable in his than in most cases to describe as the defects of his qualities. He did not suffer those whom he was perhaps too quick to dismiss as fools gladly, or even politely. "He was", wrote his neighbour and close friend, Francis Etherington, in his biographical study, "at no time an easy man to work with. He made great demands on the patience of his friends, for he never quite knew the weight of his own fist or the sharpness of his tongue." His opponents dreaded his mordant wit; even those who were on his side sometimes felt him to be irresponsible in his use of it; while some of his devotees, by their delight in it, too much encouraged him in this direction. "We were content", wrote Scott Holland after his death, "to laugh at his jibes and jokes, and we took him on his lighter and more perilous side; and he, perhaps, allowed us to do so too much, and loved to confound our respectabilities, and to startle our pomposities, and to shock our conventions, and to provoke our silly indignation." "To some," wrote Gilbert Binyon, who well remembered him, "he was extremely attractive, an enchanting soul, a real leader; ... but there may have been others who felt less inclined to join in the shouts of laughter which his writings irresistibly provoke than to wish he dealt with the Bishops and his fellow clergy more in the manner of the Fabians when dealing with capitalist politicians, ignoring their absurdities and prescribing what they ought to do."[1] But anyone less like a typical Fabian than Marson it would have been hard to find, then or now.

Again, the causes he so vigorously espoused were generally highly unpopular then, while they may seem unimportant now because they have so largely become victorious. Dying as he did in the spring of 1914, it is understandable that Marson should seem very much a "pre-war" figure in an age more drastically transformed in half a century than any other in modern history. Why then should he be remembered?

To this we may reply: Why should the Church remember any of her saints? This is no irrelevant rejoinder, if only because Marson in his equal dedication to his priestly and prophetic vocations, in his unfailing courage in the face of adversity and hostility and contempt, and in his self-denying and deeply charitable devotion to the oppressed, the weak, and the simple, manifested throughout his life some truly saintly qualities. But the rejoinder is not irrelevant for a more general reason. The Church remembers her saints not only in due gratitude for the exhibition of that spiritual energy and moral resourcefulness which are so fundamentally a part of what we mean when we speak of holiness, but with more practical considerations in mind. They were "lights of the world in their season", and to recall them and catch illumination from them gives—or ought to give—us when we know enough about them,[2] the sort of encouragement and refreshed initiative which we urgently need for our own day. If our problems are—or often seem to be—vastly different from theirs, they may not be less, and we shall certainly require all the inspiration we can get to stand up to them. One way in which God aids man is by communicating his grace to him though other men, and the lives of the saints are a vital part of the treasury of the Church. "I thank my God on every remembrance of you", we say of those loved but now for a time lost to us. There were not a few who have said this of Charles Marson.

2

What follows here is not, and could not be, a "Life" of Marson, though it owes an incalculable amount to an unpublished biography written by the Reverend Francis M. Etherington thirty or more years ago, which I have been privileged to read.[3] The particular context of this book prevents my doing any sort of justice to this many-sided man, even if space allowed me to do so. It can say little either of the opening or the closing years of his life; of the details of the numerous curacies through which he passed, with singular but significant rapidity, in the early years of his ministry; of his life in South Australia which followed on his first incumbency at home; of his deep reading in the Patristics; of his marriage and family life; of the study of English folk song in which he pioneered the way for Cecil Sharp, or of the regrettable differences that arose between them. We are primarily concerned in this book to recall the witness of four priests, all remarkably versatile men who (with whatever disproportion of emphasis, as some may feel), between the 1880s and the 1930s, saw "the Banner of Christ in the hands of the Socialists", as one of them (Thomas Hancock) proclaimed in a once famous sermon. Marson, born a dozen years after Stewart

Headlam and a similar period before Conrad Noel, provides in some sort a link between them. If it is on this aspect of his life that this essay concentrates, it is not without full realization that its subject was much more than a social, still less a political agitator. Marson never forgot that he was before all things a priest, "one of the obscurer servants of the Catholic Church in England", finding "his position to be satisfactory and joyful, even to the edge of triumph", and his whole drive and inspiration came from this. Nor was he one who, if it could be imagined that he should have found nothing further to agitate about, would have been (as one sometimes feels of "agitators") at a loss to know what to do with his life. For he was, as were many others prominent in the Guild of St Matthew, a Christian Humanist in the truest sense of a term not always very satisfactorily employed. Paul Stacy wrote of him fifteen years after his death:

> I cannot remember any conversation with him that would have been called ordinary; everything he said either informed, arrested, pleased or amused.... From Plato down to fishing and the meaning of plants, or the property of herbs, and multitudes of matters besides, he could speak either from deep and wide scholarship, or from the shrewd and canny knowledge of experience.

It was said of Burke that nobody sheltering from a storm under a tree with him for ten minutes could have gone away without the conviction that here was a remarkable man. Such, it would seem, was the impression that even a chance meeting with Marson would have conveyed—and as we know, often did.

Charles Latimer Marson, the third child and eldest son of a family of eight, was born on 16 March 1859 at Woking, where his father was curate in charge of the parish of St John's. Charles was a family name, but the christening of his child Latimer testifies to the fact that his parents had evangelical sympathies. C.L.M., for all the vigorous Catholicism into which, slowly yet in the end suddenly, he developed, showed no resentment over his second name. He knew Latimer to have been a valiant champion of the oppressed. Moreover, as he characteristically observed of Latimer and his fellow-martyr, "We must not let the folly and ignorance of modern Protestants blind us to the fact these two men were, in many respects, at least as Catholic as their opponents and would probably themselves have burnt their modern admirers with the greatest alacrity."[4]

"The relationship of father and son", Mr Etherington tells us, "was always one of deep affection, with a comradeship that was sustained by their strong sense of humour." Despite the constant friction which developed between them, as the boy went through one iconoclastic phase after another, the parent "did his son the compliment of treating his opposing opinions as worthy of the sword rather than the sneer". His mother was a less attractive character, a stern, unbending Protestant, "of the stuff of which martyrs are made, and not mothers usually", wrote her son. But, he continued,

I learnt from her two things: the vital importance of a creed, whether for good or bad, not only to oneself but to one's whole neighbourhood; and the immense power which one determined Will can wield over us, the mass of irresolute and purposeless folk. I accepted the coercive and negative spirit of such teaching, but utterly refused the positive part of it. I felt nothing but weariness and exasperation when in the company of the "Lord's own".

In fact, after her death when he was nine, and the strength of her will was removed, the influence of her teaching largely contributed to drive him into infidelity. "By the time I was in the Fifth Form I had expanded and snapped the evangelical bond", and he made no objection when others described him as "the atheist". All this, and other youthful extravagances at Oxford, where he matriculated in 1878, no doubt caused his father some distress, but he lived to see his son come through them, to return to the Faith before he left the university, and take orders, under Broad Church influences, in 1882. The old man died, as Vicar of Clevedon, in 1895, the very year in which his son, then aged 36, became a country parson in the same county and diocese as those in which his parent had served for two dozen years.

3

Marson was later to write of himself at Oxford that though he loved the place and made some strong friendships there, he was "extremely unhappy and alternatively reckless and morbid. With an enthusiastic nature, I could find nothing to be enthusiastic about." The pleasures of youthful iconoclasm had ceased to satisfy him, and he wrote at the time, "I believe I shall have to fall back upon religion for comfort." But no form of belief which was not suffused with courage and sincerity, and in touch with the needs of the time, would make an appeal to him, and at first he sought this amid the Broad Churchmen. The chivalry of Bishop Colenso impressed him; "he was the first man who suggested to me that it is possible to be a Christian without being intellectually a coward or a shuffler". A meeting with Dean Stanley, however, provoked less enthusiasm; he was not drawn to his "meagre little liberal creed". Attachment to a creed was the one thing he had found of value in his evangelical upbringing. "The beliefless belief of the liberal", he wrote, "leaves him merely a wanderer in life."

This was no role for Marson. He left Oxford, to plunge into the new systematic grapple with poverty which Samuel Barnett was organizing from St Jude's, Whitechapel, and which was to lead to the establishment of Toynbee Hall. Perhaps he felt then that "those who do the work shall know the doctrine", and he had no doubt that his work was to "battle for the Have Nots against the Haves", though whether as a journalist or as a priest he was not at first quite clear. Arrived in Whitechapel with three close friends from Oxford, in 1881, he found himself ready for ordination in the following year, and equally ready to call himself a Socialist. Taking his title from St Jude's, he remained there for two more years, and he began his ministry in no uncertain mood:

> I know for certain [he declared] that the world can be redeemed by the mere application of Christian principle. I am surfeited with all the middle-class patterings while the poor rot just because we are not brave enough to quarrel with usury, anarchy, competition, swindling, banking, etc.

It is a comprehensive agenda for a crusader, but Marson was never one to set his sights low.

He left Whitechapel in 1884 for a curacy at Petersham. ("You will appreciate what a scoundrel I am to have slid into such a berth as Petersham while London seethes and sloughs in foulness; here the aristocrat flourishes, the poor are trampled and genuine Christianity is unknown.") But he was allowed only a few months to nourish a "guilt complex" in this situation before he was "kicked out by a drove of Tories as a seditious heretic". His "heresy" seems to have proved even more shocking to the pious than his "sedition", and some who wished him well urged (as did Bishop Walsham How in the course of a warm-hearted letter) that he should be "patient and more reticent", dispositions which never came easily to Marson. There were two more brief curacies before he went at the end of 1885 to St Agatha's, Shoreditch, one of the most miserable and poverty-stricken areas in East London at that time. The strains which this imposed on him and the self-denials which he accepted (for despite his "anti-Puritanism" he never shrank from any austerities which he felt to be incumbent on him[5]) resulted in a severe illness which made it clear that, at any rate for a time, he must seek a ministry in the clean air of the countryside. Before 1886 was out, he had accepted the living of Orlestone, a village on the inland edge of Romney Marsh.

The omens might seem to have made this a wholly auspicious appointment. His predecessor in the parish had been George Sarson, a priest of strong character, firm convictions (largely congruous with those of his youthful successor), and great mental gifts—his local nickname was I.G., signifying "Intellectual Giant". Moreover, he was a friend of Stewart Headlam, and it was through Sarson that the new rector was brought into touch with that "bravest of captains, and most skilful of the swordsmen of the Holy Ghost", as Marson was, with characteristic flamboyancy, to describe him a quarter of a century later. Moreover, the patrons of the living, two brothers named Oliver, were Broad Churchmen in the Maurician tradition, "remarkable", we are told, "for their physical grace and their devotion to all that was best in the Liberal culture of the day", and "attracted not only by Marson's liberal religious outlook, but by his personal charm, his informed wit and his abundant vitality". What more could such a parish want of its priest, and what more could this priest want of his parish?

It soon became evident that there were two things which Marson did want and on which he showed himself determined to take an unexpectedly strong line. The first concerned the relation of the villagers to those set over them. Benevolent as the Olivers certainly wished to be towards "their people", in fact their administration was traditionally paternalistic in spirit; and since they seldom resided in the village, this necessarily depended upon a bailiff with whom Marson soon found himself at odds. After but a few months as rector we find him writing to a friend:

My heart aches and burns here at the degradation of village life.
These poor folk of mine are swirking and sweating to produce £1500
a year for one person, and similar sums for others, and their own
children go short and half-clad, and they none of them have time to
read, think, dance, play music or games. They are mere mill-horses.
... Yet these are men and women made in the image of God and co-
heirs with all his children of the earth and the fulness thereof....
They are so tied down that they do not even know what Liberty is.
How can we help them?

It was soon evident that the superficial tranquillity of this rural
spot was going to be considerably disturbed by its dynamic rector,
and such lack of "patience and reticence", not surprisingly, brought
rebuke from his spiritual superior, the Bishop of Dover, who wrote
to him that

the natural fruit of "socialistic tendencies" is painfully visible on the
Continent and to a less extent (as yet) in England. I earnestly hope
that our Church, in our schools and elsewhere, may use both hands
to stem the mischievous current.

It was already clear to Marson within six months of his arrival
at Orlestone that if he was to stay there, he would have a full-scale
battle on his hands, inside the parish and out.

But there was a further factor in the situation which may have
been still more unexpected to the parish and in particular to its
patrons. Marson had arrived there explicitly as a Broad Churchman;
within, it would seem, almost a matter of weeks, he transformed
himself into a vigorous and wholehearted Anglo-Catholic. Previously he had got into trouble through his "liberal" opinions; now
he was challenging a parish with Catholic ones. What was one to
expect next from such a man? Of course there was to be no "next";
Marson in these months at Orlestone had been groping for the final
and secure position which had so far eluded him. There is indeed
some mystery about this apparently so rapid development; what
were the agencies, personal or intellectual, which brought it about
we do not precisely know, for clear as he made the essentials of the
position at which he had arrived, he was never, it seems, very clear
about this. Some have thought that Stewart Headlam's marriage
of Catholic faith and practice to Maurician theology may have been
a primary agency, but Marson can scarcely have had time to get to
know Headlam well or even fully to digest his teaching. But what-

ever brought about the development, it was decisive for all his
future life, and something must at this point be said about it.

4

Chesterton wrote of H. G. Wells (whom he liked better than might
have been expected) in his *Autobiography* that whenever he met
him, "he seemed to be coming from somewhere, rather than going
somewhere".[6] Marson's friends down to this time (say about his 27th
birthday) might have had a similar impression of him. Whatever
ideas he entertained, whatever company he sought out, his choice
was inspired less by a specific desire for action or allegiance than by
some mood of reaction. He was not even consciously exploring; he
was, rather unconsciously and undeliberatedly, exposing himself
to influences on the quality and validity and ultimate claims of
which he was prepared to postpone a clear decision for the time
being. Amid such influences was that of Roman Catholicism. At
Oxford, while he was still slowly emerging from his "infidel" phase,
he attended Benediction and to the horror of some of his family
("Charles is coquetting with the great whore of Babylon", wrote an
aunt), sent an impression of the experience to a newspaper:

> How impressive it is! How utterly subversive of protestant delirium!
> Not so much that the ritual is striking, which it is, but because here
> and here only, rich and poor meet together without the ceremony of
> Sunday clothes and religious fuss. All are equal, all are knit together,
> the sceptic with his doubts, the harlot with her sins, the moral man
> with his virtues, the believer with his creeds and confusions—for once
> merely human.... The Roman Catholic Church is in the deep of the
> ocean of man, "built below the tides of War", serenely unconscious
> of the waves of controversy which stir, clash and foam upon the sur-
> face.

There was in this no hint—and still more no intention—of his
preparing to declare a definite ecclesiastical allegiance. As he said
himself in later life, "he was only trying to make his protestant
public hear the other side". But by the time he reached Orlestone
such a possibility does seem, for however brief a period, to have
presented itself to him. He wrote confidentially to a woman friend
(17.5.86):

You will not cease to love me, I know, wherever the whirl of the time stream takes me, which I think may be to Rome, because Rome calls on men to give up all and follow her, and when you do follow her she knows how to use your wits and strength, whereas this wretched bourgeois Church is all in confusion and sets greyhounds to swim and spaniels to course and her pugs to bait bulls and mastiffs to be nursed by gentlewomen.

Yet this surely is the language of frustration rather than of spiritual travail and intellectual conflict. Marson was feeling himself to be a square peg in a round hole and the victim of a "bourgeois" Church; all had promised so well in this Kentish village, so attractive after the horrors of Shoreditch, and now he found himself trapped. How to get out? He had already written for advice to Cardinal Newman, with whom he had become acquainted through a chance encounter as a small boy in Birmingham. But he had got no encouragement from him. No one knew better what a "conversion" of this kind involved, and he no doubt perceived that the bafflement which Marson was experiencing was not inspired by considerations which would justify it in such a case. The Cardinal's reply was as wise as it was brief:

I thank you for the kindly way in which you speak of me, and would be of service to you, if I could be.

But I have no experience enabling me to give you advice, and think you should know more of the doctrines and usages of the Catholic religion before taking the step of professing it.

But what essentially were those "doctrines and usages"? Were they necessarily "Roman" at all? Newman's letter seems to have set Marson back upon his heels and forced him to find his way forward no longer in a mood of escape and impatience but less subjectively and on firmer foundations. Somehow or other from this summer onwards he did find his way forward, partly it is thought by an intense study of the Fathers, to a position which allowed him to perceive a Church of England not inextricably entangled either with an "Establishment", which he always violently repudiated, or with the godlessness of a capitalistic class system, and yet Catholic in all essentials. He had found in the writings of St Bernard the declaration that "Rome is the Mother of Churches and not the Mistress". This was a position which Marson was ready to accept:

We may feel kindly and reverently towards the Pope, and look upon him (as I hope we do) as a great Christian Bishop, as the natural Primate and chairman of Christendom . . . but we cannot possibly pretend that his claims of dominance are to be admitted.[7]

Nor was the Reformation something wholly to be deplored. It had to be understood, and "it was a solid fact that when the work was over in 1662 we had left us a Catholic Liturgy, the full deposit of the Faith and an unbroken succession".

Marson's considered position on all this was, of course, set forth much later—we do not know exactly how much later, since the dates of the papers which were ultimately to make up *God's Co-operative Society* (published in 1913) are not indicated in that volume. The thirty-three pages at the beginning of the book state in reasoned argument the position at which Marson seems in all essentials to have arrived by the advent of his twenty-ninth year, before he left Orlestone. His fundamental standpoint is wholly Nicene: the Church is One, Holy, Catholic, and Apostolic. "No other conception of the Church than that of one Church may ever be entertained"—least of all that of an "invisible" one, which he dismisses (since it is open to every kind of subjective interpretation) as "a treacherous foundation". But "without unduly or idolatrously exalting the nation, we may ask that it should find a place, though only a subordinate place, in the Christian economy". This of course in no way justifies an "Establishment"—an absurdity in a non-Christian polity and a disaster when controlled by mere statesmen", which "must be snapped from the limbs of the Church". But the medieval papacy failed to meet the justifiable demand for "a reformation of Head and Members" in a variety of ways, and not least by persisting in the centralized control of national Churches. It is against this background that "we need neither to abuse or laud the Reformation in England but first to understand it". "Perhaps we can go so far as to say that the domination and autocracy of the medieval Popes served a great purpose in earlier times. It kept us from insularity." But "to precipitate a conflict between honest patriotism and the Catholic Faith is not only unwise, but actually irreligious". To remember this should help us to be more tolerant of forms of devotion different from our own than we are wont to be. "The customs of worship which are not our customs are, on our own principle, to be left to the nations which admit them to accept or to criticize." For ourselves, despite "the violence, disloyalty and insolence of the Puritans which ought to be better understood than

it is", nothing fatal to our Catholic heritage prevailed. "We are
the sons and successors of men who dared to be entirely Catholic
and yet set bounds to despotism."

Here in broad outline, and chiefly in Marson's own words, are the
elements of his ecclesiastical position, stated with pungency and
wit in these pages, and fortified by numerous quotations from
Patristic, medieval, and Caroline sources. But beyond this he was
to learn from Headlam and Sarson to relate the philosophy of their
teacher, F. D. Maurice, to the sacramental principle of the Catholic
Church and the Book of Common Prayer. Baptism and the Eucharist are not only, not mainly, private and personal appropriations of
grace. "Baptism is not only a spiritual regeneration but an incor-
poration into a visible human society. Sacramentalism in the doctrine of the Lord's Supper definitely implies that the fellowship of
the altar becomes null and void unless that principle of sharing is
carried away from the altar into the human fellowship of the world
in which that altar is placed." So did his biographer, Etherington,
summarize the teaching characteristic of the whole Guild of St
Matthew, while proceeding to develop this far more fully than space
can be found for here.

But if Anglo-Catholics can feel reassured of their position, they
can never be satisfied to repose upon it. A valid reunion must ever
be sought, not only for the sake of Christian integrity, but because
the world now outside the Church is robbed of what it needs to see
and experience while Christians remain divided. One of Marson's
most witty and sardonic—and a critic might perhaps add, somewhat
uncharitable—papers, an onslaught on "Bibliolatry", ends with this
noble passage:

> Is the reunion which we desire, for which Christ prayed, to be accom-
> plished first outwardly and then in the realm of the spirit? Would the
> blessed consummation take effect merely if the successor of St Augus-
> tine renewed his filial duties to the successor of St Gregory? if the
> successor of St Gregory again adopted a liberal and fatherly and
> modest attitude towards the successor of St Augustine? The problem
> evidently goes deeper. The new life must begin in the unseen womb
> of the soul. It must be fed by prayer and charity and nourished by
> a wholesomer, bolder thought, circulating in the life-blood of the
> Church until it is fit for the ruder airs of birth in the outer and more
> actual world. All things point to this conception as already accom-
> plished. It is our part to neutralise the poisons of individualism, which

may mar and destroy the hope of the future—to prepare and to expect the new trust, so that when the truth comes it shall not bewilder us, but be very welcome. That seems the peculiar mission of Churchmen of our generation.[8]

It may seem still more clearly, in this day of the recalled Vatican Council and the Ecumenical Movement, to be the mission of churchmen now and of Anglo-Catholics not least. We may indeed see this mission on a still wider canvas than Marson did—or could. But we should strive to see it with his clarity and pursue it with his zeal.

5

"To the average layman in the Church of England," wrote his biographer, "and certainly to his parishioners in Orlestone, the nice distinction involved in the claims of the Roman Church as to jurisdiction were not apparent. The outward signs of Catholicism, wherever they were met, meant popery, and in Orlestone the dread of the Scarlet Woman was now added to the fear of the Red Flag."

Marson well realized this, and was resigned to leave there on finding that not only the patrons, but his bishop (of Dover) felt that he should move on. "Either University", he wrote in October 1888, "would suit me best, within reach of books, and with enough work to do to prevent blue mould from quite covering my exterior. In such peaceful work I should be content to pass my days." His fate, however, was to be very different. He wrote to his old friend, Robert Chalmers, in the following February that he was "under sentence of transportation" to Australia, having accepted a curacy at Glenelg, a suburb of Adelaide. It is fairly clear that the decision was for him a sacrificial act—he was to accompany his invalid brother Frank, who had been ordered to seek a more benevolent climate. But he had written before this choice was made, "as Lacordaire said, if the clergy do not expect a life of sacrifice, who should?" Before leaving England in May he had made a still more significant decision; he had become engaged to a sister of two old friends of Oxford days, Miss Clotilda Bayne, who was to follow him to Australia in due course.

"This world", Marson wrote at this time to his fiancée, "is not a place to grow whole forests of happiness in." It is from his letters to her that we learn most about him during the following twelve months, for he was a profuse and vivid correspondent at all times. He wrote during the voyage out that it was "dreadful to have no Mass, especially when mutual loss and sacrifice are needed", as on long voyages in a closely packed vessel they are. There was indeed a chaplain on board, but he was uncooperative, apparently feeling that "Morning Prayer" was all that his congregation could reasonably expect from him. Eventually Marson insisted that the liturgy should be celebrated, but when it was, he was "sickened by the want of beauty and reverence". But the more Puritan among his fellow-travellers were, in their turn, shocked to find him playing whist on a Sunday evening. "At last a Scotch female rushed up and told me it was the Lord's Day and asked if I was not ashamed of myself. I said, 'Madam, I belong to the Church of England', and played out a splendid hand of trumps, so that she fell back routed by nonchalance." There is something wholly typical of Marson in both these attitudes to "Sunday Observance".

All his life Marson made both friends and enemies easily—and effortlessly. It was particularly so during his years in South Australia. The personal charm of this arresting, vital, and spontaneous man, with his "large mobile mouth, grey eyes with an indescribable twinkle, and rich, husky yet musical voice", was irresistible to most people of all classes so long as relationships remained on the personal level. But when they moved on to controversial planes where it was generally considered that restraint and tact were called for, and not least in a "minister", as the clergy were then commonly described in Australia, it was quite a different matter. The "patience and reticence" which Bishop Walsham How had recommended to him half a dozen years before represented an attitude so foreign to him that it seems he did not so much consciously dismiss methods and policies which they would have suggested; to adopt them simply never occurred to him. When Marson found himself, as he believed, faced by injustice, spiritual lethargy, hypocrisy, and a materialistic outlook, he had no other idea than to make an immediate frontal attack on them. Though he admired Australian pluck and particularly its exhibition in the open air life beloved by the people to whom he had come to minister, he did not, at first at any rate, find much else to praise.

Public life and public morals [he wrote to Miss Bayne] are utterly corrupt. Private life is hideous and hypocritical. The largest profession of piety is allowed to be made by people of equally large and equally open profligacy. The usurers and rent raisers eat up the people and Stiggins, Chadband and Co. bless them all heartily, and are blest in turn. Our priests compromise matters and no voice is raised to warn people that God cannot be fooled by shoddy work and shoddy morals. . . .

I know that unless we can get sincerer faith and exacter justice and some cremation of cant we are bound to die of the plague which our evil deeds breed for our punishment. I do not think you have any idea of how fervently I feel this and how misbeliefs are the abscesses which are exhausting the spiritual life of our people.

If the young lady had not, she cannot have known her future husband very well. And she must have looked forward with some apprehension to the sort of environment into which her marriage, six months after this was written, was to take her.

Marson's sermons were scarifying, both ecclesiastically and sociologically. "You sat and shivered", writes Etherington, "as blow after blow demolished the moral foundations of your father's income and your husband's livelihood. References to the servant question made you thankful that your own were not in church; denunciations of Protestantism made the necks in the pew in front of you grow deep purple, and the whole service meant such an explosive mid-day dinner table that it remains in your memory like a nightmare." But it was when he reached the question of the treatment of the Aborigines that Marson plunged his sword deepest into the uneasy conscience of his hearers. He wrote to Miss Bayne at the end of the year:

It is missionary Sunday and I have had three sermons to do. The last one was on the "blacks" and our treatment of them, and I got very hot about that, and got wild and said just what came uppermost— reproach, jest, entreaty and appeal. The audience listened . . . hung on the words, were impressed, but angry. That inspires one you know, and the result is that I feel robust again in health and in good spirits. . . . God grant it may stir some of the audience to a more chivalrous participation in the Catholic life—of rebellion and reconstruction.

Tonight I feel as though our ultimate goal was to live and die among the blacks in the interior. . . . I was to plead for this mission, but I cursed it altogether and cried for justice and chivalry at home. Look at the facts. . . . Constant massacres and venality and contempt for those folk. Their tribal organizations broken up, their game all killed, their lands annexed. . . . Their sons are made slaves of and all by people who talk about the love of Christ, and profess piety. This cursed colony was arranged in Exeter Hall, where with cant and insolence S. Australia was founded, irrespective of its real owners. Faugh! How sick it makes one.

It is not surprising that this tempestuous man had already clashed with his ecclesiastical superiors, and especially the Bishop of Adelaide, G. W. Kennion. At their first meeting in July they had got across one another. He has been described as "a courtly man—one might say a courtier—saved only from pomposity by good breeding and accustomed to insinuate a precise attitude of superiority when dealing with the inferior clergy". This was not the sort of Father in God whom Marson would be likely to treat with filial deference.

The Bishop and I quarrelled at lunch and I got in a rage with him and thrust Gore at him with mockery. He defended the indefensible behaviour of whites against blacks. He pooh-poohed St Thomas Aquinas upon the *justum pretium* which both buyer and seller ought to find and co-operate in finding out. Ergo, I thought him an ass and unworthy of his office, and he thought me a beast, irreverent and doctrinaire. I hated him and he me!

If all we know of Marson was derived from these letters, it could not be said that, for all his zeal and courage, such reckless aggressiveness, so little inclination to make allowances for the crude acquisitiveness not unnatural in the descendants of colonists who had had tough struggles to gain a foothold in a new country, so much self-assertion and egotism, would add up to produce a very sympathetic figure. Yet we know from other sources that it was by no means only acrimony and friction that were characteristic of his contacts with those to whom he had come to minister. One who knew him well paints a very different picture:

He had the power of effective detachment, and when he came into personal contact with simple people all controversial barriers disappeared and he became the ministering priest and friend. . . . Whether he was playing with children, talking to the sick or giving advice, the particular thing he was doing commanded his full attention and gave the recipient of his friendship the true impression that Marson had received pleasure himself.

Indeed, the common people heard him gladly. He not only gained their willing attention when he spoke in public, but he mixed easily with them in games at a club he founded. "They are so shy of priests, and no wonder", he wrote to Miss Bayne. "Folks have hectored them terribly and unsympathetically I find." As his biographer well puts it:

> Marson was able to conquer the working man's natural distrust of the priest, because he knew there was reason in their distrust. To do a service to one's neighbour in such a way as to establish a right to thrust religion on him was to Marson not only unfair to the neighbour but unfair to religion.

This ease of approach to simple folk always remained with him. When he went to diocesan conferences, or the like, instead of lunching at the hotel he would go into some small beer-house and have a glass of beer and some bread and cheese, probably with cattle-drovers, and they never resented the presence of the "father" after a few moments of his conversation. The same courage that compelled him to speak boldly before bishops and his peers sent him into the public house in his cassock. And all this without assumption or condescension.

6

In May 1890, Clotilda Bayne, known to her intimates, as to Marson, as Chloe, came out to Adelaide, and on 20 June, the feast of Corpus Christi and the anniversary of his arrival in the country, they were married. Were this essay primarily a biographical study, more would have to be said of the domestic and intellectual aspect of their early married life than can, or needs to be written here. It must have been a hard time for her. They were both highly intelligent people, but as Marson's biographer says, "the joys and troubles that they had to share were not confined to the small and safe kingdom of a home [which, moreover, had to be run on a very strict budget], but included the adventures, and more particularly the dangers, of their mental and spiritual pilgrimage. Their love of literature [in which subject Chloe had taken the tripos at Cambridge] and their deep religious sense were not accidents, but of the very essence of life." Marson had long left behind the Broad Church Evangelicalism in which she had grown up; he was now a declared Socialist while she was still a Liberal, an attitude to life which he particularly disliked and suspected as involving a tendency "to divide society into two classes, those who were to teach and improve and those who were to be taught and to be improved". Again, Marson was about as extroverted a person as could well be, and he thought her too introspective. "Look outwards", he had written to her during the period of their separation; "again I am preaching to you, Chloe dearest, to be more objective." He had never seen their marriage as involving an easy life for her:

> You are being dedicated to God anew [he wrote a month before their wedding] and to the co-operation with and the strengthening of one of his faltering priests. For you this step is one of pain and anxiety and difficulty—a hard mission, an ascetic life—need of every muscle of the body, soul and spirit, and at the end of the day perhaps only tired limbs and tears.

At the end of the day there was, moreover, another problem which few busy young husbands foresee but many brides experience. The woman, alone for most of the day, finds the returning "breadwinner" too exhausted and perhaps too preoccupied to be the man to whose companionship she has been looking forward. Marson wrote of this to his father:

> She finds it unexpectedly difficult that I am away so much and am tired (and unsociable, I fear) after the day's work is—not over, for it is never done but—scrambled at *pro tempore*. I have seldom an hour to chat in and if I am at home someone's sure to drop in and spoil our *tête à têtes*.

Yet whatever the difficulties with which the young wife had to contend, in a not attractive setting in a wholly strange country and parted from all her old friends, their strong love for each other, despite all their differences and controversies, held the marriage firmly together. And "the general happiness of the parish was increased by the presence of a lady not only witty and learned, but young, pretty and dainty".[9]

It was a reinforcement which by this time Marson himself was no doubt feeling that he badly needed. His rector, Canon French, was tiring of the strain of working with a curate who seemed to be always in hot water. Marson's engagement was due to terminate in June 1891, and French made it clear that he did not propose to renew it. Marson himself was in two minds whether he wished to stay in Australia or return home. "One shrinks from having all the new life buried like as the old life has been," he wrote to his father, "but Clo is all of another mind, being fresh imported. . . . But folk here are kindlier than in England, at least I have been treated kindlier and fairer here." Even so, the reaction to the news of his impending departure must have surprised him. A petition was at once organized asking that Marson should not be allowed to go. Though organized in a hurry, as many as 310 signed this and only six refused to do so. "The folk I offended have nearly all come round to be my friends and quite all returned to the Church", he wrote again to his father. "As this parish seems fairly unanimous there is a pretty fair prospect that French will ask me to stop. I sincerely hope he will not." Clearly his rector hoped that he would leave and proposed a list of conditions to which Marson would have to agree *in toto*. These the curate found impossible, and French "accepted his decision".

But before Marson could book a passage home, his parishioners made another effort at least to keep him in the diocese. They hastily raised a fund to provide a year's stipend for Marson at a mission church at St Oswald's, Parkside, and more than 400 persons combined to forward news of this to the Bishop, begging him to make the appointment. Considering the tough manner in which Marson had dealt with him at their first meeting, Bishop Kennion greeted this suggestion in a very generous spirit. Apart from laying down a few broad conditions as to methods of worship, he promised him that

> there would be no unnecessary interference. . . . In all practical work among suffering and poor you might count on my co-operation (if that co-operation be worth having) and I should think it my duty to stand by you in rows which might ensue just as I should expect you to stand loyally by me in acting on the lines of the Archbishop's judgment [on matters concerning worship]. . . . Though I may not, and I do not (as far as I know) agree with your theological views, I know I have no monopoly of truth, and I fully recognize its many-sidedness.

Marson could hardly fail to respond to such a gracious reaction to the wishes of his supporters, and in July he moved to Parkside, where he was given a warm welcome. The Bishop's restrictions on ritual could hardly have been very oppressive since, apparently without objection from episcopal or any other quarters, he introduced the use of incense into the services, the first Anglican priest in Australia to do so.

But with the arrival of the new year it became evident to him that his health was making it impossible to stay in that country. The enemy was the asthma which was ultimately, some twenty years later, to kill him.

> Every night [he wrote in January] I am awake with it, and if I jog on as I am now doing, I shall get angina pectoris or syncope, and give in altogether, so we have almost resolved to book for home next April.

A month later he reported:

> The moment I got back from the bush the enemy caught me again and with renewed torture.

It was clear that he could not remain at his post.

> But I am heartbroken about it. The work exactly suits me, and the Church has gone forward by leaps and bounds. Then the situation is so peculiar. I have been placed here as the pioneer of a whole school of Church folk and placed by the generosity and enthusiasm of my friends. To desert the post seems treason, but after all one must look for signs of Divine guidance and those beckon me away.

His wife's health was none too good either, and they had now an infant daughter to add to their responsibilities. Bishop Kennion seems to have been as genuinely regretful at the news of Marson's departure as was the priest himself. He can hardly have guessed that only three years later they were again to stand in the same relationship to one another. He wrote to Marson:

> That you would have accomplished much good work for Christ and His Church had you been able to stay longer with us I feel convinced. Though I believe more of the evident success of your work is to be attributed to your own earnestness and self-denying life than you would be willing to allow.

And so in the Spring of 1892 Marson returned to England. Considering that he had been less than three years in Adelaide he had clearly made a remarkable impact there and won the admiration and understanding of very many to whom he had spoken with a forthrightness which would hardly have been forgiven in a lesser man.

7

The three years which Marson spent on his return from Adelaide, almost all of which were passed in the metropolitan area, were, from the point of view of this study, the most significant in his life. They were so if only because it is during them that he became most widely known, that his work for the cause of Christian Socialism, especially through the Guild of St Matthew, was chiefly done, and that he formed the more mature outlook on such matters which lay behind his later writing upon them. It is indicative of the force of his personality that he should have been able to have made so strong an impression on so many in so short a time. As has been already suggested, this impression was not wholly favourable. This is not to be wondered at. The very word "socialist", which Marson never hesitated to use of himself, was at this time to most in the "comfortable" classes a stumbling-block and to economic orthodoxy foolishness. Others who might have agreed, in some measure at any rate, with his standpoint and his aims found his manner too flamboyant for their taste. These, they would have felt, were serious subjects, "no laughing matter"; but it was seldom that Marson, for all his zeal and profound sympathy for the oppressed, left his audiences without something that irresistibly drew laughter from them. Chesterton in one of his stories wrote of a politician who when he could think of a joke made one, but when he couldn't looked solemn and said, "This is no time for jesting." Wit sprang so spontaneously to Marson's lips that there seemed always to be a time for it.

But that wit was often barbed. The writer was told of such an occasion by one who was sitting next to him at a public meeting. A somewhat rhetorical speaker, with a rather oleaginous manner, was telling of circumstances when he believed himself to have been unjustly thrust into the "forefront of the battle". Rubbing his hands together, he exclaimed dramatically, "I felt like Uriah!" Marson had been finding this exhibitionism rather trying and at this point in a very audible confidence, he ejaculated "Heep he means". It is not believed that this comment reached the ears of the speaker, but it did those of not a few of the audience.

Marson was fortunate, on arriving in England, to find the saintly Bishop Westcott anxious to do his best for him, and he at once secured for him a curacy in a mining village in his diocese. Marson seems never to have regarded this post as more than a temporary one; it offered no home for his wife and child, and a doctor advised him against settling in the bleak Durham climate. He wrote in gloomy mood to a friend: "I cannot get a berth. The Church of England, as usual, looks on my sort as vermin to be chased with pokers—no, not the Church but the apostate clergy, the Church's enemies and ours, who tie and gag and bleed her." However, he did within a few weeks "get a berth", and one that it might have been supposed would suit him, at Christ Church, Clapham. Here was a fully "Catholic parish"; in certain respects, however, it seemed to Marson too idiosyncratically so:

> Father Abbott [he wrote] does not quite suit me as a vicar. I love splendid services and his perfectly frank and above-board ways, but I consider that we are bound in honour not to transgress the rubrics. He rides over the necks of rubrics in a way that I think is anti-nomian. . . . In ecclesiastical matters I am anti-Roman; but he is philo-Roman. So I am content to be looked upon as a moderate man and a scrupulous Anglican. . . .
>
> [But] no one will have me except Father Abbott and I am far too grateful to wish to cross him for his anarchic views. . . . As I say, Abbott is a brave and strong man and says that he entirely disregards all socialist views. I am at full liberty to preach these to the top of my bent if I think them right.

But if his vicar gave him this "full liberty", it seems that the congregation were by no means ready to do so. Arrived in July, he was forced to leave in the Spring of the following year (1893), "kicked out for socialism", as he wrote bitterly to his father. Yet he seems to have suspected that it may have been as much his manner as his matter which had led to this. "If only I could have inherited or acquired your loveable ways when I acquired your pugnacity", he confessed to his parent, "our external troubles would be few."

Again it was Westcott who came to Marson's aid. "It is a tribute to his discernment," wrote Etherington, "that he was able to see the devotion and the depth of Marson's character and to value it, in spite of the many youthful extravagances which made it difficult for his would-be friends in high positions to help him." In April

1893, Marson received a letter from Frederick Temple, then Bishop of London, clearly written with some misgivings:

> I have licensed you because I had a very warm letter from the Bishop of Durham in your favour and also because I thought you had been hardly treated.... But your own account of yourself is not quite what I like, and I think you ought to try to learn to be a little less sure of your own powers and merits.

Perhaps Marson realized that there was some justice in this stricture; but he may have remembered it on a later occasion when, being rebuked by Temple for the temerity of his views, he replied, "Yes, my Lord, I too have had my salad days." This sly reference to the Bishop's theological temerity in his contribution to *Essays and Reviews* thirty years before seems to have been taken by Temple in good part.

The licence above referred to was to St Mary's, Charing Cross Road. This church, which for two centuries had had a varied history, was—regrettably—pulled down in this one to be replaced by an art school. In the 1880s and 1890s it was not only a centre of the Anglo-Catholic revival, but closely associated with the leaders of the Guild of St Matthew and the distinctive interpretation of the Faith associated with the Headlam circle. Its leader appeared here regularly to celebrate the liturgy, and to preach, as he was hardly allowed to do anywhere else, the brand of sacramental, socialistic, and anti-Puritan teaching which he had evolved ever since his early days in Bethnal Green. The nominal vicar was an absentee and the "curate-in-charge" was in effect completely so. Marson's predecessor, W. E. Moll, was not only a whole-hearted Church Socialist but an active propagandist for the Labour movement and later, while vicar of St Philip's, Newcastle, for the newly formed Independent Labour Party. Marson had no need here, as he had always had to do before, to break new ground or to pioneer suspect ideas and practices, whether ecclesiastical or sociological. He had come into what was for him a goodly heritage; he had only to make the most of it. And so, for a golden year from the Spring of 1893, he certainly did.

For Marson was now in his element. He settled in a fine seventeenth-century house (No. 13, Soho Square) with his wife and child, and made it a centre where all like-minded folk, and young ones most of all, could drop in to enjoy the vitality of his company and the vivid talk which derived from the wide scope of his interests. He himself loved the cosmopolitan atmosphere of his surroundings, so different from the "stuffiness" only too characteristic of most of the parishes in which he had previously served. It offered everything he wanted, except one thing which had eluded him right through his ministry—security. That was not guaranteed, and in 1894 it suddenly vanished. The money for his stipend had been provided by a sympathetic barrister, one Henry West, Q.C. He died in this year and Marson found "his occupation gone".

He moved to another St Mary's—a church which in later days was to have a notable place in the history of the Christian Social Movement. For it was here, in Somers Town, that the mind of Basil Jellicoe, while he was still a layman working for the Magdalen College Mission amidst its surly squalor, was suddenly illuminated by recollection of the prophetic declaration: "They shall build the old wastes: they shall raise up the former desolations." The wastes and desolations were only too much in evidence when Marson went there, and though he found an active church life and a colleague, Fr Fyfe, "whom he knew well and loved much", the surroundings depressed him. Whatever the poverty of Soho, the area had an atmosphere of vitality and gaiety; here all was drabness and discouragement. There was a touch of the "manic-depressive" about Marson—he was easily elated and rather quickly downcast. This did not matter much if these moods were not too greatly prolonged. But in Somers Town depression tended to get the upper hand.

It was not surprising. Marson's new dwelling-place was a sad contrast to the dignified comfort of Soho Square. A friend coming to see him there found him grimly catching the bugs which infested the walls and, not unnaturally, in the depths of dejection. Suddenly his face lighted up as he squashed one of the unpleasant creatures between his fingers. "There's one consolation though," he said, "these bugs are remarkably like Dr. —— [a Nonconformist leader towards whom Marson had a particular antipathy] to look at; one does get *that* satisfaction in killing them."

He took a leading part in one campaign while he was in Somers Town. This was a strike of cab drivers, many of whom lived in this parish, and from his own experience he knew how bitter was their struggle to make ends meet. He wrote to the *Daily Chronicle* in May 1895 :

The friends of the living wage have an excellent touchstone in this cab strike, and it is certainly time that they rallied up in support of the men. ... Often for days together this winter the driver has only been able to earn the hire for his master, leaving nothing for himself. The men are tired of working for no wages, or next to none, and a cabman's day, I would remind you, often means as much as sixteen hours. ... There is no better alms than that which helps men to fight better in the cause of justice. Will not our friends help forward this honest and orderly demand for a fair and living wage?

These are not the words of an "irresponsible agitator", as Marson was sometimes, quite unjustly, thought to be by those who mistook his zeal for a crude and unthinking partisanship. As his biographer insisted, "his sense of justice demanded fair treatment for the absent party, no matter in what camp he was fighting, and by separating prejudice from principle he was often able to be an interpreter between those whose interests appeared to be in direct opposition".

The hardships endured by his parishioners were by no means unknown to Marson himself, though these were often voluntarily incurred. His Lenten austerities were always severe. Percy Widdrington, living with him in the country three years later while being tutored for his final schools at Oxford, reported that "Marson does not eat meat for the whole forty days, doesn't smoke, take snuff or drink; we both felt very ill yesterday". This may have been supportable in a country environment; it imposed much too heavy a strain on a man far from fit working in a slum area. The Vicar of St Pancras, Luke Paget (afterwards Bishop of Chester) hearing of this severe discipline, wrote to him confidentially to protest against it:

March 9th, 1895.

Dearest Marson,

Two independent witnesses have told me that you are keeping Lent in such a way as to really endanger your health and seriously weaken yourself. ...

I can't believe, try my hardest, that you are right in going so long without meat, or that the gain, be it discipline, or be it the sheer good of obedience, is proportionate to the risk you run, the anxiety you give your friends, or the real crippling of work that such rigour often brings.

The strain of his life in Somers Town did indeed prove more than he could sustain. A country living in Somerset was offered him (by the then Prime Minister, Lord Rosebery) and this he accepted. Though he cannot have foreseen it then, it was the last move he was ever to make. A totally new life was opening for Charles and Chloe. They took with them the good wishes of those among whom they had lived in London and one gift which Marson must have found particularly touching—a silver pyx subscribed for by the cabmen whose cause he had championed. "It has a significance," wrote Etherington, "for it shows that the priest was not lost in the social campaigner."

8

When Marson published the volume of collected essays and addresses which he entitled *God's Co-operative Society*, he added as a sub-title, "Suggestions on the strategy of the Church". The phrasing is significant. The opening paragraph of the book, though relating primarily to doctrinal matters, is indicative of the author's attitude in respect of everything with which he dealt in it.

> It is almost an ungracious task to attempt anything like Church defence, for the true and only safe Church defence is Church attack.... The Church policy of the future should be such that we should hear much of the defence of atheism ... and of all forms of individualism in religion, but little or nothing about Church defence.

Marson might have taken as his motto the words of a once popular song "Accentuate the positive; eliminate the negative". However critical he might be led to be, it was always reconstruction on an assured Catholic foundation that he had in mind.

When he was dealing with ecclesiastical issues this (if his interpretation of the Faith was accepted) was relatively simple. It was not only that sixty years after the emergence of the Oxford Movement he could count on having a confident and well-organized Anglo-Catholic army on his side. His own deep reading had given him a firm grasp of his authorities. He could, of course, be strongly opposed, but he could not be simply neglected; denounced but not dismissed. But in the field of social justice his task was much more difficult. Since the disintegration of the original Christian Socialist group in 1854 this cause had found few champions in the Church of

England and received no organized attention for some thirty years. So far as anything resembling "socialism" existed, it was associated with atheism, positivism, or the vague aspirations of ethical idealism. Headlam's little Guild of St Matthew was founded on the welding together of Maurician theology and Catholic doctrine, and had been developed in close relation to the struggles of the working class in London through the long depression which lasted from the middle of the 1870s to the very end of the 1880s. But the Guild was pitifully small, and so much under the domination of its founder as to present a distinctly idiosyncratic character in church circles. Its appeal had been largely to the "gentiles" without rather than to the "faithful" within. It was only in the 1890s, under the "respectable" though always courageous, leadership of Westcott, Scott Holland, and Gore that a calculated effort to reach "the man in the pew" was made by the Christian Social Union.

It was natural that for a man of Marson's dynamic, even flamboyant temperament it should be the G.S.M. which gained his primary allegiance. He must have attached himself to it in his Orlestone days, as his predecessor there, George Sarson, had earlier done. At St Mary's, Charing Cross Road, he was at the very centre of its spiritual and intellectual inspiration. But there can be little doubt that he brought to this nucleus at least as much as he gained from it. There is little that is obviously derivative in those chapters in *God's Co-operative Society* which are devoted to the relation of the Church to social justice and the workers' movements. These occupy pages 66 to 115 of the volume and consist of three papers, "The Church and Social Problems, I Present and Future, II Past", and another on "The Church and Labour".

In the second of these, Marson is careful to explain that he turns to the past "in no slavish spirit".

The past is past because it was outgrown. Every cry with "back" in it is self condemned. ... If we look to the past, it is to see not the actualities which have disappeared, but those inset ideas which are everlasting. We look to last year's fruit not because we complain that it is moulded away, but to see what we may expect of the tree that bore it. ... If the Church now and in the future is to speak socially and politically she must obviously speak as one true to herself.

He quoted from a passage in Newman's *History of the Arians* less familiar then no doubt than it has since become.

If the primitive believers did not interfere with the acts of the civil
Government, it was merely because they had no rights enabling them
legally to do so. But where they have rights the case is different (Acts
16. 37–9), and the existence of a secular spirit is to be ascertained not
by their using these, but their using them for ends short of the ends
for which they were given them.... The duty of using their rights
in the service of religion is clear; and since there is a popular mis-
conception that Christians, and especially the clergy as such, have no
concern in temporal affairs, it is expedient to take every opportunity
of formally denying the position, and demanding a proof of it. In
truth the Church was framed for the express purpose of interfering or
(as irreligious men will say) meddling with the world.

Let us see, Marson asks, "in what direction the primitive believers
Newman speaks of, would have used the rights which were denied
them". And he opens his chapter on "The Past" with the defiant
declaration that "The teaching of these primitive believers leads us
to see that they would have exercised their powers in the direction
of the frankest Socialism".

There is perhaps no more complete chameleon in the English
language than the word "socialism". "When I use a word,"
Humpty Dumpty said, in rather a scornful tone, to Alice, "it means
just what I choose it to mean—neither more nor less." Our "progressive" Humpty Dumpties have been using the word "socialism"
in this way for over a century. Marson came nearest to a definition
in this chapter in a rendering of some words of St Basil, who, he
said, never concealed that

the Word calls us to socialism (τὸ κοινωνικόν), brotherly love and
obedience to Nature, for man is a political and gregarious animal. So
in the common polity and mutual society, generosity is a necessity
for the uplifting of the needy.

"Under all the ceaseless insistence upon almsgiving", Marson
continues, "lies the Christian doctrine of the injustice of the world
and God's purpose for a better state and a juster order."

What he was seeking to establish in this chapter above everything
else was that contemporary society had developed upon a series of
assumptions and practices which bore no relation to Christian doctrine and tradition through the ages right down to the sixteenth
century, and that the great mass of Christians were living in this
world without the slightest intention of "renouncing" its values or
of transforming its character. Beginning with the New Testament,

he proceeds through a long catena of quotations from the Fathers
and the medieval teachers, ending with a prayer from Queen Eliza-
beth's private Prayer Book of 1578 "for them that be in poverty"
from which we take these phrases:

> Thou, O Lord, providest enough for all men, with Thy most liberal
> and bountiful hand; but whereas Thy gifts are, in respect of Thy
> goodness and free favour, made common to all men we (through our
> naughtiness, niggardship and distrust) do make them private and
> peculiar. Correct Thou the thing which our iniquity hath put out of
> order: let Thy goodness supply that which our niggardliness hath
> pluckt away.

Marson concludes his chapter by writing:

> Thoughts so widely, so deeply, so long held by the Christian Church
> ought to be not only tolerable but intensely dear to the minds of
> Churchmen. It might naturally be thought that bishops and arch-
> bishops would bless the promoters of modern Socialism, would pray
> for them in public, subscribe liberally to their Societies, and insist
> that all who discuss such questions should do so in the light of the
> Incarnation.

The combination of gravity and irony in this passage is very
characteristic of Marson. It is clear that dearly as he longed to see
the banner of social justice in the hands of the Church's leaders, he
believed it still to be, as Thomas Hancock had proclaimed thirty
years before, in the hands of the Socialists. Since this was so he was
ready to align himself with them.

9

Notwithstanding what has just been said, Marson's primary appeal
was always to churchmen and above all to those who claimed to
stand in the Catholic tradition. The Tractarians had shown the way;
they had brought back the associative principle to English religion,
but the extension of its application to political and social questions
was not their task. "They had no notion that Church principles
which began at the altar, stopped at the south porch or the lych
gate." But the movement, he felt, had got bogged down in piety,
ritualism, and an introverted ecclesiasticism. "The fate of the Evan-

gelicals has befallen the Puseyites. The disciples have lost the conquer-
ing and extending spirit. They are content with their fathers' win-
nings." This was not altogether just in the days of Father Stanton
and Father Dolling, any more than it would have been the whole
truth later in the days of Conrad Noel and Basil Jellicoe. But
there was too much truth in it in the former period as there was
still in the later one, despite the work of the Catholic Crusade, the
Anglo-Catholic School of Sociology and the Christendom Group.

"The absolute inefficiency of the individual to help himself by
himself," wrote Marson, "the consequent need of a society, a club,
a country, a Church—whatever we call it—that was the root principle for which the Tractarians contested. In things spiritual this
leads to all their principal doctrines." And in a vivid paragraph,[10]
too long to quote here, he makes this application to the whole
sacramental system of the Church. How, he then inquires, can "a
man who has been sojourning in his own country, the New Jerusa-
lem, and learned his fraternity, its unity with itself, lightly or
logically see the predatory society outside and conform to it immediately and without qualms. . . . The most serious charge which can
be brought against our modern High Churchmen, is that the things
they tolerate and support outside the Church clearly prove that they
have not seen what they think they see inside." This radical criticism is integral to Marson's argument.

"The world", he goes on to declare, "is in suspense waiting for
the clear guidance of the only authority which can pronounce dogmatic verdicts, the Church of Christ. That Church is at present
manacled and gagged. The greatest question of the time is whether
she will ever obtain the use of her hand and tongue to speak the
clear, saving word, for lack of which the whole earth is in jeopardy."

We must always remember, of course, in reading Marson's
declarations on these matters that they were made more than half
a century ago in a world vastly different in many respects from ours,
both in its religious and in its secular outlooks and circumstances.
The great gulfs of catastrophe represented by world wars and world
"depressions" and crises yawn between now and then. The Church,
however we interpret the term, *has*, to no small extent, "obtained
the use of her hand and tongue", through papal encyclicals, Lambeth
declarations, and a World Council of Churches. But that the world
outside is at all consciously "in suspense waiting for the clear guidance" of the Church was already very doubtful then and could

scarcely be anywhere asserted now. If the Church is more alert and alive to the ills, and to some extent to the mistaken aims and social idolatries of society than was the case at the beginning of the century, this does not mean that she has, or is at all generally expected to have, more influence in face of them now than she had then. How far the Welfare State is a product of the Christian social conscience and of decades of devoted voluntary service by Christian social workers, it would be quite impossible to assess. How far, again, such a unique figure as William Temple (whose father licensed Marson to St Mary's, Charing Cross Road, with so much misgiving), who was quite as ready as Marson was to describe himself as a Socialist in the decade before the First World War, would have found the incumbent of Hambridge ready to accept him as the sort of bishop—and archbishop—he had been crying out for, when Temple rose to leadership after that war, we cannot usefully guess. Certainly "the whole earth is in jeopardy" now to an extent and in ways which Marson could not possibly have foreseen when he wrote; nor is it clear that the most "dogmatic verdicts" on the circumstances which have brought it to this pass would have been listened to in recent years even if they had been explicitly formulated. Nevertheless, it is surely true to say that the Church is far more conscious of the need to attempt such a role as Marson presented for her in the 1960s than she was in the first decade of this century.

When we read Marson's diagnosis of the situation in his paper on "The Church and Labour", we realize how greatly the society he there accurately describes—and justly denounces—has changed since his day. Consider these sentences from his opening paragraphs:

> There are, of course, two nations in every modern country. It is merely a truism to say this. But the Churchman, who stands for a City that is at unity with itself, must face the fact that he is fighting for the moment a losing battle; for the two nations are drawing apart, industrially (which is dangerous) and mentally (which is disastrous). . . . The one nation feels its power grow, the other its power decay. Each draws apart from the other. The former becomes masterful and sometimes incredibly insolent. The latter becomes sullen, despairing, even anarchic. . . .
> Does any picture in *Punch* make the poor otherwise than contemptible, half cretinous, and wholly ridiculous?

Whatever the flaws in our allegedly "affluent society" today—and

there are plenty of them—no one could expect to be taken seriously
if he were to draw such a picture of England in the 1960s. Our
country has still its divisions, but they are rather of fortune and
occupation than of "class" in the old sense; there are much more
than two "nations" in this island today, and they are not "draw-
ing apart" but increasingly merging into each other. Where snob-
bery is complained of, it is often more intellectual than social in
character (for example, the description "very Third Programme").
The power of the working class can hardly be said to be "decaying"
(though the rapid development of automation and computer
mechanics may soon leave it no longer on a "seller's market"), and
few but those grievously victimized by pension problems and the
housing shortage are "sullen and despairing".

Nor are the character and responsibilities—or, for the most part,
the failures—of the clergy identical with those which Marson
delineated. Having complained that under the plutocratic domination of Edwardian England "the great nation [of workers] is un-
touched by Art, uninterpreted by Art, and ignored by Art with a
growing completeness", he continues thus:

> There remains religion to interpret each nation to the others. She has
> ambassadors always moving to and fro between them, with fenders
> to deaden the shocks and jars of the constant collisions . . . or to put
> the matter in its true light, to remind both sides that they do not be-
> long to the capitalist fashion of this world, which must pass away
> (the sooner the better) but to a world wherein dwelleth justice. . . .
> [But] they almost wholly ignore these pressing duties, and are gen-
> erally unaware of their unique position. There are more civil gov-
> ernors who know the gravity of the situation, who try to do justice in-
> differently and truly, than there are clergy who have discovered even
> that justice needs to be done in thought and heart as well as in law
> and civil conduct. We have a class ministry.

Of course none of this is so true now as it was then. Yet it is still
perhaps worth while listening and assenting, with whatever modi-
fications time may now necessitate, to what Marson went on to say:

> It is of the first importance that our clergy, the *ecclesia docens*, should
> study humbly and patiently the lives of the poor, which they do a
> little; and the views of the poor which they never do. Then they must
> themselves explain their views to the class to which they belong (in
> the ugly worldly sense of this word "class"). Before they improve the
> poor man's mind they must know it and tell it. Then it will follow

that all the things which do or can protect the disinherited will be their delight. They will try to know and to understand Labour leaders (most pathetic of men, with all the woes of Moses and but a little of his vision). They will be openly in favour of the existence, strength, and health of Unions. They will support all laws, imperial or local, which make for the health and are against the helplessness of the governed.

This interpretative duty and opportunity is a point repeatedly insisted upon by Marson in this paper.

The clergy and the clergy alone can, if they have the grace of the Holy Ghost, not only hear the cry of the poorer nation, but can reach the ears of the classes and carry the truth to them. As priests they are and always have been bound to be ardent social reformers; but as modern priests they are now bound also to be interpreters. We have missions from public schools and universities to Bethnal Green and Southwark; we really need settlements and missions from Seven Dials and Hoxton to Oxford or to Eton. The fish porters cannot well reach the perishing hundreds in the West End clubs, nor the Railwaymen's Union evangelise the sorely necessitous in the grandstands. But even the most timid archdeacon or the panic stricken prebendaries might bear witness to the patience, dignity, wholesomemindedness, bodily grace and mental sincerity of their humbler (splendid word!) parishioners.

The irony and hyperbole of these passages were characteristic devices with Marson, not only, where necessary, for "scattering the proud in the imagination of their hearts" but for awakening the faithful, and above all their pastors, to obligations of which they were scarcely aware and opportunities the existence of which had never occurred to many of them. Because these exhortations seem "dated" to us now, and the specific pleas for social justice appear hardly to be relevant to the needs and issues of our own time, we may be in some danger of forgetting two things. First, and no doubt less important, that it was the "shock tactics" of the "socialist" priests and preachers at the end of the last century and the beginning of this, of men generally regarded in the Church as irresponsible and almost impious "extremists", which had not a little to do with preparing for a new mood among the clergy such as was already evident in the work of the National Mission only three years after Marson's death, and with whatever checks and inadequacies, has wonderfully developed since, through such a varied band of prophetic leaders as Neville Figgis, Studdart Kennedy, William Temple, Basil Jellicoe, and John Groser.

But more important is it to remember that the Church must always be on the watch to detect those features of a social order in which "public opinion", and even "enlightened" opinion, may spy no dangers, often because it may need a discrimination based upon Christian doctrines of Man and Society to do so. This is not the place to suggest what in our time such features may be, and no attempt will be made to do so. But some words from the paper on "The Development of the Church" with which Marson closed *God's Co-operative Society* may be borne in mind in this connection:

> The plea of the foregoing essays is not for making evolutionary advances in the Church, because conscious efforts in this direction are usually vain, and if they could be effective they would most likely be disastrous. It is rather a plea for observation, for taking into account and ordering ourselves for the developments which are coming from within, which are now made possible from without. It is a plea for what is there, and so can become visible and actual; for what is not there or it would not need to become so. It is not a plea for development, but a plea that the development which the wit of man has not contrived and the wisdom of man has not accomplished should be recognised and welcomed: and further developments should always be expected and allowed for.

Christian terminology speaks of the Church Expectant, but the Church Militant must be expectant too. It must believe itself to be challenged to shed an illumination on social situations such as can never sufficiently come from any other source. It was to awaken the Church of his day to the existence of this obligation that Marson struggled always, and not wholly without success. His example is there for us in our day to learn from, and to follow.

10

"The parish of Hambridge", wrote Mr Etherington who, living in a neighbouring one, knew the whole district well, "lies in the lowlands of South Somerset about sixteen miles from Taunton and Bridgwater and between Langport and Ilminster. It is a land of gentle streams, and life runs in measure with the streams, quiet and unhurried. To those from more turbulent places it may even seem sluggish, but to the listener it seems to say with mild reproof that rush and noise are avoidable accidents."

Marson had lived all his life in much "more turbulent places", and it is not strange that he found the transition from metropolitan life a difficult experience. As his biographer writes:

> The quick wit of the street life, the ready neighbourliness born of the comradeship of urgent poverty, the resentment of class-feeling bred of the close jostling of riches and rags found no counterpart in this new charge. Here resentment was not restless and even sinners seemed as sluggish as the streams. Piety was passive and wit seemed wanting. And Marson was miserable. . . .
>
> It was a far cry from those meetings of cab strikers called in snatch moments at Somers Town to the conferences of the venerable parish pump order in Hambridge, and the result was a bewildering gloom for the ardent reformer and episcopal suspect.

Somers Town to Somerset; it is the sort of transition which has brought dismay and frustration to many a priest who has found that it takes years of patient waiting to find himself accepted by a rural parish, and a man of Marson's restless energy and questing mind was particularly ill fitted for the new role he must learn to play. After six months he confessed that "a country flock is too hard for me to understand", and after three years he found "no advance in friendliness among the rustics and no signs of the higher life anywhere. . . . I don't know how to speak my message to these folk." This was a new experience for him. Always before he had known how to strike a spark out of those to whom he spoke; sometimes a spark of enthusiasm but more often, of course, a flare of antagonism. Either way he had got a "come back". But now he had to learn *from* them and *of* them before he could speak *to* them.

His first break-through began to come through the medium of the Nativity Play which he instituted in his second winter at Hambridge.

> He gave the village people the theme, and set them to do the situations with their own speech. He then noted and collected the lines and produced the result of this communal effort. There was no need to manufacture an atmosphere or coax the past with an elaborate stage setting. The actors translated the theme into their own surroundings and experience naturally and without explanation.

Moreover, despite whatever initial disappointments he experienced, Marson was both a diligent visitor and a welcoming host. In the country, folk, whether officially "church people" or not, like to be called on and regard their pastor's visit, and to some extent an open invitation to his home, as their right and privilege. "There is a substantial remnant of sacerdotal respect in our country parishes", wrote Mr Etherington of this matter thirty years ago. Of such respect confidence and even affection can slowly grow if the priest knows how to earn it, and Marson, aided by his wife, gradually did. He found how to teach his people through hand and eye, introducing meaningful ceremonies into his ministry, as for example, by his practice of washing the feet of three small boys on Maundy Thursday he indicated that he was amongst them "as one that serveth". And he taught them, as time went on, to regard the parish altar as the centre of the community's life, and that, as Etherington writes,

> The priest is acting not in isolation but for and with his people, and he is offering with the Bread and Wine all the daily toil and joy of which bread and wine are the symbols. In the Mass the walls of the church disappear and the altar becomes the centre of all the labour that is going on in fields and shops and home.

So in due course Marson "got through" to his people and—just as importantly—they got through to him. His last book, *Village Silhouettes*, finished just before his death though published afterwards, is striking evidence of this. He opens these so sympathetic sketches with some sentences of self-reproach for his failure to penetrate sooner to an understanding of his rural flock. The book, he said, had a serious purpose:

> It is to bear some testimony to what the author has discovered—how shameful and blind to have discovered it so late!—the greatness, the sweetness, the unexpectedness and the cleverness of God's common people in the green of the world.

No acknowledgement could be more handsomely expressed than this. It says nothing of what he learnt to give on his side, and we know enough of his long and persevering pastorate to know how much this was, though there is little space to say more of it here. The title of Marson's incumbency at Hambridge was the odd one of Perpetual Curate, and perpetual in one sense it proved to be, for though he chafed against its limitations and spoke at first of seeking "any excuse to shy Hambridge and to become a burglar

or a Dean", he never for a moment desired the sort of "promotion"
that others felt was his due. He had not a spark of worldly ambition.
"You must be very serious about all practical matters if you want
to be worldly", he wrote once. "It is awful slavery and not a bit
worth while. . . . It is tiring and boring and unnatural and there is
no sense in it." If it came easy to Marson to put first things first,
it was because he had never put them anywhere else, and in few
lives can there have been better exemplified the service that is perfect
freedom.

II

Occupied as he always was with the problems of his parish and
devoted as he came to be to his parishioners, it is not to be supposed
that Marson's interests were, or could have been, confined thereto.
Hambridge was the base from which he exercised a vigorous and
often contentious influence over the diocese of Bath and Wells and
in some measure over many other parts of the country. Much less
can be said of all this here than would require to be said if this essay
claimed to give a rounded account of the life of this many-sided
man and of his writings. His energetic share in what he himself
always felt to be misleadingly described as the ritual controversies
of the time; his persistent repudiation, not only of the fact but of
the very idea of an Established Church; his sardonic exposures of
what was then widely accepted as "religious education" and of the
grave inadequacies in the training of the clergy; his somewhat idiosyncratic outlook on the claims for the "emancipation" of women
—much could be written on all these things which cannot be
included in a treatment of the man in his character as a rebel
against plutocracy and a bearer of prophetic witness to the social
implications of the Faith. Nor can anything be said of his discovery
of Somerset folk-song and his co-operation—until an unhappy and
rather childish quarrel divided them—with the far more famous
pioneer in that field, Cecil Sharp, with whom he had first struck
up a friendship in Adelaide many years before. And scarcely any
account can be given of his books, ranging from *The Psalms at
Work* and *The Following of Christ*, which were published in the

middle 1890s, to an anonymous work, *Angling Observations of a Coarse Fisherman*, which appeared ten years later.

But Marson's outlook, at any rate as he himself saw it, was so much of a piece that before taking leave of him it is necessary to glance at some of these activities, and in particular at those which soon made him a leading figure in the diocese. Etherington tells us that "at that time the diocese of Bath and Wells was well in the forefront of the Catholic movement, and contained many churches that were known beyond diocesan boundaries as Catholic outposts." The arrival of Marson must have given a strong—if sometimes an embarrassing—reinforcement to those championing this cause. Equally it must have given rise to no little apprehension in the mind of the recently appointed diocesan. For this was none other than that former Bishop of Adelaide, Dr Kennion, who might naturally have supposed that in saying his friendly farewell to Marson there he was hardly likely to be further troubled by this "turbulent priest". "One may feel some sympathy for the Bishop", wrote Etherington, "when he found that one of his first duties was the induction to Hambridge of Marson, who had been appointed by the Crown under Lord Rosebery at a time when the see was vacant and so had not been appointed by the Bishop, as the Bishop himself took occasion to point out at a later date." They were to be in recurrent opposition during the nineteen years remaining to Marson after his arrival in the diocese.

Etherington gives a graphic picture of the scene characteristic of a Diocesan Conference during Marson's period at Hambridge:

Picture a June day in the Chapter House at Wells: the platform filled with men of authority, even of distinction, and their immediate following; the floor thronged with clergy and lay representatives. . . . The Reverend Charles is known by his next door neighbour to be engaged in prayer. His name is sent to the President as desiring to speak. When it is announced there is a grim and disapproving look noticeable on the faces of the great ones at the High Table, and a settling down to endure. The sharp yet husky voice begins with some quip that causes a stir of nervous apprehension or naughty anticipation. Then come the lashing strokes and the indictment, stinging words and pointed parables, and the dignified armour of the great ones rattles beneath shrewd blows. And men are heard to whisper to one another, "He really does go too far." "It is rather strong language to use." "He only damages his case by putting it so crudely." Yes, but his neighbour knows that the words were not spoken without prayer, and the strokes not given without pain and fatigue and a sinking at the heart.

For all the apprehension Marson created he did not speak without effect. A remarkable example of this is afforded by the paper Marson read in 1898 preparatory to moving a resolution in support of Socialism. This was seconded by the famous Canon Stuckey Coles, a native of the diocese and very influential therein. The support of such a seconder no doubt contributed to the astonishing result that the motion was lost only by the casting vote of the Chairman—Bishop Kennion.

When the new century opened, the Church was plunged into controversy over what was popularly—and as Marson always strongly insisted erroneously—described as "ritual disorders". In 1904 a Ritual Commission was set up to investigate "excesses and digressions" in this field. An agent of the commission visited Hambridge, and his report afforded Marson a magnificent opportunity of describing exactly what he did at his High Mass (of All Saints) and why he did it. Having done so, he ended with a characteristic challenge:

> I beg leave to point out that the lives of Christ's poor people are starved and stunted; that their wages are low; their houses often bad and insanitary and their minds full of darkness and despair. *These are the real disorders of the Church.*[11]

In the whole of this protracted, often bitter, and quite inconclusive controversy Marson was urgent to establish true "priorities" and to fight not on the essentially secondary matter of ritual but on what he regarded as vital issues. In this he was in close agreement with Headlam with whom he was in consultation at this time. "If we fight with chandlery or chasubles on our banner," he wrote to a friend, "we shall be smashed and our chasubles with us and all the land gained from the protestant sea will be swamped again."

We may take first the point made in the quotation above about "the real disorders of the Church". In a draft Marson made for an "open letter from the Clergy and Communicants to the Archbishop and bishops", which, unhappily, one feels, did not get beyond private circulation, he starts by "uttering a strong filial remonstrance and an affectionate appeal", and continues:

> That you have been given a high worldly position, dear Fathers, is surely because it is understood that you will be peculiarly sensitive to

spiritual wickedness in high places, and help us and all men to with-
stand the assaults of the world by using all such powers as are en-
trusted to you, for the furtherance of Christ's Kingdom, the Church,
and for the heavenly and universal justice which is therein embodied.

Yet in an age of luxury and distress, when this our beloved country
is sharply divided into Haves and Have-nots, we do not hear you
speak Gospel words of rebuke against the usury and waste and callous-
ness of rich Christian robbers; nor yet the words of consolation, hope
and protection to the poor, the unemployed and the miserable in the
one true fold.

But at least, he goes on to urge, we might expect that if "we
cannot see the bread which perishes rightly divided by and amongst
Christ's people . . . yet we can and must make it possible for all men
to have the Bread which came—and comes—down from Heaven".

So we ask, or rather we demand of you, that you should make it
plain that you will listen to no complaints on minor matters of modes
or dress, of gesture and of ceremonial, until you be first assured and
certified that every human person under your charge shall have the
offer of free access to the Holy Ghost in Baptism, the offer of forgive-
ness of sins upon Confession, of strength and endowment in Confirmation, and of the full benefits of Christ's Passion in the most
necessary and comfortable Sacrament of the Lord's Supper.

The second point on which Marson was urgent to insist is dealt
with later in the same document, by a protest against a "prelacy"
which prevented the Church being governed constitutionally.

They tell us, reverend Fathers, that you are seeking to obtain from the
secular powers a more Roman authority over us, your sons; that you
wish to impose new oaths upon those who accept benefices, and would
recast our Ordination Vows of obedience, making them to be vows of
obedience to a Diocesan, without Synod, as to a Corporation Sole, as
to a King unconstitutional and without Parliament. But is not this to
cede the whole ground and claim to Popery? Can Englishmen, who
could bear a one-man rule, distant, safeguarded and hallowed by tradition, be expected to find use for a fallible Pope in each Cathedral city,
beyond whom there is no ecclesiastical appeal? New powers often
diminish old authority. Was it not so in the history of the Holy See?

The third point for which Marson strove at this time, and not
only against his antagonists but amongst his Catholic allies, was that
the fundamental doctrinal matter at issue was the Real Presence in
the Blessed Sacrament. When the Commission's Report appeared in

1906, he stressed the significance of its reference to the practice of saying before the administration of the elements to the people, "Behold the Lamb of God", as constituting a "grave charge" against those who did so.

> This is the point to fight upon. It is the pith of the whole matter. Is God's Lamb there? Is He to be beholden? Yes or No? If Yes, why not say so? This is an encroachment upon pure spirituals, abetted by the Archbishop, and a deliberate attempt to rob us of the only vision that is worth seeing.

The matter dealt with in the pages immediately preceding may seem to have taken us somewhat far from the main purpose of this volume. Yet it is quite essential to an understanding of the central inspiration of the men dealt with in it, men widely regarded as "eccentric" (and indeed sometimes so perhaps in their flamboyant gestures and manner of presentation), to be clear upon what was the driving force that impelled them. Assuredly it was nothing so tangential as "ritual".

12

Marson had "the pen of a ready writer", not only metaphorically in the sense that the Psalmist coined the phrase, but actually as his pen was put to paper. He was never more successful than in his correspondence with his many friends; Lord Morley even declared that "he was the best writer of English letters since Addison". In his books he was not always so successful; even friendly critics described some of his prose as "slapdash", and his writing sometimes tended to be too whimsical and periphrastic. But when his heart was wholly in his work and the theme called for vigorous treatment, he could be brilliantly effective, and this was perhaps never more the case than in the famous pamphlet on the emptily factual and spiritually barren teaching which passed for "religious education" at the beginning of the century, a subject which moved him to a truly righteous indignation. This publication developed out of an address given at Oxford in 1894 for which he took a title indicative of the sterility and remoteness of what he was denouncing, *Huppim and Muppim*, which few who came upon it were

likely to recognize as the names of two of the sons of Benjamin.[12]
This address was printed in the *Commonwealth*, then edited by
Scott Holland, and sparked off, as Marson must have hoped it
would, a vigorous controversy as to the value of what was likely to
be—and commonly was, even in church schools—served up to
children as "undenominational religion". Though neither adver-
tised nor reviewed, the pamphlet "got upon its own legs", said its
author, "and ran and then flew abroad". It has remained almost the
only well-remembered piece of Marson's writing. Twenty years later
it was included in his book *God's Co-operative Society*.

"It does not matter a bit," declared Marson provocatively, "as far
as religious education goes, whether we have secular provided
schools or whether we have non-provided schools or no schools. It
does matter very much indeed that we should recognize that real
religion is not being given now." The syllabuses in church schools
were often as bad as any others. He specified one which "sketches
out a nine-year course and is so dexterously arranged that under it a
child may reach the age of ten without getting as much sacramental
teaching as a medieval weanling got in a week". When his pamphlet
was republished some years later, he declared that "some educators
are still to be found who boast that the infants under their hands
have had a complete course of lessons in the insects of the Old
Testament", probably, he adds in a characteristic footnote, "leaving out the only really important insect, the worm that dieth not".
"While our clergy proclaims the glories of Huppim and Muppim
and Ard the people are destroyed for lack of knowledge. . . . They
know all about Abraham except the way to his bosom; all about
David except his sure mercies; and all about St Paul except the
Faith which he preached and which justified him."

Ard being yet another son of Benjamin, Marson a little later took
his name as a title for a further pamphlet which thrust the examination of the whole subject a stage further back by a scrutiny of the
"religious knowledge" required of their intending pastors. He
speaks highly of the zeal and high level of intelligence of the priesthood before declaring that "it seems obvious that Huppim and
Muppim must have been bred in the bone of the clergy, before these
could come out so conspicuously in the flesh; and therefore the
coign of discomfiture is to be looked for in the training given to
the clergy themselves. Let any man compare the theory of the
English Ordinal with the actual recruiting and training of the

English clergy, in each grade, and he will be surprised to find that these have little or nothing in common."

This Marson proceeds to do. After arguing effectively that the trouble begins in the public schools, he goes on to declare that "the deacon is not examined in any of the matters which should be his main concern". So would seem to have been the case half a century ago if the questions set to them, as quoted by Marson, are at all representative. "Where was Nob? Examine the foreign policy of Ahab. Comment upon 'Moab is my washpot'. Explain the term 'Shawm'."

> Not a word about reading, voice-production, music, not a suggestion of slums, sweating soupkitchens, balance sheets, truck acts, sanitations, allotments, diseases and school teaching.... Not a question as to how to christen a child validly, an art which might be thought to be of some use to deacons....
>
> The priests' work according to the Ordinal is to teach, feed, and search out, to forgive sins and to bless.... But does the priest know his proper work? Obviously he knows every craft under the sun except priestcraft.

As to bishops—but, as always, Marson is particularly sardonic at the expense of the late Victorian episcopate, and on how its members become such. ("Is it possible that the wrong man chooses the wrong men for the episcopate?")

> There seems to be no provision for training bishops, no Staff College, and it is not our use to supply an honest shrewd man to jog one elbow, while a trained theologian jogs the other, which was the medieval plan. It has been suggested that the Athenaeum Club really supplies all these needs, although even that may be disputed.

Much of this, of course—and happily—seems quite outdated now. But, since it is so, we may well ask how much may be attributed to such gadflies as Marson who had the courage to speak plainly about these "negligences and offences" and the gift to do so effectively. It is a main purpose of this volume to suggest that it is often "reckless extremists", such as these men must have seemed to be to their generation, who are in fact to a large extent the agencies through which changes which, to a later one, seem to have been a natural evolution are brought about.

This of course is the writing of a man still in his thirties, though since things seemed to him to be little better in this respect in his last years, he was ready to reproduce it, with all its railing—and raillery—with his other collected papers. But his long years in the country tended to give his prose a calmer, gentler tone. He came to love his rural setting, but he praised it not as merely natural but as "nature bitted and bridled and used for human ends... What is really lovely and glorious in nature is best seen and known where human nature is present and is master, when man determines the limit and orders the disarray." And so when he composed the pieces which were later collected for his last—and posthumous—book, it was the men and women of his parish he chose to write about. *Village Silhouettes* was illustrated by real silhouettes cut with no little art by Marson's own scissors. And those of whom he writes are clearly real people, if described with rather more whimsy than would be acceptable today. There is room here for only one example of his later manner, where he writes of the village inn as the meeting place of a true community.

> It has a romance about it. It is so pleasantly bare in the real and interesting part of it. The smooth wooden tables, the fire, the settles, the welcome to the world, the fraternity of it. . . .
> There is no exclusive club here, no nice people, aristocrats of wit, virtue, money, blood or taste. There is none of that smug, proprietory castle notion of home here. It is a cosmos in little, it is common land for common folk, a public house, as public as Paradise will be when pasts are not thrown up against us, and all things are unappropriated and for use.

Here is Marson, the "socialist", speaking of man's true relationships as clearly as he ever did in some violent sermon in Australia or to his harrowed cab drivers in Somers Town.

13

Despite much happiness which the vicar of Hambridge came to find in his later years there, these years were clouded by an ever advancing shadow of ill health. His asthmatic condition did not improve, and Etherington tells us that "both the complaint and the constant remedies he had to use played havoc with his constitution". In 1907 he wrote:

> I am a wretched roarer who spends a slice out of every night blowing

like a whale—practically dying—but to little purpose, I fear, and sacrificing smokes to the Furies.

Two years later matters were worse. He wrote to a friend:

I'm at low water. The ladies sent for a leech, who said "bad strain to heart" and gave me dynamite and other concoctions. I crawled about and had bad bouts and am still a wraith. . . . It makes one feel queer to be told one has been playing at hide and seek with the last enemy. It gives one a kind of monoplane view of our funny world, which seems so pleasant and dear . . . all that one just has glimpsed at in the great illuminated Service Book of Life.

The glimpses were to last for another four years. But on New Year's Eve of 1913 he wrote to refuse an invitation from a friend in London:

I have had a terrible time (i.e. one that scared me) for they supposed I was to fall into that nasty ditch between the world where a man neither lives nor dies neatly. But kind friends have hauled me out and I am being refitted for another run, I am thankful to say, and am beginning to find out how delightful it is to be alive.

Alas! No London for me. Must rush back to my disordered parish as soon as my legs have any rush in them.

But the run was to be a short one. Two months later on 3 March 1914, after an afternoon of visiting, part of it spent amusing some children with his scissors and paper, a violent attack drove him home where, having first to endure some hours of great suffering, he died. He was only 55.

It was his close friend Etherington who said the Requiem Mass for him four days later. At the funeral which followed, his much-tried bishop spoke the words of committal and paid a generous tribute to "the consistency of his character, the devotion of his life and the fearlessness with which he spoke out". Cecil Sharp was among those who stood by the grave.

"It is a privilege to live with Marson, as his knowledge is encyclopaedic and his wit wonderful. I can't help feeling that I shall look back on this time as a very memorable period in my life and every day I am more and more impressed with his grip on life and his qualities as a parish priest." So wrote a young man living and studying at Hambridge to his fiancée, a man who was himself to exhibit great qualities as a parish priest, both in town and country—Percy Widdrington, then twenty-three. It is interesting that Wid-

drington should have discerned Marson's pastoral gifts at a time
(1897) when that pastor had by no means satisfied himself that he
had learnt how rightly to exercise them in his rural parish. Widdrington has told of how Marson scandalized many of his parishioners by bringing a gipsy family into the Vicarage to save the father
of it from dying in the open from pneumonia. It was a characteristic
gesture of that *caritas* which lay behind all his thought and was
inspired by his faith. Twenty years after his death a woman who
remembered him with the warmest recollections wrote to the man
then compiling his (alas, unpublished) biography. She began her
letter with the words. "He was very kind to the poor." Of all
memories of him it was perhaps this which he would have been
most happy to have recalled. And no tribute could have been more
faithfully earned.

NOTES

1. *The Christian Socialist Movement in England*, pp. 171–2.
2. Which is not always the case, indeed, even of some of the apostles themselves. And the inclusion in pietistic "Calendars" of the names of persons
   from primitive and medieval times of whom practically nothing is known
   is not calculated to make the reality of sainthood more widely understood in a post-Christian age.
3. In this, his son informs me, he was much aided by Dr Maud Karpelis,
   o.b.e., who "did a tremendous amount of work" in helping with its presentation. Mr Etherington was at this time Vicar of Minehead.
4. *God's Co-operative Society*, p. 20.
5. "I am no ascetic in theory", he once wrote, "and yet I never get quite
   enthusiastic about a spiritual leader who has not some ascetic traits in
   him."
6. *Autobiography*, p. 223.
7. *God's Co-operative Society*, p. 16.
8. Ibid., pp. 33–8.
9. Chloe is remembered by Fr Francis Etherington, son of the author of the
   Memoir on which this essay so much relies, as "an extremely witty and
   eccentric woman, who made him laugh to an extent that was almost painful on her visits to Minehead Vicarage".
10. *God's Co-operative Society*, pp. 74–5.
11. This is reproduced in full in the second (1930) edition of *God's Co-opera-
    tive Society*.
12. "To know these worthies", Marson declared, "is a fair example of the
    knowledge which still passes muster as religious education "

Conrad Noel, 1869–1942
Catholic Crusader

ROBERT WOODIFIELD

I

Conrad le Despencer Roden Noel was the youngest of the four
men with whom this book deals. In his *Autobiography* he said: "By
the irony of fate, for I have never had any love for monarchy,
limited or unlimited, I was born at 2.25 a.m. on 12 July 1869 in a
house on Kew Green, one of the royal cottages inhabited by ladies
in waiting to Queen Victoria and lent to my father, Roden Noel,
during the period of his service at court, by his aunt, Lady Jocelyn."
As one of the "old aristocracy" (his family really had "come over
with the Conqueror") and brought up in Court circles, and influenced, no doubt, by his father, who developed radical views and
consequently relinquished his post as Groom of the Privy Chamber,
he no doubt knew what he was talking about when, years later, he
referred (in the *Manifesto of the Catholic Crusade*) to "that nest
of flunkeys, the Court"!

A considerable part of this essay will consist of a fairly comprehensive setting forth of Conrad Noel's theology, because, in my opinion,
this was at once the most important, and the least known or understood, thing about him. He was not a "learned theologian", but his
theological thought was alive, original and creative.

His religious background was very mixed. His father, who had
been brought up with the idea of his being ordained to the ministry
of the Church of England, came to have "so many doubts about
the doctrines that were then supposed to constitute Christianity"
that he gave up this idea; but, after a period of atheism, he came to
"a recovery of faith and an intensely reasoned belief"—influenced by
a group of people which included F. D. Maurice and F. W. Robert-
son.

His mother was an Evangelical who, with her son and daughter, attended a church the vicar of which "although not one of the most extreme of the brimstone order, did from time to time suspend us over the everlasting burning". His father, "fond as he was of his Evangelical wife, could not stand the religion of the torture chamber . . . and sought out happier temples".

And his aunt, Lady Gainsborough, who had a good deal to do with Conrad's upbringing, as he lived with her during the winters which, owing to his mother's ill-health, his parents spent in Italy, was a Calvinist who, "while she doubted the salvation of most of mankind . . . was very doubtful of her own", which uncertainty "lifted her above the level of most Calvinists, who are smugly satisfied about their own future, and as smugly certain of the damnation of the rest".

It is evident that his mother's Evangelicism and his aunt's Calvinism never made the slightest appeal to Conrad; they did, in fact, repel him. But, as evidently, his father's "intensely reasoned belief" did appeal to him. He described that belief in an article, in the *Humane Review* early in this century, on "Roden Noel, Poet"— from which I quote:

As regards the orthodox Christian creeds, he was nearer to orthodoxy than the conventional Christian world would suppose. . . . He had, in fact, little quarrel with the creeds, but regarded an intellectual capacity for swallowing supposed events, Christian or otherwise, as having very little to do with faith. Faith was not assent to the fact that such and such a person went up into the clouds, or down into hell. If there were sufficient proof for it, by all means accept it, but faith was, in the language of the Epistle to the Hebrews, the very life-stuff of things longed for, the impregnable conviction of things not seen—i.e., not of events at present unverifiable, but of things which never were, never are, and never will be seen—things of their very essence invisible; the unseen, intangible realities of justice, mercy and truth, which underlie the world of sense, and alone give it consistence and being. . . . Human life he interpreted in terms of deity, and the only deity he knew was the Human God, as seen in the life of heroes, martyrs and saints, of men full-grown, full developed, who had entered into their kingdom. He felt that God is immanent in, but transcends, and is in that sense distinct from, the universe, but that for us all knowledge of deity must come through the channel of nature. He was orthodox enough to believe in the true manhood of Jesus Christ, and *therefore* in his Godhead.

In this description of his father's basic belief Noel was also revealing the mystical root of his own. But he came to give to what might be called his father's "liberal and humanist" Christianity a more "Catholic" basis and expression. He did, in fact, begin to do this even as a boy. For as his father had "sought out happier temples" in which to worship than the Evangelical church which his wife attended, so eventually did he. At St John's, Upper Norwood, he learnt to love the externals and the "atmosphere" of Catholic worship—a love which, years later, he was to express so beautifully at Thaxted. But he never became an "Anglo-Catholic"— that is, a Tractarian or "Puseyite"—in *theology*; his father's "liberal and humanist" theology had made too deep an impression on him for this to happen. He became, what he called himself, a "Liberal Catholic". When, in the early years of this century, the "Modernist" movement arose in the Roman Church, and influenced some Anglicans, he sometimes called himself a "Catholic Modernist"—although, like the Roman Catholic Modernists themselves, he did not much like the term (he referred, in *Byways of Belief*, to "that wise movement with the stupid name, Catholic Modernism"). He greatly admired Father George Tyrrell, the leading Modernist in this country, and was in general agreement with his position as set forth in such books as *A Much-Abused Letter, Through Scylla and Charybdis, Medievalism*, and *The Church and the Future*; but he regretted that in writing his last book, *Christianity at the Crossroads*, Tyrrell had been so much influenced by Schweitzer's *The Quest of the Historical Jesus*.

Noel's Liberal Catholicism involved him in difficulty on the very eve of what was to have been his ordination to the diaconate. It had been arranged that he should go as curate to an extreme Anglo-Catholic church, All Saints', Plymouth. Although his theology differed considerably from that of its vicar, Fr Chase, he had been attracted by the homeliness and naturalness and "continental" atmosphere of its worship, and because it was "certainly the church of the destitute". One rather wonders how long the difference between the Vicar's teaching and his own would have made it possible for him to have remained there. But this difficulty never arose. For on the very morning of the day on which he was to have been ordained he was summoned to an interview with the Bishop, Dr Ryle, who told him that "after wrestling with the Lord all night in prayer, it had been shown to me that it would be dangerous for you to go to All Saints' ". But "I pointed out to him that although I loved the service at All Saints, I by no means shared all Fr Chase's views". "Ah, that's the trouble," said the Bishop, "for you add to his Romanism your own pantheism, and pantheism is a heresy." So ended Conrad's first attempt to enter the ministry of the Anglican Church. He returned to work—as he had been working for some time—as a layman with Father Dolling at St Agatha's, Landport, Portsmouth.

With reference to Dr Ryles's reasons for refusing to ordain him deacon ("pending further instruction"!) his father said, in a letter to the Bishop:

> The doctrine in which my son understood that your Lordship thought him heretical is, as he believes, the very doctrine urged upon him by Bishop Westcott as a most important one to be believed—the Immanence of God. The Romish doctrine as regards Holy Communion my son certainly does not believe. . . . He might be led to modify his views . . . but whether he would ever be led to exchange them for the Evangelical opinions to which your Lordship probably refers when you speak of the "simplicity of the faith as it is in Jesus" is, of course, problematical.

With reference to this episode Conrad says in his *Autobiography*:

> When the Bishop said that it would be dangerous for a young man like myself, at the beginning of his career, to go to such a church as All Saints' at Plymouth, he had this amount of justification, that many years later Charles Chase made his submission to Rome, and perhaps that was always the home of his spirit. What he failed to see was that although I was attracted by the continental aspect of All Saints', its ever open door, its votive offerings, the sailors and dockers who worshipped there, and repelled by the heavy respectability of the Anglican Church in general, my trend was not really towards Rome, but towards a more rational and modernist interpretation of the Catholic Faith.

Noel was eventually (in 1894) ordained deacon in the Chester diocese, and his first curacy was in the parish of Floweryfield (in which there were no flowers and no field). There he started a series of lectures on Sunday afternoons on "Catholic Socialism". "These lectures were boycotted by the ordinary congregation, but thronged by men and women who had never previously been to church. The audience included many Nonconformists, and also agnostics and atheists." The churchwardens complained to the Bishop of Chester,

Dr Jayne. "In his interview with me he expressed indignation at my invitation to outsiders to hear the lectures. . . . Had I no respect for the wishes of the proper congregation, and did I prefer a pack of atheists to them? 'Are you prepared to make yourself acceptable to your congregation? Are you going to get on with them or not?' —to which I replied, 'I am not'." The result of all this was that the Bishop refused to ordain him priest, and, against the wishes of the vicar, ordered him to resign his curacy at Floweryfield; which he did.

For two years he was out of work as far as the Church was concerned. In those years he did a great deal of public speaking, mainly at Socialist meetings, and became well known in the Socialist movement, especially in the North. Then in 1897, through the intervention of Canon Charles Gore, he obtained a curacy under Canon Hicks at St Philip's, Salford, and at last, in 1898, was ordained priest—four years after he had been ordained deacon, and six years after Dr Ryle's last-minute refusal to ordain him to that office.

The long delay in getting priested was due to his Liberal Catholic theology, and to his preaching Socialism, as regards its essential principles and values, as the expression of that theology. Years later he set forth such a theology, and its close connection with Socialism, in a lecture on "Socialism and Theology" which he gave at the 1912 Annual Conference of the Church Socialist League. The lecture was published in the September 1912 issue of the *Church Socialist*, from which extracts are given in the second part of this essay.

Noel's role as a preacher of "Catholic Socialism" antedated by fully a dozen years the formation of the Church Socialist League in 1906. So in the 1890s he was—naturally and inevitably—a member of the Guild of St Matthew.

But although a member of the Guild, his name is not so much associated with it as are those of the other men with whom we are concerned in this book. He does not, in fact, seem to have been very active in it—according to his standard of activity. And his *Autobiography* suggests that his enthusiasm for it was not unbounded. He, of course, agreed wholeheartedly with the essentially "Liberal Catholic" theology that was prevalent in it, particularly as it was expressed by its warden, Stewart Headlam—he mentions *The Socialist's Church, Priestcraft and Progress, Lessons from the Cross, The Laws of Eternal Life,* and *The Meaning of the Mass.*

(In their *The Development of Modern Catholicism*, Wilfred Knox and Alex Vidler said that the Guild's "task of 'getting rid of the prejudices of Secularists' involved nothing less than the working out of a Liberal Catholic theology".[1] Noel was also in thorough agreement with Headlam's and the Guild's anti-Puritanism. His own little book, *The Day of the Sun—A Plea for a rational Sunday*, was publicized and sold by the Guild. And he joined with Stewart Headlam, Gilbert and Cecil Chesterton, Hilaire Belloc, and, I think, Percy Dearmer, in forming the Anti-Puritan League—which had a short life but a gay one. (When Noel's *Byways of Belief*, which included a chapter on "The Heresy of the Teetotallers", was published, one reviewer described the author as "one of the beer, dogma, and democracy school"!)

But he was not satisfied with the Socialism of the Guild. In comparing it with its successor, the Church Socialist League, he said that the latter "was much more Socialist than the older Guild of St Matthew. . . . The weakness of the Guild was that beyond a general support of the working class movement it confined itself to land reform, and was dominated by the teachings of Henry George. . . . It was the more thoroughgoing Socialism, which included the problem of the land but did not shirk the question of interest, which made the Church Socialist League a necessity."[2]

As a very young member of the Guild (for about the last two years of its life) I do not agree with this criticism of it. It is true that Headlam himself, and some, but not all, of its members, did regard the "land question" as being, for practical reasons, of *primary* importance, and supported Henry George's policy for dealing with it. But it is not the case that they were "unsound", from the Socialist point of view, on the "capital question". All members of the Guild, I venture to say, wanted what is the basic objective of all Socialists—a society in which ownership of the land *and other* means of production is not concentrated in the hands of a few; in which, therefore, these essential means of living are accessible to all without the intervention of a profit-seeking owning class; and in which all co-operate in using these things for the common good. And all held that these basic Socialist principles are also basic principles of a Christian social order. These principles found expression—and where not explicitly expressed were obviously assumed—in the Guild's publications. In particular, they were quite explicit in the leaflet *The Guild of St Matthew: What it is and who should join it*, which bore all the marks of having been written by Headlam himself. This leaflet was as socialist with regard to capital and interest, as well as to land and rent, as the most orthodox Socialist could desire. (My copy of this leaflet has been lost or "lent", so I cannot quote from it. But my recollection of what it said, in effect, on the point in question, is clear.)

I have already described how Noel's first attempt to be ordained deacon was frustrated; how, when at last he had become a deacon (in 1894) he was discharged from his first curacy, and was unemployed, as far as the Church was concerned, for two years; and how, with the help of Charles Gore, he obtained a curacy at St Philip's, Salford, where, after a year as deacon, he was ordained priest. There he was fairly happy, under a more or less sympathetic vicar, Canon Hicks (later, Bishop of Lincoln). His happiness was only slightly marred by the fact that Hicks was not only a teetotaller himself, but was an ardent crusader for teetotalism! After two years at Salford Noel went to Newcastle as an assistant priest at St Philip's. There, at last, he was really at home, with two Catholic Socialist colleagues, the Vicar, W. E. Moll, and his fellow assistant priest, Percy Widdrington. The three of them carried on a vigorous Catholic Socialist propaganda, in the church and in the parish. Two years later he came to London, and for five years was assistant priest to A. L. Lilley at St Mary's, Paddington Green. Lilley (who later became a Canon of Hereford) was a Socialist, and a thoroughgoing Modernist—a friend of Fr George Tyrrell, and *the* Anglican authority on the Roman Catholic Modernist movement. From there he joined his friend Percy Dearmer, also a Socialist and a Liberal Catholic, at St Mary's, Primrose Hill. Three years later (in 1908) he left St Mary's to become the full-time organizing secretary of the Church Socialist League.

The Church Socialist League was formed in 1906, shortly before the death of the Guild of St Matthew, mainly by members of the Guild—W. E. Moll, Percy Widdrington, Egerton Swann, Cecil Chesterton, Lewis Donaldson, and Conrad Noel, to name a few. In its basis, Socialism was defined as "the fixed principle according to which the community shall own the land and capital collectively, and use them co-operatively for the good of all". Probably most members of the League in its early days, including Noel, held that the application of this "fixed principle" would in practice involve

"State Socialism"—that is, the direct control and "running" of practically all industries by the State or municipalities. But an increasing realization of the almost inevitable danger of bureaucracy in such a system (of which Headlam had been well aware), a realization stimulated by the publication of Belloc's *The Servile State*, and other writings of Distributists, Syndicalists, and Guild Socialists, helped to draw the League away from that brand of "Socialism" (which I prefer to call "State Collectivism") towards some more truly democratic form of Socialism, and eventually it became practically a "Guild Socialist" body. The main idea of the Guild Socialists was that while the community should be the ultimate "owner" of the means of production, the actual control and carrying on of each industry should be in the hands of the workers ("by hand and brain") in that industry, only ultimately subject to the general co-operative ordering of society for the common good. The National Guilds League was formed, by G. D. H. Cole and others, to propagate this "guild idea", especially in the Trade Union movement, and to work out schemes for implementing it; and many members of the Church Socialist League joined it—at least two of whom, Maurice Reckitt and Conrad Noel, were elected to its Executive Council.

The affinity of this "guild idea" with the main idea of the early Christian Socialists is worth noting. As C. F. G. Masterman said in his book on F. D. Maurice:

> Socialism came to Maurice . . . in the form of encouragement of association or co-operation among the working classes themselves. It was not the formation of little secluded Utopias he desired, leading the communal life. Nor did he ever appeal to the State to come in to organise the industrial class. But he thought that, by uniting the workmen themselves into Co-operative Producing Associations, he could eliminate the profits of dead capital and abrogate the ferocity of the competitive struggle. [Such associations] might become universal; and, when universal, would overthrow the tyranny of capital.[3]

Towards the end of the last century Noel had become well known, especially in the industrial north, as a "free-lance" speaker on any Socialist platform on which he was invited to speak—which were many. But when he became the organizing secretary of the Church Socialist League, he toured the country speaking mainly at meetings arranged by the League, or on other platforms in its name.

At this time he was at the height of his powers as a public speaker —and that was very high indeed. It was as a speaker, rather than as a writer, that he excelled. He usually wrote well, and sometimes superbly (as some of the quotations given in this essay show), but it was as a speaker that his extraordinarily dynamic and colourful and many-sided personality found supreme expression. In his speaking, in the pulpit and on the platform, fire and passion, persuasion, satire, reason, and humour were blended, all conveyed by variations in voice which it was a joy to hear, and by gestures which it was a joy to see. With reference to him as a speaker Dr Wilson, his bishop at the time of his death, said at the requiem for him at Thaxted:

> I remember Conrad Noel when I was a young student. I remember him giving an address on the political principles which were dear to his heart. I remember the fire in his eye, the flash, the zeal, the passionate enthusiasm of his words as he advocated those principles which, in those days, meant the extinction of every hope of professional success, but such a thing as professional success never crossed his mind.

In 1910 Noel was offered the incumbency of Thaxted, Essex, by its Socialist patron, the Countess of Warwick. There he remained until his death in 1942, having placed Thaxted "on the map" during those thirty-two years.

Thaxted church is very beautiful but, like so many lovely old churches, it was cluttered up with a mass of "ecclesiastical" furniture when Noel went there. He at once proceeded to act on his own motto—"To beautify a church, *take things out of it!*" The result was a spaciousness in chancel, nave, and aisles which revealed the full architectural beauty of the building. But he and his wife, Miriam—whose taste in such matters was sure and faultless—also put things *into* the church—beautiful hangings, banners, and altar frontals, all making a perfect blend of colour; and Miriam herself made many of the vestments, full and graceful, which were worn at Mass.

In ceremonial Noel adopted, in its main features, the "English Use", which Percy Dearmer had revived at St Mary's, Primrose Hill and which during his time as assistant priest at that church he had come to appreciate, for he regarded it as being at once more simple and more beautiful than what was then the "modern Roman"

Use, which most Anglo-Catholic churches had adopted. But he altered the 1662 Prayer Book order of the Mass to the more traditional order, in doing which he differed from Dearmer, who was strictly a "Prayer Book Catholic". (But Noel's statement, in his *Autobiography*, that Dearmer "even insisted on reading one of the lengthy exhortations to Communion at every Sunday Mass" is not correct. I attended St Mary's regularly for some years when Dearmer was its vicar, and frequently after Noel came there, and I can say definitely that one of the long exhortations—the one which ends with an invitation to confession—was read *only* on the Sundays immediately preceding the three Great Festivals of the year.)

The music—in which Gustav Holst,[4] during the years that he lived at Thaxted, gave much help—was a combination of plain-song and polyphonic, and was led by a group of singers in the nave, accompanied on festivals by an orchestra. The Litany was sung in procession before Mass on all ordinary Sundays, but at festivals a "People's Procession" was substituted, in which the people joined in behind the ministers and servers, some carrying banners preceded by lights, girls wearing gaily coloured veils, and they, and the children, carrying flowers and branches—the whole thing being indescribably gay and beautiful.

I mention these things that Noel did in Thaxted church (and the list is by no means complete) in order to bring out what was such an essential part of his nature—his love of beauty and gaiety and drama.

I should add that his successor—and son-in-law—Fr Jack Putterill, has continued on the same lines as regards the services in Thaxted church.

In spite of Noel's early enthusiasm for the Church Socialist League, the time came when he was not satisfied with the theological position of the League; and his dissatisfaction grew until, in 1918, he resigned from it, and began to form the Catholic Crusade. Whereas the C.S.L. had been open to anyone, whatever his theology, who was "a member of the Church of England", the new society had as its basis such a "Liberal and Humanist" Catholicism as I shall set forth in the later pages of this essay.

The outlook on life which such a theology was held to involve was expressed in *The Manifesto of the Catholic Crusade*. This was a flamboyant production, and very "revolutionary" in tone, but beneath the flamboyance and revolutionary language was thoroughly balanced thought. Examples of this were: the balance between the need for individual and group freedom and initiative, and the common authority of the community in civil and industrial life, and in the life of the Church; the balance between "personal and common ownership", to encourage "initiative in fellowship"; the balance between national independence and international interdependence, and the condemnation of narrow nationalism and empire, each of which upsets that balance; the balance between the principle of absolute pacifism in all circumstances and violence in some circumstances—"persuasion is the first weapon, and violence the last, in the Christian armoury"; the balance between the enjoying of "dancing, colour, and merry-making", and the striving for social justice; the balance in seeing the need for "the swift decision of the present" to have its roots in "the matured conviction of the ages" as expressed in "common traditions"—and so on (for I have not exhausted the list).

When I first read the *Manifesto* it at once reminded me of what Chesterton said in *Orthodoxy*:

> There was never anything so perilous or so exciting as orthodoxy. It was sanity; and to be sane is to be more dramatic than to be mad. It was the equilibrium of a man behind madly rushing horses, seeming to stoop this way and that, yet in every attitude having the grace of statuary and the accuracy of arithmetic. The Church ... swerved left and right, so as exactly to avoid enormous obstacles. ... In my vision the heavenly chariot flies thundering through the ages, the dull heresies sprawling and prostrate, the wild truth reeling but erect.[5]

I referred just now to the "revolutionary tone" of the *Manifesto*; and this was more or less typical of much of the Crusade's propaganda. But this "revolutionism" was not a particular *policy* for bringing about the root change in society—the revolution—which all Socialists, and some who would not accept that label, want. What the revolutionary language of the Crusade's propaganda expressed was a sense of urgency in working for that revolution—not "waiting until the great Slug-God Evolution evolves something, or Progress pushes you down into hell"—and not having too much respect for law if it seemed that something positively good could be achieved which would not otherwise be achieved, or something evil prevented which would not otherwise be prevented, by some direct, if unlawful, action. (An example of the kind of action that the Crusade would certainly have applauded, had it then been in existence, was that of the Poplar Guardians, under the leadership of that great Christian Socialist, George Lansbury, in breaking the Poor Law in order to secure more decent treatment for the people under it, and being sent to prison for doing so. As they themselves said, in a statement issued at the time, they were "guilty, and proud of it".)

The first public meetings held by the Crusade were in November 1919, on the subjects, "Why the Catholic Crusade supports the Russian Revolution", "Why the Catholic Crusade welcomes the Irish Republic" (which was then in rebellion against the British Government and its armed forces), and "Why the Catholic Crusade demands an English Revolution". All these meetings, at which Conrad Noel was the main speaker, were crowded—and Scotland Yard was also represented!

In supporting the Russian Revolution Noel was in line with the majority of Socialists, for although they no doubt welcomed it with varying degrees of enthusiasm, they all regarded what had emerged from it as preferable to Czardom. Noel himself welcomed it whole-heartedly. So great was his enthusiasm for it that he saw the Lenin dictatorship not only—as did most supporters of the Revolution—as a practical necessity in the circumstances, but actually as a true form of democracy, which was that of a "creative leadership" expressing the "latent will" of the people. This was a conception of democracy which made even some members of the Catholic Crusade uneasy. If Noel was still holding this view at the beginning of the Stalin dictatorship, he was soon disillusioned!

During the twelve years of its life the Catholic Crusade carried on a vigorous propaganda, through public meetings, taking part—with "Catholic" symbols—in unemployed and other marches, initiating rent strikes against the owners of slum property (as Fr Groser did in Stepney), and other activities, both in the Church and in the working class and "revolutionary" movements. Noel himself, for example, was Chairman of the British Section of the League against Imperialism, to which, also, many Catholic Crusaders belonged.

As has been the case with so many "left wing" societies, the Crusade eventually split on the Communist issue, which came to a head when the majority of the London group, of which Fr John Groser (then Vicar of Christ Church, Watney Street, Stepney) was the leading member, decided to support the Labour Party candidate rather than the Communist candidate, Harry Pollitt, at a by-

election in Stepney. Noel adopted a middle position between the
contestants, not only because he wanted to save the Crusade from
dissolution, but because that really was his position in this matter.
Nevertheless, this dispute eventually killed the Crusade.

After the dissolution of the Catholic Crusade, Noel and others
formed the Order of the Church Militant, with the idea of carrying
on similar work, but this never seemed to acquire the vigour which
to a great extent had characterized its predecessor.

For thirty-two years, until within a very short time of his death,
Conrad Noel preached at Thaxted such a theology as I describe
in this essay, with its resultant outlook on life, and way of life for
society. But "Didn't he preach personal religion?" it may be asked.
He certainly did. For him, "religion" which is not personal would
not be religion. But also, "personal religion" which is not essentially
social would not be personal religion. He acknowledged no separate
"sides" in the Catholic Religion—a "personal side" and a "social
side": for him these "sides" were one and indivisible, and he held
that the attempt to divide the indivisible spells disaster—as it has
done and is doing—to religion and life. But if the question "Didn't
he preach personal religion?" means was he not concerned with the
conscious relationship of the individual to God; with his character
as an individual; and with his relationship, other than "political",
with other individuals? then the answer is that he was very much
concerned with these things—as everyone knows who often heard
him preach, or who went to him for confession and advice, or who
knows his excellent manual for confession, *Sins and their Cure,*
or, of course, who knew him at all intimately.

With a man like Noel as vicar there are bound to be many "inci-
dents" in the course of thirty-two years. The best known of these
was the trouble that arose over the presence of the Red Flag and
the Sinn Fein Flag in Thaxted church. In the early days of the
1914–18 war—which he supported as being, in its resistance to
"Prussianism", on balance a "just war"—he had placed the St
George's Flag, as the flag of England, in the church. After the
1916 Easter Rebellion in Ireland, and the formation of the (illegal,
from the British Government's point of view) Irish Republic, he
placed in the church also the emblem of that Republic, the Sinn
Fein Flag, as witnessing, in the particular case of Ireland, to what
Noel held to be the general Christian principle of the right of

nations to self-determination. But—as we have already seen, in talking about the Catholic Crusade—while recognizing the value of national distinctions, he held that the truly Catholic outlook involved also the need for the inter-dependence of all the nations of the world. So he added to the two national flags in the church the flag which had for long been the recognized symbol of a world commonwealth of nations—the Red Flag, later inscribing on it the words "He hath made of one blood all nations". (Maurice Reckitt made a factual mistake in saying—in a footnote in his biography of Percy Widdrington—that this flag had been placed in Thaxted church as the flag of the Soviet Union, for it had been placed there before the Russian Revolution had taken place. But it is true that when the Soviet Union came into existence and adopted the Red Flag as its emblem, Noel certainly did not withdraw the flag.)

The actual trouble arose out of the support that Noel was giving to a miners' strike, in 1921, and his denunciation, from the pulpit and elsewhere, of the mine owners and the Government. This was given a good deal of publicity in the national, as well as in the local, press, and it was then that an enemy publicized the presence of these flags in the church. The result was that for some weeks a number of young men, many of them of the gangster type that, a few years later, would almost certainly have joined the British Union of Fascists, descended on Thaxted and its church, tearing down the flags and replacing them by the Union Jack—Noel and his supporters promptly reversing the process each time. There was some mild rioting, both in the church and in the streets—which was prevented from becoming more than "mild" by the presence of some hefty ex-policemen (men who had been discharged from the force for demanding the right to form a police "trade union", and for striking in support of their demand). These men kept an eye on the church and the vicarage to prevent damage being done to them, and any violence being done to the vicar—which was threatened, perhaps with serious intent. The enemy held frequent open-air meetings (which Noel and his supporters did not attend), and paraded the streets carrying Union Jacks and shouting slogans, and hurling insults at Noel, or any of his known supporters, if they happened to pass.

Eventually the opposition gave up the active fight, and proceeded to make plans for taking the matter to Court—which they did about a year later (in 1922). By this time the British Government had recognized the Irish Republic, so only the Red Flag was involved in the Court case. Noel, of course, lost the case, and was ordered to remove the flag from the church. After some thought, and consultation with his friends, he decided to obey the Court order.

Another "incident" that might be worth mentioning was the holding of a Procession of the Host through the streets of Thaxted, and the giving of Benediction with the Host from the steps of the old Guildhall (in June 1919). Owing to Noel's advertising of the procession in the church press and elsewhere, and to the publicity which his opponents had given to his Bishop's prohibition of it, a large crowd had been drawn into the little town. The opponents, who included a number of Kensitites,[6] tried, unsuccessfully, to break up the Procession, and even to snatch the Host from the hands of the priest who was carrying It.

Arising out of this, Noel wrote a small book, *Uplifting the Son of Man, Being notes on the spiritual and legal bearings of Processions of the Host.* As regards the "legal bearings" his argument seemed to me to contain a good deal of special pleading! On the "spiritual bearings" he said:

> In Thaxted the little community which worships at the Parish Church has made some attempt to recover that personal devotion and revolutionary zeal which are equally necessary to the reality and wholeness of the Faith. In Processions of the Host ... one may find a living illustration of this union of ideas, and a demonstration of the fact that wherever our Lord is present to do battle with the powers of the world, he meets with the same furious opposition which darkened his path in Galilee. Hearing that there was to be just such an opposition to our Procession—arising not from simple Evangelicals, but from rowdies of a neighbouring town backed by four or five residents from whom our movement had already received more violent opposition in the matter of Social Justice—we were the more determined to lift up our Lord in the public ways as the God of Justice and Comradeship. In face of the threat of our opponents that the Blessed Sacrament should never return to the church again, we remembered that as our Lord met without fear or shame the scoffs and threats of his enemies in Palestine, so now he would have his followers bear him aloft amidst the Hosannas of his friends and the curses of his foes, for "I, if I be lifted up, will draw all men unto me."

There is, perhaps, in this a touch of the romanticism that was part of Conrad's charming make-up. No doubt some of the opposition was "political", but I suspect that much of it, if not most of it, was opposition to what was regarded as "Romish idolatry"!

But Thaxted also had its lighter side. I recall with pleasure—and some nostalgia—the parties which would spontaneously gather in the local public houses (denounced by the "Puritans" of the town), and the dancing on the vicarage lawn on Sundays (denounced by the Sabbatarians—mostly the same people). The dancing at Thaxted included, but not exclusively, folk and morris dancing, which Conrad and Miriam had revived. But there was nothing self-conscious or solemn about this; ordinary people, especially young people, obviously enjoyed it. As Kingsley Martin said in an appendix to Conrad's *Autobiography*: "The dancing was fun, and if Conrad wanted to revive what romantics believe to have been the feeling and tradition of the Middle Ages, he was not unsuccessful. It would be a superficial observer who dismissed Thaxted as 'ye olde'."

2

In the beginning of this essay I said that a considerable part of it "will consist of a fairly comprehensive setting forth of Conrad Noel's theology, because, in my opinion, that was at once the most important, and the least known or understood, thing about him". It is commonly thought, or assumed (probably because he was the vicar of a church with "advanced" ceremonial, and habitually used "Catholic" terminology—such as "Mass"), that he was an Anglo-Catholic—which, for most who accept that label, still means essentially a Tractarian—in theology. This "fairly comprehensive setting forth" of his views, largely in his own words, will show how far he was from holding that theology. I will start by quoting from a lecture on "Socialism and Theology", which he gave at the 1912 Annual Conference of the Church Socialist League, to which reference was made in the first part of this essay.

He began by saying,

It has been contended in some quarters that there is a tendency to identify the Church Socialist League with a particular type of theology held by only a few churchpeople, and that this tendency is very dangerous. And it must frankly be admitted that persons like myself do wish to see the League centring round a particular body of theological doctrine, although they do not wish to exclude from membership those who are by baptism actually members of the Church, but do not at present see their way to accept the full proportion of the Faith.

He went on to give examples of the kind of doctrines, mainly Tractarian and Evangelical, of which he said:

God forbid that we should exclude any one of them. But God forbid that any one of these theologies should become the theology of the League, for not one of them forms a basis for Socialism, nor is rooted in a philosophy in the least consistent with Socialism.

But, "There is a theology which not only agrees with the fundamental assumptions made by Socialists, but which actually explains and enriches and confirms them: all other theologies darken counsel." He went on:

Supposing that men and women are as much the offspring of God as I am the son of my father, and that their happiness and fulness of life depend upon their response to that fact in heart and mind and deed; supposing that God requires the response or responsibility of men and women, and not the machine obedience of sub-human automata, and therefore had to give them an embryo will and consciousness with the dangers attaching to these things, that in time they may freely and of themselves desire him in the commonwealth of each other; supposing that by an act of deliberate refusal, or by slackness and omission, they had chosen darkness rather than light and were very far gone from original righteousness, so that they found themselves living in discord and at sixes and sevens, quarrelling, grasping each one for himself, slandering and hating, so that they had ceased to believe that they were the divine family, or no longer desiring to act as such; and supposing, further, that they were not so far gone but that divine prophets might from time to time arise from the deep wells of their essentially divine nature, because God had not ultimately given them over to believe a lie, but was present with them and in them and only hidden from their eyes by the dark mountain of their own sin; supposing that he were for ever pouring forth his grace to meet the faintest suggestion of desire and of grace on the part of human-kind; and supposing that at last, out of the depths of the race's being, which is identical with the being of God himself,[7] there arose a Deliverer, able to recall them to the nature and meaning of God, because he was divine actually when they were only divine potentially and were behaving like devils, and able to recall them to the true nature and meaning of humanity, because he was man actually and they were only men potentially, and were behaving like unmanly, inhuman demons: would not this great body of truth be bound to express itself, where people actually believed it, in something very like Socialism?

After saying that "the Kingdom of God is the whole world of men and women become conscious of commonwealth and living for the common good, the world, that is, according to God's original will and plan"; that the Church is "the divine instrument of this regenerated world"; and that eternal life is not "an unending existence beyond the grave", but that "it consists in 'the knowledge of thee, the only true God' and in the service of mankind, which is the outcome of such knowledge", he went on:

Supposing that Christ lived this life which is eternal, and recalled men to commonwealth, giving them fulness of life in measure as they responded to the call; supposing that he foresaw that the hatred of commonwealth would kill him unless he were willing to betray the truth that was in him, but foresaw, also, that by death alone can come the resurrection from the dead; supposing that he chose the few who had ears to hear and hearts to respond, that they might be the nucleus of a Divine Fellowship in the world; supposing that by death he entered into the unseen but ever present world which, to those who do respond, is closer than breathing and nearer than hands and feet; supposing that the sign and sacrament of his new-found power and presence were his outward and unmistakable appearance among them in joy and his visible exaltation into the innermost core of the universe, which is the heart of God; supposing that the world began to respond to this new power, its sign and sacrament to them being its visible presence in the faces and lives of the early Christians; supposing that the whole earth is so full of the glory of the Lord that the meanest things are not common or unclean, and that the means of our every-day nourishment and gaiety, the very bread and wine, are themselves but the outward signs and manifestations of God's very Body and Blood; supposing that men and women partaking of food set apart and consecrated by God's own ordinance to convey God's own self in the fellowship of a meal, were to persuade them that in him all things consist, and that without him noughtsoever is; supposing that human life were at its best so heroic and so God-like that men began to worship those who had fought the good fight and were covered with glory; supposing that the heaven of the saints consists in the service of the sinners, as co-partners with God and saviours of the race; supposing that the God-penetrated democracy, the Church, for the sake of holy order, chose from its divine and priestly ranks certain men for special functions and administrations in the same, and as organs of the body's life: would not this further body of doctrine find its expression in something very like a democratic common-wealth? And if not, why is it that anti-Socialists who dwell comfortably in the present system do comfortably accept the conventional and popular theology of Romanists, Puseyites, Broad Churchmen and Evangelicals alike, and reject this particular body of doctrine?

I do not expect that the League will accept this body of theology at once, but I do expect that it will examine it with the utmost care, and on the assumption that however strange a thing may seem, it may turn out to be but the newness of the old tree putting out its fresh leaves, inspired by the Ancient of Days who says "Behold, I make all things new". I do not expect the League to accept this suddenly, but I do expect it to accept it ultimately, or to perish among forgotten and worthless things.

This is a long quotation, but I include it because it presents in one statement a fairly clear outline of Noel's theology. As I reproduce it here I am reminded of the remark made by his friend (and, in the early days at Thaxted, assistant priest) John Grant: "Conrad puts life into Catholic theology, or, rather, *shows you the life that is in it.*"

This provocative article aroused heated controversy in the Church Socialist League. Those Anglo-Catholics who held strictly to the Tractarian theology regarded it as being especially an attack on that theology, and in their turn denounced it for its "Modernism" and "Pantheism". The most prominent of these, Arnold Pinchard, resigned from the League in protest against it.

With reference to this article, and also to Noel's expression of his theological views elsewhere, another prominent member of the Church Socialist League, Egerton Swann, himself an avowed Modernist and in substantial agreement with those views, criticized what he regarded as Noel's too free use of the word "Catholic" as applied to his distinctive theology. Thus, in reviewing *Byways of Belief* (which was published about this time) he said:

If one accepts so avowedly Modernist an attitude as Mr Noel's (like most Modernists he is not very fond of the *name*), one is hardly justified in speaking of "the Catholic Faith" as though this meant some clear, definite, and well-understood content. "The Catholic Faith" will mean, on Mr Noel's principles, to every man the cycle of his own individual beliefs. . . . Of course it is easy to say that we hold all the essentials or fundamentals of the traditional Catholic Faith, and only reinterpret consistently with keeping our hold on these. But then everyone will differ in detail as to what is and what is not essential. Mr Noel, if he were to describe in detail and with scientific accuracy all that he does and does not believe on the various matters most debated among Christians, would probably shock terribly the great majority of professed "Catholics" by some of his doubts or negations. . . . This consideration makes it especially dangerous to speak of "*the Catholic faith in its fulness*" when one really means one's own particular reinterpretation of the Catholic Faith.

Egerton Swann had certainly "got something" there; but the same difficulty seems to be inherent in *any* use of "labels"—including that of "Christian" itself. Do not professed *Christians* "differ in detail as to what is and what is not essential"? Some would say, for example, that the doctrine of the Virgin Birth of Jesus is essential in the Christian Faith; others would say—as Swann, as well as Noel, did say—that it is not *essential*.

My mention of the doctrine of the Virgin Birth reminds me of Noel's review of Dr Neville Figgis's book *The Gospel and Human Needs*. Figgis had claimed that this doctrine, and that of the "Empty Tomb", are essential to Christianity, and asked, as rhetorical questions, whether, without these, it "would be very much to live by" and "anything at all to die for". With reference to this view, Noel asked:

What is really the value of the various clauses of the Christian creed? Is the statement of the peculiar birth of Christ really worth dying for? Or is this statement something after the nature of scaffolding to building, or husk to kernel? Which is the more important, the peculiar birth, or the Incarnation which the supposed or actual virgin-birth is meant to safeguard? . . . I often wonder what the irruptionist conception of God is. Would they have thronged about the Christ without ever suspecting that he was God-like and supremely adorable, until someone assured them that he had been born in an extraordinary way, and that his body was destined for a levitation into the sky? . . . Or was there something about the Galilean to drag from the very hearts of simple people the conviction "Never man spake as this man", to assure them that they were in the presence of a divinely Human Being? . . . Would the irruptionists have believed that there was everything divinely delightful in Jesus, or could they not have believed until one rose from the dead? . . . What are the divine values behind the supposed phenomena?

And criticism such as mine does not deny the occurrences. It merely minimizes their importance and suggests that belief in the eternal values of the Catholic Faith is not dependent upon them. ... For myself, an ordinary, dull, sinful human being, but at the same time with a vague reminiscence of my divine origin and my home in heaven, and an occasional inrush of conviction that we are all sons and daughters of God, the faith of that very ordinary man, the dying thief, a faith propped up by no external wonders but the wonderful, godlike heroism of my Divine Brother, the Very God of Very God and the Very Man of Very Man, the heroism of the only perfectly natural man that the world has as yet produced—faith in him and the blessed saints and heroes of our race is enough. Through man we reach up to God, for God is *perpetually* "intruding" himself into this world, and is himself its very Substance. Every wayside flower is a sacrament of his Body and Blood, and every human heroism a Revelation. This is the Catholic Faith, which except a man believe faithfully, without doubt he will shrivel into mean and narrow death.[8]

In spite of this criticism Noel said, in this review, that there was "very much of charm and value" in this book—which is what he found in all of Figgis's writings. And for his part, Figgis told me (when, some time later, he came to Thaxted to preach) that he considered Noel's to have been the best review of his book that he had seen. They had, in fact, great respect for each other, and Noel deeply regretted Figgis's untimely death—and regretted, too, that since his death he had been so unjustifiably neglected.

With regard to the doctrines of the Virgin Birth and the "Empty Tomb", I should say here that by the time that Noel came to write the *Life of Jesus* (which was published twenty-seven years after this review of Figgis's book), while still being more or less agnostic as regards the former (he went no further than to say that "it might well be a fact"), he had come to attach much more importance than he had done to belief in the Empty Tomb. In the chapter on "The Mighty Resurrection" he set forth at some length a view for which he claimed that it made the empty tomb "no longer a difficulty; it would be the tomb with its corpse that would now be scientifically unthinkable". Stated very briefly, this theory was that because, in the case of all other men, their "central personalities" are sinful, they are, at death, unable to hold their bodies together, or any longer to use them. But,

Conceive of a man inheriting from a mother blessed above women a splendid body, and from the first moments of childhood preserving his will uncorrupt, and co-operating energetically with the God of life and saving health, growing in wisdom and stature as the years go by; is it not likely not only that he would radiate health and sanity and all wholesome things from the core of his being, but would be able to do so because in his case the outer was as the inner, quick and responsive, and in complete union with that inner creative personality.... Is it not conceivable that where the central personality has all along been creative and healthy and unitive, not only that such a personality could not be holden of death, not slain by inner disloyalties, but that having suffered and been slain only by external forces, it should be able to return into the outward and visible and "material", and once more to hold it and energize it and use it in the transformed and transmuted shape that tradition describes as the Resurrection Body of Jesus? ... It may be objected, does not such a Christ become so utterly unlike ourselves as to be valueless? The answer is that such a Christ is infinitely more like ourselves than we ourselves are. When we sin, we are—to use a popular expression—"not quite ourselves", and the state of the body which results from sin is not quite our own body. We are ourselves only when we become as God meant us to be. We must measure our true and enduring selves not by the base and faulty measure of the unspeakable thing which we have at present made of ourselves, but by the true and human measure of the full stature of the Christ, the goal of human nature, its interpretation, and our Proper Man.[9]

So Noel had now come far from "minimizing the importance" of belief in the Empty Tomb. But he would still, I am sure, have recognized the essential orthodoxy of those Christians who, while not convinced of its truth as an historic fact, or while "minimising its importance" as such, wholeheartedly believe, on the authority of the common experience of the Christian community all down the ages, the essential truth which it expresses—the truth that Jesus, in the fullness of his divine-human nature, had not been holden of death, and is ever a life-giving Presence in our midst.

I have quoted Noel as speaking of "the depths of the race's being, which is identical with the Being of God himself", of God as "the ground of our being", and as saying that "God is *perpetually* 'intruding' himself into this world, and is himself its very Substance". Because he stressed so strongly the doctrine of the divine immanence he was often accused of being a pantheist; but this was untrue. For him the immanence was, in Dr Temple's words, "the immanence of the Transcendent". In reply to someone who had reproved him for teaching the *transcendence* of God (!) he said: "Surely the Catholic doctrine rightly insists on transcendence and immanence, on the doctrine of man turning his face towards the sun, because his sunlike nature craves more light, and the doctrine of the inrush of that transcendent light into the expectant souls of men."[10] He saw the Eternal Word or Son as being at once the eternal Self-Expression of the transcendent Father, and the eternal Archetype and Ground of creation, and of the human creation in particular. So he would speak of the Eternal Son as the "Eternal Humanity" in God, in the image of whom, and through whom, created humanity came into being, and in whom it is ever grounded and ever "consists". This "Eternal Humanity" in God, ever underlying created humanity, finds partial expression whenever, and in so far as, men yield to the urge of his Holy Spirit—the "Spirit of good impulse"—within them, and was supremely manifested, within the necessary limitations, physical and mental, of a perfect human being in this world, in Jesus.

Noel set forth this conception in a paper on the incarnation which he read at a conference of "Catholic Modernists" at Thaxted in 1912. Here are a few quotations from that paper:

> The Eternal Word ever contained the Eternal Humanity in whose image we are made.

> God the Son became under time and earth conditions *a* man because he was *Man* from all eternity. *Man* is the "only-begotten Son of God", and from all eternity one with the Father. Therefore we, in accepting the Christ and becoming one with him are only returning to our own proper God-human nature.

> In some real sense Humanity pre-exists as the only-begotten Son of God, but in spite of this pre-existence the birth (as Jesus) was as real and human a birth as any other birth has ever been.

> Jesus the Christ was God-Man manifested as an individual man; we are individual men who fail to manifest God-Man.

> The doctrine of the Trinity is three eternally distinguishable properties or *foci* in the Unity—three different, but inter-dependent, activities eternally essential to God's nature. The orthodox doctrine is that in Jesus there was a close and essential union of what we now know as a human being with the Being of God the Human, or God the Word; and, ultimately considered, that in the union of these two natures is one of the eternal activities or *foci* of God.

N. Berdyiev expressed the same idea when he said that "the eternal face of Man abides in the very heart of the Divine Trinity itself. The Second Hypostasis of Divinity is Divine Humanity."[11]

William Temple said: "In him [Jesus] we touch the Divine Humanity which was always in the Godhead but only then [in the Incarnation] made fully manifest. The Everlasting Son of the Father, the Humanity of God which is eternally obedient to the Divinity of God—if the expression may be allowed—took flesh in the fulness of time, that, seeing him, we might learn to love God."[12]

And Noel's descripion of F. D. Maurice's teaching is relevant here:

> Here in England the rich Catholic tradition, in distinction to Evangelicism and Puseyism, was recovered by F. D. Maurice, who insisted that the Incarnation was no intrusion of God into an alien world, but was the supreme manifestation, in a particular human life, of that Eternal Word or Son who is the underlying Reality in whom the whole human race is rooted, who, prior to, and apart from, the Incarnation, is ever "in the world" as the Life and the Light of men.

The view that Noel held of the relationship of the whole human race to God involved a view of the Church, and of baptism as the sacrament of admission into it, which differs from the Roman and Tractarian view. For the latter view—to put it very briefly but not, I think, inaccurately—is that admission into the Church by baptism raises the baptized out of the "natural" state of "mere manhood" into the supernatural state of sonship to God through union with Christ, which there and then *becomes* a fact. Baptism—that is, according to this view—gives to the baptized person a relationship to God which was not his before, and which is not that of human beings as such. As a leading Anglo-Catholic theologian, Dr Eric Mascall, has put it, "A baptismal rite which asserted or assumed that men are already children of God by their natural birth would stand condemned."[13] But that is precisely what Noel's theology did assert. For he held, as we have seen, that the whole body of humanity is, as an objective fact, whether men believe it or not, whether they live according to it or not, grounded in God the Son and, therefore, that all men are, in their essential nature, sons of God the Father, and indwelt by God the Holy Spirit. The Catholic Church, with its sacrament of baptism, is based upon, and witnesses to, this basic truth about all humanity, of which it is the divinely ordained representative. Baptism does produce a change, but the change is one of environment, not a change in the relationship of the baptized person to God. Born into a world in which the true and essential relationship of mankind to God is to an enormous extent obscured and distorted and made ineffectual by the individual and collective sins of men, a child is, in baptism, outwardly and visibly claimed by Christ in his Church for what, *as a human being he essentially is*—"a member of Christ, the child of God, and an inheritor of the Kingdom of Heaven";[14] and is re-born into the new environment of Christ's world-redeeming Body, the Church, wherein he may be helped by its teaching, and by the intensified grace of the universal Spirit in its sacraments and fellowship, to live accordingly, and to take his part in the work of world-redemption.

Noel summed up this view in an instruction in the Thaxted parish magazine, the *Country Town*, in which he said:

> In Baptism everyone is claimed, just because he is a member of the human family, as a member of Christ, the child of God, and a part owner in the Kingdom of Heaven.... We therefore claim mere infants, unconscious of right or wrong, of God or evil, as God's children, and put the seal of Baptism upon them to register them as his offspring, by virtue of their being human creatures, and so bring them into the fellowship of the Church from the very beginning of their lives.... There is nothing irrational or magical about regeneration or re-birth, which simply means the placing of the human plant in the new environment of fellowship. Baptism declares and effects: it declares our divine origin, and helps us to act up to it by uniting us in the strength of the Fellowship.

Elsewhere he asked:

> Of what use is this new birth when you are, as a fact, grafted into the inertia of Laodicea, into the deadly complacency of Slowcombe-in-the-Marsh, into a small coterie of self-conscious Britishers, shallow Italians, or superstitious Spaniards? Scarcely do modern parishes care about the establishment of God's Kingdom; what even do they care about the children re-born into their midst, as witness the post-Reformation scandal of solitary baptism, which bids fair to eclipse the pre-Reformation scandal of solitary masses? ... If the tree be dead, what chance of life has the engrafted twig? If the immediate parish be apostate, avaricious, pharisaic, the immediate soil choked with stones and weeds, God's scheme of the "common salvation" through the interplay of gracious souls is altogether thwarted. This is all appallingly true, but it is also true that, in spite of the worst periods and

most lifeless localities, we are baptized into something beyond the immediate period and environment. ... We are not baptized into Paul or Apollos, into the head of this or that sect or church, but into Jesus Christ and the whole company of Catholic men, the living and the dead, nourished by the rites, sacraments, gospels, traditions of the living Church, limbs of the new Adam, regenerate men, heirs of all ages.[15]

Not only are all men children of God: they are also God's priests. In another article in the *Country Town*, replying to some local Congregationalists who had talked about the "sacerdotalism" taught in the parish church, Noel said:

In Thaxted Church I venture to say that more sermons are preached against "sacerdotalism" than in Bolford Street chapel. ... Why do we speak of the Priesthood of *Humanity* where the Congregationalists speak only of the Priesthood of *Believers*? ... Jesus has revealed the true nature of all human beings to be the sacrificing and forgiving nature, that is, the *priestly* nature. By *nature* they are priests, not by conversion or belief. By belief they make good their priesthood, but do not create it. To say that Christ has abolished the sacrificing priest-hood is to utter the most monstrous lie, and along with that lie is preached the awful heresy that he is our substitute, whereas he is our representative. In Christ is represented and focused and brought to a head and manifested the priestly nature of the whole human race. That is why we talk of the Priesthood of Humanity.

And what is true of Christ in this connection is true also of his Church. In the Church, too, as the visible Body of Christ, is "represented and focused and brought to a head and manifested the priestly nature of the whole human race". This is brought out in the sacrament of Confirmation. "Just as in Baptism the fact that all human beings are God's children is declared and made clear, so in Confirmation the fact that all human beings are God's priests is made clear." And this universal truth is further represented and focused in the sacrament of Holy Orders, in which, "for the sake of Holy Order", certain men are ordained to be the representatives and the mouthpiece of the whole priestly body of the Church in the administration of its sacraments. Noel's view was that the ordained priesthood derives its authority not, as "orthodox" Roman and Anglo-Catholic teaching has it, direct from the transcendent God, whose "grace and truth" are dispensed by it to an essentially subordinate and passively receptive laity, but from the transcendent

God through his Spirit immanent in the whole body of the Church, the "Catholic Democracy", which is itself the sacramental instrument of the Holy Spirit immanent in the whole body of humanity. The first of these views he called the "caste" view of the official priesthood; the second he called the "democratic" view—which he claimed to be the truly Catholic view. (This immanentist and democratic view of the authority and function of the official priesthood was set forth by Father Tyrrell in *Through Scylla and Charybdis* in the chapter "From Heaven or from Men?" In his copy of this book, Noel has written in the margin, "This true Catholicism Tyrrell hoped would be appreciated in the R.C. Church. Its authorities expelled him for preaching it."

The principle of the manifestation and focusing of the eternal and the universal in the temporal and the particular, which governed Noel's interpretation of the incarnation itself, of the Church, baptism, confirmation, and holy orders, governed also his interpretation of the doctrine of the Real Presence in the Blessed Sacrament. He held that in that sacrament the Eternal Son who, as the "Eternal Humanity" in God,[16] ever underlies the whole human and material world, and who in time became incarnate as Jesus, manifests and focuses his universal presence in particular representative products of that world, bread and wine, set apart to be consumed in his Spirit of brotherhood and equality in a Common Meal. In that Sacrificial Meal the Catholic community, representing the whole body of mankind, "presents before the Father the Very Man, the very ground of our being and assurance of our liberation",[17] having in mind his particular manifestation and supreme redemptive activity in the life, death, resurrection, and ascension of Jesus, and looking for the coming of his Kingdom; and with him and in him we offer "ourselves, our souls and bodies" to the Father for the service of God and man—which is the building of God's Kingdom on earth.

In a composite book, *The Great State*, edited by H. G. Wells, Noel contributed an essay on "The Church in the Great State". In it he based his picture of what he hoped Catholic teaching and worship would become, on an imaginary visit to a cathedral in the future (which bore a remarkable resemblance to Thaxted church!) Here is an extract from that essay:

> From the moment when the child is initiated by Baptism into the life of the Fellowship until the last rites of the Church are administered in the hour of death, the sacraments of friendship are his nour-

ishment, and the graces of fellowship uphold him. Present at Mass
from earliest childhood, he makes his communion only after having
received the sacrament of Confirmation, that effectual sign of the
priesthood of mankind. ... In the sacrament of "Holy Order" some
are consecrated as delegates and spokesmen of the whole human priesthood, and in this Parish Mass of Christmas one felt that the consecra-
tion of the Bread and Wine at the hands of the bishop was not the
act of a sacerdotal caste, but of all the people; for as the great bell
tolled at the supreme moment, not only the congregation but the
whole country-side was linked together in that act of adoration, when
the everywhere-present God is made manifest in the friendship of
those who eat and drink in common, and in the nourishment and
energy, the gaiety and intoxication of life, as symbolized by the life-
giving bread and the genial wine.[18]

I feel the need to say something about Noel's views with regard
to one other sacrament, the sacrament of marriage, and the legiti-
macy or otherwise of divorce for Christians. He certainly held that
marriage is meant to be a lifelong relationship, and that people
should enter that state with the intention of making it so. But he
had not the mind of a rigorist in this (or in any other) matter. In
discussing the subject (in the *Life of Jesus*) he said, with reference
to the question of separation as the alternative to divorce: "There are
cases when lifelong separation places an intolerable strain on a
young woman or man, and where it might be wiser for the Church
to grant the right of re-marriage both on the lower ground that 'it is
better to marry than to burn' or on the higher ground that some
really lifelong comrade or mate had at last been found."[19]

With regard to the contention that the Church "has settled this
matter once and for all by its strict rulings", he said:

It may be questioned whether this is really the case. ... No general
council of the universal Church has ever thoroughly examined the
question or pronounced upon it; but the Church has universally laid
down that the ministers of marriage [i.e. the man and the woman]
are the contracting parties, and not the priest who blesses the marriage;
so that the "what God hath joined together" of the marriage service
refers not to the blessing of the Church, but to the love and comradeship of the bride and bridegroom. Supposing this love never to have
existed, or to have ceased to exist after every effort has been made to
maintain it, is not the marriage thereby dissolved, and ought not the
Church to grant a divorce or a decree of nullity? ... We would not
presume to dogmatize on the point, but would urge that Christendom

should seriously review the whole matter in the light of modern biblical criticism, in the light of common sense, and under the guidance
of the Holy Spirit who has been given to guide us into all truth.[20]

The direction of his own sympathies is obvious.

With regard to the "after life" of human beings Noel was a Universalist. His belief in the ultimate salvation of all men was based, not
only or mainly on such scriptural texts as "I, if I be lifted up, will
draw all men unto me", and "As in Adam all die, even so in Christ
shall all be made alive"—which he regarded as being open only to
the Universalist interpretation—but, more fundamentally, on his
belief in the essential divine sonship of all humanity, and, consequently, his conviction that it is God's will that all shall eventually
come to fullness of life in his Family, and that the failure of even
one person to do this would be the defeat of God. So he rejected
the official Roman doctrine (held also by "orthodox" Anglo-
Catholics) according to which men's ultimate fate, for good or ill,
is fixed at death, and that it is only those who, at that moment, are
"faithful" and repentant who are destined for heaven and enter
purgatory to be prepared for it, while the rest pass for ever into the
state of "eternal death". In *Jesus the Heretic* he quoted the *Catholic
Dictionary* as saying that "the place of purging is reserved for souls
who depart this life in the grace of God. . . . Purgatory is not a place
of probation, for the time of trial, the period during which the
soul is free to choose eternal death, ends with the separation of soul
and body." It is true that Rome allows the severity of this doctrine
to be somewhat mitigated by the plea of "invincible ignorance", and
that broad-minded Roman Catholics press this plea to the utmost
possible extent. But there seems to be no escape from Noel's conclusion that according to the official teaching of the Roman Church
(and, again, the teaching of "orthodox" Anglo-Catholics) men's
fate for all eternity, for eternal life or eternal death, is fixed at death.
He used to say of people who held this doctrine that they observed,
not All Souls' Day but Some Souls' Day.

    With regard to Anglo-Catholic teaching in this matter, he re-
ferred, in *Jesus the Heretic*, to Dr Pusey's acceptance of Roman
doctrine, but added that "even in the beginning of the Anglo-
Catholic revival, Dr Pusey's rigorist doctrine was opposed, not only
by such liberal Catholics as Maurice and Kingsley and, it goes without saying, by the whole Broad Church school, but also by such

famous Anglo-Catholic leaders as Dr Gurney, vicar of St Barnabas, Pimlico, and Dr Littledale, and later by the writers of *Lux Mundi,* that classical work which turned the Anglo-Catholic tide into broader seas".[21] But I feel bound to add that even today many Anglo-Catholics have not plunged into those "broader seas"—not only as regards this particular matter, but in their general theological position.

William Temple once said that the idea that "at the moment of death all is irrevocably settled; whatever be the state of the soul at that moment, in that state it must unalterably remain" is "a once prevalent delusion for which neither in revelation nor in reason is there a shred of evidence".[22] Being in complete agreement with that statement, Noel held that at death *all* men enter purgatory, in which, through wider and deeper and, if necessary, painful experience they will grow into that fullness of life—that eternal life of fellowship with God and man—which is heaven. As he said in a sermon preached at Thaxted on All Saints' Day 1912:

> The love of God, as a consuming fire, burns up the dross in human souls, purging all our iniquities, that the pure gold of human nature may shine forth in everlasting brightness. So we pray for the dead, not that they may escape the purging process, but that the purging process may be shortened only by their submitting their wills to the cleansing fires of experience and repentance.[23]

In the *Life of Jesus,* quoting our Lord's words "I, if I be lifted up, will draw all men unto me", he went on:

> How else could his victory be achieved? It would be no triumph for Christ or the Father if a single soul remained outside the fellowship of heaven, cursing and unconsoled. . . . A future world where men still for ever and ever resisted God would be the triumph of satan and the defeat of God.

And in reply to the "free will" objection to Universalism he said:

> True, the Church had to safeguard the doctrine of the freedom of the human will. God forces no man in this life or in a life to come to act righteously or to love him. How could he? Who shall command the heart? But neither life nor death can entirely quench the Holy Spirit in the individual soul. . . . After long ages the love of God will melt the hardest heart, even if it be "so as by fire".[24]

Noel made much of the doctrine of the Communion of Saints. In an exposition of the doctrines of the Apostles' Creed he said:

We believe in the communion between the living and the dead; in the power of the living to help the departed, by prayer and intense desire, on their way through purgatory or the fires of experience towards their home in God; and in the power of departed heroes, whose heaven lies in extended ability to help those who remain within the limitations of this world.[25]

The unseen world was for him very much a *peopled* world, and he made much both of prayer *for* the departed ("faithful" and otherwise) and of prayer *to* them—especially, but not exclusively, to the "departed heroes" whom we call "the saints". (He commended the custom in the Eastern Church of praying not only to the "saints" but also to the "ordinary" departed, and thought that the Western Church made too much of a gulf between the two.)

He ended the All Saints' Day sermon from which I have already quoted, thus:

I appeal to you who have ears to hear and eyes to see. That you should hold your dead in your memories, that you should know them to be among the living, that you should feel their presence and be uplifted by their grace and goodness to heroic deeds—this is my prayer for you. By this great and proportioned Faith of the ages, a Faith into which you are re-entering with added knowledge and larger experience, you shall live; in its light you shall yet see light and shall yourselves be as lights to lighten the darkness of England's dreary night, in the faith and love of God who not only ascends into heaven, but descends into hell, who liberates the spirits in prison with a love that is deeper than the depths beneath, for "If I climb up into heaven, thou art there: if I go down into hell, thou art there also. If I take the wings of the morning, and remain in the uttermost parts of the sea, even there shall thy hand lead me and thy right hand shall hold me."

Conrad Noel's distinctive interpretation of Catholic doctrine was essentially in the F. D. Maurice tradition, although it was also a development, in both the "Liberal" and the "Catholic" directions, within that tradition. What Wilfred Knox and Alec Vidler said, in their *The Development of Modern Catholicism*, of Stewart Headlam and the Guild of St Matthew generally—that "they had as their background the theology of Maurice" but "went further than he did in their Liberalism, no less than in their Sacramentalism"[26] —was emphatically true of Noel.

This general type of theology has been called (as Maurice Reckitt informed us in his *Maurice to Temple*) "snug incarnationalism" by the "younger theologians". While not agreeing with these younger theologians (now not so young) that this theology is out of date, I would admit that since the First World War it has to a considerable extent been supplanted by a theology which, as Dr Vidler has put it, makes "sharp differentiation between nature and grace, or between the natural and the supernatural, or between humanity and redeemed humanity"—which differentiation, he says, "Maurice did not accept." [27]

The present situation seems, in fact, to be comparable to that which obtained when Maurice and his few supporters confronted the greater part of the religious world, "Catholic" and Protestant, of his time. As Maurice himself said:

> Romish and Protestant divines, differing in the upshot of their schemes, have yet agreed in the construction of them. The Fall of man is commonly regarded by both as the foundation of theology—the Incarnation and death of our Lord as provisions against the effect of it. Now St Paul speaks of the Mystery of Christ as the *ground* of all things in Heaven and Earth, the history as the gradual discovery or revelation of this ground.

But, "the fall of Adam—not the union of the Father and the Son, not the creation of the world in Christ—is set before men in both divisions of Christendom as practically the ground of their creed". [28] Again, Maurice said: "No man has a right to say, 'My race is a sinful, fallen race', even when he most confesses the greatness of his own sin and fall; because he is bound to contemplate his race in the Son of God." [29] And "The truth is that every man is in Christ. The condemnation of every man is that he will not own the truth." [30]

Needless to say, neither Maurice nor anyone whose theology is in his "incarnationalist" tradition has ever minimized the fact of sin and its appalling effects on human life, individual and social—who could? I have quoted Noel, for example, as referring to "the unspeakable thing that we have so far made of ourselves". But it was "of faith" for him that the natural basic union of God and man, manifested in the incarnation, while obscured and distorted, cannot be *destroyed* by sin, for it is eternal in the Mind of God.

3

For Conrad Noel the basic principles and values of Socialism were
the necessary expression, in the political and economic sphere, of his
theology. And the doctrines of that theology that are most directly
relevant to that sphere are (a) the basic unity of the whole human
race, in spite of the surface disunity caused by sin, as ultimately
rooted and grounded in God and as the Family of God; (b) the
permanently distinct entity and eternal value of each individual
human being as a member of that Family; and (c) the sacramental
nature of the material world in which, and by means of which, man
lives.

The unity of the human race as the Family of God involves the
brotherhood and equal value of all men; and the distinct entity of
each individual as a member of that Family involves the need and
the right of every human being to the utmost amount of freedom
as is consistent with the same need and right of all other human
beings. These two doctrines together, that is, involve that one and
indivisible trinity of spiritual values which is summed up in the
old democratic watchword "Liberty, Equality, and Fraternity",
which, as Noel said in *The Manifesto of the Catholic Crusade,* "are
not 'extras' and 'implications', but essential articles of the Faith,
without which creed and worship are turned into deadly poisons".

Out of these doctrines will necessarily come the desire for a social
order in which, despite differences of sex, nationality, race, and
colour, all men and women *live* as the equal children of the one
God that they essentially *are*; freely co-operating in using the earth
and its products for the common good of all, and thereby sacramen-
tally expressing the living God in whom both mankind and the
material world are ultimately rooted, and whose Spirit is in all men
as the very Spirit of "Liberty, Equality, and Fraternity".

The economic life of such a social order must be based (a) on the
principle that ownership and control of the things to which all must
have access in order to live—the land and other "means of production"—should not be concentrated in the hands of a few; and
(b) the principle that all should co-operate in using these things for
the primary purpose of supplying the needs of all, with as much

scope for individual and group freedom and initiative as is consistent
with ultimate co-operation.

These principles, Noel held, are essential to the Christian social
outlook, and it is with them in mind that Christians must look
at and judge existing society, and towards the bringing about of a
social order based upon them that they must work. For these principles, while of course requiring application in very different ways
according to different conditions and stages of social development,
are themselves permanent principles of economic justice, fellowship, and freedom; and, he held, they are recognized as such in the
main Jewish and Christian social tradition.

In the Jewish Law Noel saw the principle that ownership of the
essential means of living should not be concentrated in the hands
of the few—the principle of the "classless society"—expressed in
such laws as those of the Landmark, the Sabbatical Year, the Year
of Jubilee, and the prohibition of usury. For these laws were designed to prevent the permanent accumulation of the ownership of
land and farms (then practically the only "means of production")
in the hands of the few, and the consequent division of the Jewish
nation into classes of owners and non-owners of those things. And
he saw the Jewish prophets expressing this principle in their denunciations of those who remove their neighbour's landmark, lay
house to house and field to field, and who take usury from their
neighbour.[31]

Jesus, born into this tradition, was brought up by a mother whose
outlook was expressed in her rejoicing at the vision of the mighty
being put down, the humble exalted, the hungry filled, and the rich
expropriated. Later he himself expressed this democratic and equali-
tarian outlook in his whole attitude to the poor and the rich re-
spectively ("blessed are ye poor" : "woe unto you that are rich");
in his condemnation of greed for riches (the serving of "mammon");
in his identifying himself with John the Baptist and his "levelling"
teaching ("every valley shall be filled, and every mountain and hill
shall be brought low"); and, basically, in his appeal to the "Law
and the Prophets". Jesus did not, indeed, commit himself or his
followers to the letter of the law (for example, to such enactments
of it as those just referred to), but he did commit himself and them
to its underlying principles, which he came to "fulfil"—and to
extend to "all nations", for he saw all men, not only those of the
Jewish nation, as equally children of God. So to "seek first the

Kingdom of God and his righteousness" would, Noel held, involve our striving to bring about on earth a world commonwealth which, expressing the nature of God, would be based on the principles of "classlessness" as regards ownership of the means of living, and of co-operation in production and distribution for the common good as regards their use.

The early Christian community expressed what it felt to be the urge of the indwelling Spirit of the risen and living Christ in its spontaneous adoption of a "communistic" way of life, and its general outlook was expressed in such a saying as "let the brother of low degree rejoice in that he is exalted, and the rich in that he is made low". The same "communistic" and "anti-riches" outlook was held by the early Fathers of the Church; and the Schoolmen, while laying more stress on the value of personal property than did the early Fathers (in which matter Noel would have agreed more with the Schoolmen), were clear in their opposition to such ownership of property as involves the exploitation of other people. And the Guild system of industry, with its regulations—such as the just price—for safeguarding the common good, combined with scope for the exercise of individual and group initiative, and with its insistence upon good quality of goods and workmanship, arose naturally in the moral "climate" which the Faith tended to create.

It is true that avarice and lust for power in some men, and apathy on the part of many (as Noel put it, "inward and spiritual rascality on the part of the few, and inward and spiritual apathy on the part of the many") always made largely abortive the various ways in which, from the Jewish Law to the regulations of the Guild system, it was sought to defend the community against economic exploitation. This became increasingly true as the Church, long before the Reformation, became increasingly infected with the spirit of "the world". And after the Reformation the avowed individualism of the kind of Protestantism that eventually became dominant led to the abandonment of the very idea of a Christian social and economic order—that is, of an order which, in its structure and working, is based upon and expresses Christian principles, values, and purposes. Religion and economics, which for long had in practice been uneasy partners, were now even avowedly divorced. The concentration of the ownership of the bulk of the means of production in the hands of a comparatively small class, the uncontrolled running of industry primarily for the profit of that class, and the exploitation of the labour of the dispossessed to that end, became the characteristics of the new industrial system—which Maurice Reckitt has described as "organized avarice". That system was now unashamedly supported by most professing Christians, Catholic and Protestant. And this, not without protest from some individuals, remained the general position until the middle of the nineteenth century, when what God had joined together but man had put asunder, the Christian Socialist pioneers began again to bring together.

This lightning sketch, mostly in my own words, of Noel's ideas, of course merely hints at the way in which he saw "Socialism in Church History" (which was the title of one of his books). And he set forth fully his interpretation of our Lord's life and teaching in his *Life of Jesus*.

This book was the outcome of many years of thought and study. In the Preface he said:

> I have tried to see his life and teaching from the angle of those who actually came across him for the first time and were drawn within the orbit of his influence. Theological deductions as to his nature and his relation to the Godhead are of a later period. My hope has been to recover something of the life itself, its spontaneity and freshness, and to interpret it in relation to its actual environment.

The basic idea in our Lord's teaching was that of the "Kingdom of God". As St Mark's Gospel puts it: "Jesus came into Galilee preaching the gospel of the Kingdom of God." What is the Kingdom of God? Noel answers this question first of all by saying what it is *not*. It is not the conventional idea of "heaven", as the "place" to which individual souls go after death. It is not a private relationship between the individual soul and God, resulting in a "comfortable feeling inside". And it is not the Catholic Church. What, then, is it?

> The Kingdom of God is the world of men and women as planned in *heaven*, that is, in the ideal world of God's mind, will and intention. It is in the truest sense the real world, because it is the world as eternally constituted in the mind of God. Against it are the temporary "kingdoms of this age"—i.e. of the competitive age in which men are at sixes and sevens—which the Church has to translate into the Kingdom of unity or at-one-ment, into the Kingdom of our Lord and of his Christ, into the Kingdom in which each, by serving all, best serves his eternal self and grows into full or eternal or overmastering life.

The underlying fact is the kingdom or solidarity of men, the fact of God's Holy Family. That fact is so blurred by egoism, impurity and other deadly sins and ignorances that men arrange their lives, domestically, politically and commercially, as if the fact did not exist. The Church is a body of men converted to the fact and sworn to convert others to the fact, and to frame the social life upon the fact.[32]

This kingdom eternal in the mind of God is, through the initiative and activity of his Spirit in men and winning their co-operation, to be incarnated in the actual life of mankind and in all its affairs, individual and social, political, economic, cultural, and in its "fun and games". In so far as the eternal Kingdom is so incarnated in human life, to that extent is the Kingdom established on earth. The Kingdom is to be "built upon the eternal impulses of the whole human race".[33] It is "a world which Christ wishes men to build here on earth. Although it is not to be a man-made kingdom, for it is God-planned and God-given, yet it must be man-accepted and man-actualized by the grace of God."[34] But although we are to pray and work for the building of God's Kingdom on earth, within history, it "will be brought to its perfect fruition in the world beyond",[35] and "men shall enjoy it in the fulness of their manhood, i.e., in something corresponding to the body that now is, in a transformed body, and with outward expression".[36]

To ascertain the kind of social order which would "incarnate" the eternal values of God's Kingdom, and for which Jesus stood, Noel turned first to the Law and the Prophets. He quoted Dr Gore as saying:

The Lord assumed all that the Old Testament laid down. . . . The Law and the Prophets had been struggling for the establishment of a great social system on a great moral basis. . . . The Law is full of it, the Prophets are full of it. Now do you see that every word that our Lord said, he said to people who had all that behind them. It is the point from which he starts. Until you have got there, you have not begun.[37]

The "great social system on a great moral basis" would necessarily, Noel held, be some form of classless and co-operative world order. But how was it to be brought about? I confess that I find the answer that he gave to that question rather confusing. Thus, he sometimes seemed to present a picture of Jesus as a social revolutionary leader who is working for an upheaval which would "bring the existing order to sudden desolation",[38] and which would bring about "the new world order . . . in the near future".[39] But there is much in the book which does not seem to fit in to this picture, and it may be that Noel was expressing in this dramatic language only what he felt to be our Lord's sense of the urgency of the need to work for the destruction of an evil social order and the creation of a good one.

I am quite without the scholarly qualifications that would be needed (even if space for it allowed) for anything approaching an adequate examination and discussion of the case that Noel put forward in this book. (It is a pity that no recognized biblical scholar and critic has written a critique of the book.) But what is clear is that the basic conclusion to which the author leads is that Jesus wanted and was striving for a social order based upon his fundamental belief in human brotherhood and equality, and was therefore in the deepest sense a "revolutionary" in face of the kind of world in which he lived, based as it was on the domination and exploitation of class by class and nation by nation; and that his followers in every age, inspired by his Spirit and holding the same belief in human brotherhood and equality, must also be "revolutionaries" in face of these same evils (however different may be the forms in which they are expressed) in the world in which they live—this being involved in their vocation, which is to be fellow-workers with Christ in transforming the "kingdom of this age" into the "kingdom of our Lord and of his Christ".

Evelyn Underhill, in reviewing the *Life of Jesus*, which she described as "vivid and interesting", while insisting that "the rich and living personality of Jesus cannot be pressed into the mould of the social revolutionary", went on to say:

> Father Noel presents this reading of the Gospel with much persuasive eloquence, giving fresh meaning and vigour to well-known incidents and phrases, and casting new light on many of the sayings of Christ. It is true that some of his readers will feel, perhaps rightly, that the more mysterious incidents of the Gospel record are insufficiently stressed; and particularly that the treatment of the Passion is inadequate. But against these limitations must be set the many points at which a wholly new light, independent of theological interpretation, is cast on the personality and teaching of Jesus as given by the Evangelists. His book is strongly to be recommended to all who care for Christian realism; and especially perhaps to those who are least inclined to agree with its author's point of view.[40]

The following extract from near the end of this book sums up the essence of the faith out of which it was written:

> It is true that the Lord Jesus says: "A new commandment I give unto you, that ye love one another"; but it is not a new police regulation, but a commandment grounded in the very law of man's being as revealed in him. If it is an order imposed by the Majesty on high, who is not the very essence of men's life and of their relation to one another in an organic body, it will never be obeyed, because it never can be obeyed.
>
> But if it be the revelation of one who was in the world from the beginning, in whom all things consist, in whom we live and move and have our being, it may be hard to obey; sin and stupidity may keep us from that obedience, and it may be with infinite difficulty that we find the way home. But it will be home to which at last we come. In commonwealth we shall have found him who is our life, and who has written his laws in our hearts, and we shall be travelling back by his grace into our proper nature as revealed in him. For mankind was made by him to be the body of God.[41]

4

G. K. Chesterton, in his *Autobiography*, said:

> I cannot remember where my brother or I first met the Rev. Conrad Noel. I rather fancy it was at some strange club where somebody was lecturing on Nietzsche; and where the debaters (by a typical transition) passed from the gratifying thought that Nietzsche attacked Christianity to the natural inference that he was a True Christian. And I admired the common sense of a curate, with dark curly hair and a striking face, who got up and pointed out that Nietzsche would be even more opposed to True Christianity than to False Christianity, supposing there were any True Christianity to oppose. I learned that the curate's name was Noel.
>
> Conrad Noel, the son of a poet and the grandson of a peer, had all the incalculable elements of the eccentric aristocrat; the sort of eccentric aristocrat who so often figures as a particularly destructive democrat. That great gentleman, Cunninghame Graham, whom I knew more slightly but always respected profoundly, was the sort of uncompromising rebel; but he had a sort of Scottish seriousness similar to Spanish seriousness; while Noel's humour was half English and half Irish but always mainly humorous.

Chesterton records that on one occasion he, with Percy Dearmer,
Conrad Noel, and C. F. G. Masterman were coming away together
from some meeting, he wearing his usual "calamitous" costume,
Dearmer in cassock and "English" square cap, Noel in "correct
clerical clothes", but wearing a "furry cap which made him look
like an aesthetic rat-catcher", and behind them came Masterman
"in conventional clothes worn in an unconventional manner, with
top hat on the back of his head, pointing derisively at the three and
crying aloud: 'Could you see three such backs like that anywhere
in God's creation?'". He went on:

> I mention this fringe of eccentricity, even of eccentricity in dress, upon
> the border of the Anglo-Catholic party in the Anglican Church, be-
> cause it really had a great deal to do with the beginning of the pro-
> cess by which Bohemian journalists, like my brother and myself, were
> drawn towards the serious consideration of the theory of the Church.
> I was considerably influenced by Conrad Noel; my brother, I think,
> even more so.

Going on to talk about his brother, Cecil, Gilbert said:

> He had far too lucid and lively a mind not to be bored with material-
> ism as maintained by materialists. This negative reaction against
> reaction, however, might not have carried him far, if the positive end
> of the magnet had not begun to attract him, in the person of person-
> alities like Conrad Noel. It was certainly through that eccentric cleric
> that my brother began to cease to be anything so barren as a mere
> anti-clerical. I remember that, when conventional people complained
> of Noel's wild ways, or attributed to him worse things of which he
> certainly was not guilty, my brother Cecil answered them by quoting
> the words of the man healed by blindness in the Gospel: "Whether
> the man be a sinner or no, I know not; but this I know; that whereas
> I was blind, now I see."

So eventually Cecil Chesterton, having been prepared by Conrad
Noel, was confirmed at the church at which Noel was then an
assistant priest, St Mary the Virgin, Primrose Hill. Unfortunately,
the confirming bishop, a suffragan in the London diocese, was an
Evangelical of the "glory-for-me" soul-saving variety. As his "pi"
talk went on and on, Cecil's face became gloomier and gloomier.
The situation was saved by the vicar, Percy Dearmer, who, sensing
his friend's suffering, slipped out of the chancel and handed to
Conrad, to pass on to Cecil, a slip of paper on which he had written
"See Article XXVI", which, when they looked it up, they found to

be the Article which dealt with "The unworthiness of the Ministers, which hinders not the effect of the Sacrament". Cecil at once cheered up!

(When, some years later, Cecil, under the strong influence of Hilaire Belloc, joined the Roman Church, Conrad was bitterly disappointed. He had done his utmost to dissuade Cecil from taking this step.)

Nan Dearmer, in the biography of her husband, Percy Dearmer, tells how he and his first wife, Mabel,[42] first met Conrad Noel. Dearmer was in his first curacy (in 1891), at St Anne's, South Lambeth (under that splendid Socialist priest, W. A. Morris). "One day there was a knock on the door of 59 South Lambeth Road, and on opening it Percy found an engaging-looking tramp with a red handkerchief knotted round his throat. The tramp introduced himself as Conrad Noel, and explained that he had come to live at Rowton House, Vauxhall, the first of the improved common lodging houses to be built by Lord Rowton, and known as the 'working man's hotel'. Conrad Noel had come to South London to study conditions, and at first he had tried an ordinary common lodging house, but that had been too much even for his enthusiasm. He and Percy made friends, and from then on saw a good deal of each other." (They would have met in the Guild of St Matthew, which they both joined.)

Dr Harry Roberts, who was well known as London's East End "sixpenny doctor", said in his appendix to Conrad's *Autobiography*:

I first met Conrad Noel when I was a medical student at St Mary's Hospital, Paddington; Conrad was a curate at St Mary's Church, Paddington Green. We became close friends at once, and remained close friends till his death.... He had been operated on in early childhood for hare-lip. Curiously enough, this in no way detracted from the distinction and real beauty of his face. I shall always remember it as I saw it a fortnight before his death, as that of an elderly saint and lover who had won the secret of eternal youth.

At the Requiem for Conrad at Thaxted, the Bishop of Chelmsford, Dr Wilson, said (in addition to what I have already quoted him as saying about Conrad as a speaker[43]):

We are bidding farewell to a man who, in my judgment, was the greatest personality in this diocese. His loss is irreplaceable. He was unique. He was in a class by himself. Little people may argue and dispute regarding his political opinions... but to me he was distinctive. He was never afraid to say what he thought and to fight for his principles; that is always a sign of a great man.... What Conrad Noel did for this parish and this church many of you know better than I do; but that Thaxted church is one of the outstanding churches in England today is of itself a tribute to the man, his character, his life, and his work.

I believe it to be literally true that he was the greatest personality among the clergy in this diocese as a student, as a writer, as a religious and political leader, as a man of artistic and musical sense, and, most of all, as a saint of God. In him were assembled many and diverse gifts, any one of which would have given distinction. His courage, which was unbounded, remained to the end, and as he had lived, so he died, a brave and faithful servant of Jesus Christ. Thank God for such men, and thank God it has been our privilege to meet one such in our journey through life.

The writer of this essay first saw and heard Conrad Noel on a Sunday evening in Advent 1905, at St Peter's Church, Streatham, London. The main theme in his sermon was that "democratic" view —as opposed to what he called the "caste" view—of the priesthood which is included in my account, in the second chapter of this essay, of his general theological outlook. That view was not new to me, for I had been taught it, and the essentials of that whole outlook, by Percy Dearmer, at St Mary's, Primrose Hill, before I had even heard of Conrad Noel.[44] But I was immediately and deeply impressed by the personality of the preacher. I met him personally soon after this (early in 1906), and between then and his death thirty-six years later I got to know him intimately.

That Conrad Noel was an extraordinarily live and original and dynamic person must by now be obvious to the reader. But no words of mine, or even of his own in his writings, can convey with any degree of accuracy his natural charm and graciousness. Even in controversy, whether private or public, although he could sometimes be a heated opponent, he always remained courteous.

Conrad was a stimulating conversationalist and raconteur, with a keen sense of humour. And his humour did not desert him when he entered the pulpit. One instance of this that springs to my mind was his quoting an ancient writer as saying that in the messianic kingdom "each vine will have a thousand branches, and each branch ten thousand twigs, and each twig ten thousand clusters, and each cluster ten thousand grapes, and each grape yield twenty-five measures of wine"—and then adding, with a beatific smile, "*There's* a kingdom for you!"

He had a somewhat romantic streak in his nature, and this sometimes led him into giving a too highly-coloured account of some particular event, and into making rather extravagant and exaggerated statements. But against this tendency, on occasions, must be set the balance in his essential thinking, to which I have already called attention in this essay.

The suggestion has been made that Conrad might have been so interested in ideas and principles, and so concerned about their application in public affairs, that he tended to lack concern for the welfare of individuals. In his introduction to the *Life of Jesus* he said: "The work will dwell on the social content of Christ's teaching, but it will at the same time try to keep the balance between his plan for world liberation, and his intimate dealings with the individuals with whom he came into contact." So far from Conrad tending not to keep this balance himself, I would say that he was rather outstanding as a "revolutionary" who *did* keep it.

I remember Conrad saying that his favourite motto was that of Hugh Walpole's novel *Fortitude*—"It isn't life that matters but the courage you bring to it". He certainly brought courage to his life. There was the courage with which he always stood by his principles in face of all opposition and often bitter hostility, regardless of consequences—always, I must add, supported with equal courage by his wife Miriam (about whose delightful and, in a variety of ways, extremely capable personality much could be written; she was very much a person in her own right, and not only as the wife of Conrad Noel). And there was the courage with which he faced and endured his physical afflictions—the diabetes from which he suffered for nearly the whole of the thirty-two years during which his work was placing Thaxted "on the map"; the increasing lameness and blindness, eventually complete blindness, which resulted from that disease; and finally cancer, from which he died.

I saw him for the last time within a few weeks of his death. In spite of his condition he was still very much interested in, and talked about, a variety of subjects, with sense of humour undiminished. He had indeed "won the secret of eternal youth".

Conrad Noel died on the 22 July 1942, and was buried in the church-
yard of Thaxted church, close to the east wall, on the other side of
which is the High Altar. On his tomb-stone are the words

HE LOVED JUSTICE AND HATED OPPRESSION

NOTES

1. *The Development of Modern Catholicism* (1933), p. 69.

2. *Autobiography*, p. 60.

3. *Frederick Denison Maurice*, p. 73.

4. Holst's *Hymn of Jesus* is dedicated to Conrad Noel.

5. *Orthodoxy* (1943 edn), pp. 167f.

6. Followers of John Kensit who actively opposed what they (incorrectly)
   called "ritualism" in the Church of England.

7. This thought would be less open to the charge of "pantheism", and more
   in accordance with Noel's real meaning, if it were expressed thus: "And
   supposing that at last, from the God in whom the race is grounded,
   there arose a Deliverer...." (I say more in answer to the charge of
   "pantheism" later in this section on pp. 156–7.)

8. *Church Socialist Quarterly*, July 1910.

9. *Life of Jesus* (1937), pp. 524f.

10. *Jesus the Heretic* (1939), p. 26.

11. *Freedom and the Spirit* (1935), p. 207.

12. *Foundations* (1912), p. 251.

13. Article in the *Church Times*, 6 May 1941. (There were no qualifying, or
    explanatory, remarks in the context.)

14. Thomas Hancock expressed this view in his succinct remark that "a
    child is baptized because he is *born*".

15. Noel's pamphlet *The Sacraments*, pp. 10f.

16. See pages 157–8 above.

17. Noel's pamphlet *The Sacraments*, p. 14.

18. *The Great State* (1912), p. 322. Dr S. C. Carpenter, in reviewing Noel's
    Autobiography in 1946, said of this essay that it "had a prophetic quality.
    One reader at least has remembered it since 1912."

19. *Life of Jesus* (1937), p. 446.

20. Ibid., pp. 444–5.

21. *Jesus the Heretic*, p. 91.

22. Sermon preached at Westminster Abbey on All Saints' Day 1919.

23. This sermon was published as a supplement to R. J. Campbell's "New Theology" paper, the *Christian Commonwealth*—to which paper Noel was for a time a regular contributor.

24. *Life of Jesus*, pp. 425f.

25. *Byways of Belief*, pp. 292f.

26. *The Development of Modern Catholicism* (1933), p. 74.

27. *The Theology of F. D. Maurice* (1948), p. 79.

28. Quoted in *The Theology of F. D. Maurice*, pp. 36–7.

29. Ibid., p. 44.

30. Ibid., p. 56.

31. In his *The Social Ideal of the Bible* (p. 21) Gilbert Clive Binyon says of the economic enactments of the Jewish Law that they "were designed to prevent the growth of a class of rich landed proprietors; to secure to all the means of livelihood; the soil . . . no man was to count absolutely his own".

32. I have quoted this from an article that Noel wrote many years ago, because it expresses concisely the view which is expressed more diffusively in the *Life of Jesus*.

33. *Life of Jesus*, p. 312.

34. Ibid., p. 580.

35. Ibid., p. 432.

36. Ibid., p. 173.

37. *The New Commentary on Holy Scripture*.

38. *Life of Jesus*, p. 362.

39. Ibid., p. 364.

40. *Spectator*, 27 August 1937.

41. *Life of Jesus*, p. 588.

42. Mabel Dearmer died of enteric fever in the First World War, contracted when serving as a nurse with the British Medical Unit in Serbia—with her husband as its chaplain.

43. See p. 143 above.

44. At this time Dearmer really was a Liberal *Catholic*, as distinct from what might be called the *mere* Liberal that he seemed to have become in his later years.

SELECT BIBLIOGRAPHY

THOMAS HANCOCK

Christ and the People (1875)
The Pulpit and the Press (1904)
Both these volumes consist of sermons delivered by Hancock

A. M. Allchin, *The Spirit and the Word* (1963)
Two lectures: on R. M. Benson and Thomas Hancock

STEWART HEADLAM

The Laws of Eternal Life (1905)
The Socialist's Church (1907)

F. G. Bettany, *Stewart Duckworth Headlam: A Biography* (1926)
See also two articles on Headlam by Stephen Liberty in *Christendom*,
December 1948 and March 1949

CHARLES MARSON

The Psalms at Work (1894)
Charity Organisation and Jesus Christ (1896)
Turnpike Tales (1897)
Village Silhouettes (1914)
God's Co-operative Society (1914)

CONRAD NOEL

Socialism in Church History (1910)
Byways of Belief (1912). First and last chapters.
The Life of Jesus (1937).
Autobiography, ed. Sidney Dark (1945)
"... written during his last years of illness and blindness, not completed by
him, and apparently over-zealously amended, is sketchy in parts and not
always accurate" (Reg Groves in *Conrad Noel and the Thaxted Movement*
(1967)).

Gilbert C. Binyon, *The Christian Socialist Movement in England* (1931)
Maurice B. Reckitt, *Maurice to Temple* (1947). Scott Holland Memorial
Lectures for 1946.
These two volumes cover much of the background to which these essays
are related.